THE BEDFORD SERIES IN HISTORY AND CULTURE

The Sacco and Vanzetti Case

A Brief History with Documents

THE BEDFORD SERIES IN HISTORY AND CULTURE

The Sacco and Vanzetti Case

A Brief History with Documents

Michael M. Topp

University of Texas at El Paso

BEDFORD/ST. MARTIN'S   Boston   ♦   New York

For Bedford/St. Martin's

Executive Editor for History: Mary V. Dougherty
Director of Development for History: Jane Knetzger
Developmental Editor: Elizabeth Harrison
Senior Production Supervisor: Joe Ford
Production Associate: Chris Gross
Senior Marketing Manager: Jenna Bookin Barry
Project Management: Books By Design, Inc.
Text Design: Claire Seng-Niemoeller
Indexer: Books By Design, Inc.
Cover Design: Billy Boardman
Cover Photo: Sacco and Vanzetti Arriving at Court, April 19, 1927. Bettmann/CORBIS
Composition: Stratford Publishing Services
Printing and Binding: Haddon Craftsmen, an RR Donnelley & Sons Company

President: Joan E. Feinberg
Editorial Director: Denise B. Wydra
Director of Marketing: Karen Melton Soeltz
Director of Editing, Design, and Production: Marcia Cohen
Manager, Publishing Services: Emily Berleth

Library of Congress Control Number: 2004107919

Manufactured in the United States of America.

0 9 8 7
f e d c

For information, write: Bedford/St. Martin's, 75 Arlington Street, Boston, MA 02116 (617-399-4000)

ISBN-10: 0-312-40088-8 (paperback)
        1-4039-6808-X (hardback)
ISBN-13: 978-0-312-40088-0 (paperback)
        978-1-4039-6808-1 (hardcover)

Acknowledgments

Foreword

The Bedford Series in History and Culture is designed so that readers can study the past as historians do.

The historian's first task is finding the evidence. Documents, letters, memoirs, interviews, pictures, movies, novels, or poems can provide facts and clues. Then the historian questions and compares the sources. There is more to do than in a courtroom, for hearsay evidence is welcome, and the historian is usually looking for answers beyond act and motive. Different views of an event may be as important as a single verdict. How a story is told may yield as much information as what it says.

Along the way the historian seeks help from other historians and perhaps from specialists in other disciplines. Finally, it is time to write, to decide on an interpretation and how to arrange the evidence for readers.

Each book in this series contains an important historical document or group of documents, each document a witness from the past and open to interpretation in different ways. The documents are combined with some element of historical narrative—an introduction or a biographical essay, for example—that provides students with an analysis of the primary source material and important background information about the world in which it was produced.

Each book in the series focuses on a specific topic within a specific historical period. Each provides a basis for lively thought and discussion about several aspects of the topic and the historian's role. Each is short enough (and inexpensive enough) to be a reasonable one-week assignment in a college course. Whether as classroom or personal reading, each book in the series provides firsthand experience of the challenge—and fun—of discovering, recreating, and interpreting the past.

Natalie Zemon Davis
Ernest R. May
Lynn Hunt
David W. Blight

Preface

In the 1920s, a decade marked in the United States by a volatile postwar reaction and a series of battles over political and civil rights, the trial of Sacco and Vanzetti achieved unparalleled notoriety throughout the world. For both sides in the trial, the stakes were much larger than the criminal case itself. As far as the prisoners and their supporters were concerned, the two men were on trial not for robbery and murder, but for being anarchists and immigrants. Conversely, the judge and the prosecuting attorneys saw themselves as defenders not of a local community against violent crime, but of the United States against dangerous ideas and populations. The Sacco and Vanzetti trial encapsulated many of the central issues and tensions of the era: immigration, labor activism and radicalism, the Red Scare, and anti-immigrant sentiment.

Nor are these issues relevant only to this particular period in history. Citizens of the United States, while they hail themselves as members of a "nation of immigrants," have frequently grown alarmed by the presence of immigrants they deem too numerous or too different from themselves. Intense periods of xenophobia—the fear of people or things considered foreign—have followed every major wave of immigration into the United States, from the eighteenth century to today. Likewise, many Americans have historically viewed their nation—not entirely accurately—as one in which foreign or radical ideas and ideologies are wholly unwelcome. These attitudes too have reached particular points of intensity at certain moments of American history: just after our independence in the late eighteenth century; in the 1870s and 1880s; just after both world wars; and today.

The fundamental questions raised by the Sacco and Vanzetti case about the extent to which a society can, or should, go to protect itself against people or ideologies regarded as foreign or dangerous have become all the more pressing in the United States in recent years. Since the terrorist attacks of September 11, 2001, many Americans have looked out upon a world that suddenly seems alarmingly unfamiliar and far more frightening. If Americans' perceptions of the world in which they live have changed dramatically, however, our response to our fears appears disturbingly familiar. The Sacco and Vanzetti trial exposed flaws in the American judicial system, and fault lines in American society, that tragically are still detectable. The impulse to target people whose racial identity doesn't fit neatly with the United States' image of itself, or whose belief system is deemed different, has reemerged with a vengeance fueled by anger and fear. So too has the eagerness to rid the United States of any perceived dangers, even to the point of denying individual members of target populations basic legal rights. Once again the United States runs the risk of dismantling the very ideals it professes to be defending in its pursuit of those who might threaten it. This is not to argue that the threats the United States faces are wholly unreal. Nonetheless, the Sacco and Vanzetti trial may still have something very important to teach us about what can happen when a solution is more dangerous than the problem it is meant to solve.

Despite the fact that the case is so revealing of the central tensions of that era and our own, there is no single volume suitable for classroom use. There have been numerous volumes written on the case over the years. Most, though, are brazenly partisan arguments about guilt or innocence; few have sought to explore the immigrant and radical cultures out of which the two men emerged. My goal here is to examine not only the central features of the trial and immediate reaction to it, but also the larger context within which the two men lived and died.

The introduction first explores the immigrant and radical cultures of the times, emphasizing the diversity of 1920s America, both in its populations and its range of political ideas. It analyzes the increasing reaction against immigrants, labor activists, and especially political radicals that defined the post–World War I era Red Scare. The introduction then takes up the central features of the trial itself, including the international fervor it provoked. Finally, I turn to the legacy of the trial, exploring how and why it has remained a relevant and even volatile issue to this day.

The documents are organized along the same lines as the introduction. The first documents focus on Italian immigrants' reception in the United States, on anarchist philosophy and practice, and on the postwar reaction. The bulk of the documents relate to the trial itself—drawn from trial transcripts, from affidavits and reports of involved parties, and from published and unpublished accounts or reminiscences of the wide range of people drawn into the case. The final documents deal with the legacy of the case. I have made an effort to include the voices of Sacco and Vanzetti themselves as often as possible. Several of the documents pertaining to anarchism or written by Sacco and Vanzetti appear in print, and/or in English, for the first time.

The volume concludes with a chronology of important events related to the Sacco and Vanzetti case, which will allow students to follow the unfolding trial while keeping in mind other relevant social and political developments. A series of questions for consideration follow the chronology, helping students synthesize important themes from the documents; they work well as either discussion topics or writing assignments. I have also included a brief bibliographic essay covering the scholarship on the case and an essay outlining artistic and cultural productions based on the trial.

ACKNOWLEDGMENTS

First of all . . .

This book is dedicated to Anne Louise Collins, my lifelong friend. You have filled my life with love and riotous joy from the day I met you, and for that I can never thank you enough. Here's your book, Alice.

Next, I want to thank colleagues who provided much-needed advice and support. As always, my compatriot Nunzio Pernicone of Drexel University was enormously generous intellectually; he gave the entire manuscript a very careful reading more than once and provided me with materials from his own research. Other reviewers for Bedford/ St. Martin's—Paul Avrich, Queens College, City University of New York; Paul Buhle, Brown University; Philip Cannistraro, Queens College, City University of New York; Mark Gelfand, Boston College; Jonathan Rees, Colorado State University at Pueblo; and Mary Ann Trasciatti, Hofstra University—provided invaluable critiques of the manuscript. My thanks to all of them; any errors of fact or judgment that remain are, of course, my own. Archivists at a number of libraries over the years, especially Mary Person at the Harvard Law School Library and Joel Wurl at the Immigration History Research Center in Minneapolis/St. Paul, Minnesota, helped me explore the labyrinths of the case or the broader world of Italian American immigrants. Special thanks are due to Verbena Pastor, a librarian at the Aldrich Public

Library in Barre, Vermont, who years ago helped fuel my burgeoning interest in Luigi Galleani and the *Galleanisti*. Peter Agnew, who organized the Sacco and Vanzetti conference in Boston in 2002, Peter Miller, whose film on Sacco and Vanzetti I await anxiously, and Peter Vellon, who extended a kind invitation to me to speak as part of the Calandra Institute lecture series, each provided great help and encouragement. Patricia Rossi and especially Elizabeth Harrison at Bedford / St. Martin's not only helped guide this project to completion, but made it an incredibly enjoyable undertaking. My thanks to them as well.

Finally, all of my love and thanks to Valerie, Adam (a.k.a. "dude"), and Esme (and her immortal Emily), for sustaining and inspiring me. Without you, life would be unimaginable.

Michael M. Topp

Contents

PART ONE

Introduction: The Sacco and Vanzetti Case

On April 15, 1920, just after three o'clock in the afternoon, Frederick Parmenter and Alessandro Berardelli walked down Pearl Street in South Braintree, Massachusetts, carrying two metal lockboxes containing almost $16,000 in payroll money for the workforce at the Slater and Morrill shoe factory. They never made it to the factory. On the way, two men who had been lying in wait attacked them. Parmenter, who held on to his lockbox, was shot twice; he would die several hours later. Although Berardelli dropped his box immediately, the thieves seemed particularly eager to kill him. One apparently followed the guard, finally killing him with a fourth shot as he tried to rise from the ground. The bandit then fired into the air, a signal for the getaway car to come for him and his accomplice. They leapt into the car with the two payroll boxes and drove out of town. The robbery took less than a minute.

The crime, though jarring in its brutality, was not unusual. The United States was still wracked by unrest following the collapse of the World War I boom economy. There was a widespread perception, largely the product of frayed postwar nerves, that a crime wave was sweeping the nation. The increase in crime after the war was very slight on the national level, but in certain areas of the country new levels of criminal activity did seem to demand attention. A series of robberies had taken place in the towns still dominated by textile mills and shoe factories in the northeastern United States. In November of the preceding year, a bank in the neighboring town of Randolph had been robbed. The following month, on Christmas Eve, four men tried to rob a shoe factory paymaster in nearby Bridgewater. In fact, there had been so many robberies in the Boston area that the head office of Slater and Morrill had recently altered its payroll delivery schedule in response.

But the South Braintree case was not destined for the obscurity of most common crimes. Two men, both immigrants from Italy and devout anarchists, were arrested and convicted of the murders and robbery. Nicola Sacco and Bartolomeo Vanzetti had been virtually unknown outside their community of fellow anarchists, who like them believed that all governments were inherently oppressive. Nonetheless, by the time all of their appeals were exhausted seven years later, they were household names literally across the globe. When Sacco and Vanzetti were executed just after midnight on August 23, 1927, explosive protests erupted in major cities throughout the world. In the United States, the case was profoundly divisive. Utterly convinced of their innocence and of the monstrous injustice of their deaths, John Dos Passos, a celebrated writer of the day, wearily announced what had become increasingly obvious over the course of seven years: "All right, we are two nations." The trial had indeed revealed and exacerbated a national divide, a widening gulf between those who saw a gross miscarriage of justice and those who hailed the resolute Massachusetts justice system for having defended the United States against two brutal immigrants and their even more brutal political philosophy.

How had the stakes become so large? How had an unremarkable (if brutal) crime, and two seemingly unremarkable immigrants, advocates of a philosophy that was marginalized even in the world of Left-wing politics, become the objects of international attention and passion? How had they become symbols for many Americans—for many in the world—of the flaws in the American judicial system? They were certainly not the most likely candidates for such a role. For one thing, they were, by their own admission, "unmarked, unknown," even "a failure"—two immigrants out of millions who came to the United States at the turn of the last century, and proselytizers of an uncompromising and unpopular philosophy. For another, they were hardly the only ones for whom American justice had failed. Since the end of Reconstruction in 1877, lynch law had been pervasive in the United States as whites, especially but by no means exclusively in the South, sought to keep blacks an oppressed and unfree population. Blacks, and especially black men, were murdered "legally" and extra-legally on the slightest of provocations, real or invented. It was the Sacco and Vanzetti trial, however, that captured the imaginations of people in the United States and beyond in ways that few trials before or since have.

This trial, moreover, has remained a part of American lore. From the first, it inspired not only dry, painstakingly detailed legal arguments in defense of Sacco and Vanzetti; it also inspired myriad forms of art and popular culture. The case, and especially the two men, inspired poetry, novels, plays, folksongs, movies, and more. In 2002, the seventy-fifth anniversary of their executions, an opera about the two men opened in Tampa, Florida. Even the quickest perusal of the Web revealed dozens of Web sites dedicated to maintaining the legacy of Sacco and Vanzetti. Sacco and Vanzetti captured the attention, and the artistic imagination, of so many people for a variety of reasons.

The trial of the two men brought to a head many of the tensions swirling around the postwar United States. Massive immigration for the forty years preceding their arrest had fundamentally altered the population of the United States, as well as relations between various populations in the nation. The war heightened fears about immigrants, many of whose loyalty to the United States was questionable at best. Widespread opposition to the war had existed, often emerging out of the still strong and influential Left community. When the Bolshevik Revolution erupted in Russia in November 1917, fears in the United States about immigrants, the labor movement, and the Left merged into panic. Sacco and Vanzetti embodied the threats that many Americans felt they were facing.

There were other bases for the resonance of the case at the time. Sacco's first lawyer, Fred Moore, specialized in defending radicals and radical causes (two local Boston lawyers, Jeremiah and Thomas McAnarney, represented Vanzetti). Moore very consciously—and very successfully—strived to make the case a rallying point for labor and the Left nationally and internationally. He was able to do so because the trial as it was conducted was appallingly unfair. It revealed glaring problems in the Massachusetts legal system, certain of which were acknowledged when laws were changed in its aftermath. However, nothing at the time protected Sacco or Vanzetti from the irregularities, prejudices, and outright lies at their trial.

The Sacco and Vanzetti trial continues to generate interest and even incite passions to this day for still other reasons. The most basic one is that the case remains unresolved. The trial was so unjust, and much of the evidence against the defendants so faulty, that assertions of their guilt are difficult if not impossible to sustain. Their innocence can't be firmly established either. As more and more people have researched the trial over the last seventy-five years, this issue has grown more, rather than less, complicated. Now, with all of the original participants in the trial dead, it is arguably impossible to say definitively whether either man was guilty. The difficulty, even the impossibility, of resolving the case one way or the other makes it all the more tantalizing.

Regardless of their guilt or innocence, Sacco and Vanzetti continue to stand for many as powerful symbols of unjust social relations and their consequences. Their fate represented an extreme example of what could happen to people in the United States who were members of suspect populations or who voiced unpopular opinions. If anything emerged clearly at their trial, it was this: who they were and what they believed had marked them in damaging and ultimately fatal ways. Their fate was extreme but by no means unique. They were not the first people whose racial or ethnic identity or whose belief system determined what sort of justice they would receive in court; nor, by any means, would they be the last. This is yet another reason why the Sacco and Vanzetti trial continues to be important: it demands answers to questions that not only have not disappeared but that remain pressing in the United States today.

ITALIAN AMERICA

Nicola Sacco and Bartolomeo Vanzetti entered the United States in one of the largest movements of people in history. From the beginning of the 1880s to the early 1920s, almost 26 million people came to the United States, some in search of religious and political freedom, most pursuing economic improvement. People had been migrating from Germany, Britain, and elsewhere in Northern and Western Europe in large numbers since the 1840s, and this migration continued unabated. In addition to this migrant stream, people began to arrive in enormous numbers from Southern and Eastern Europe as well—from Russia, Poland, and Austria-Hungary, for example—and in smaller numbers from the Middle East, Asia, and Mexico.

Few of the nationality groups that contributed to this massive influx matched the numbers or the visibility of Italian immigrants in the

United States. What began as a trickle of immigration from the boot-like landmass that became the Kingdom of Italy in 1861 became a flood by the turn of the twentieth century. Between 1820 and 1880, just over 80,000 Italians migrated to the United States; in the following four decades, more than 4 million made the trip, 3 million of them after the new century began. Those that remained here settled largely, though not exclusively, in the northeastern and midwestern United States, and largely, although again not entirely, in urban rather than rural areas.

Italian immigrants usually assumed a place at the bottom of the economic ladder upon their arrival. Most Italian immigrant communities had intellectuals, artists, and "ethnic brokers," small-scale entrepreneurs who functioned as mediators between their immigrant clientele and the larger community. This immigrant population, however, was defined largely by unskilled and semiskilled manual labor, by work in the nation's mines, steel mills, construction sites, and textile and garment factories. Italian men and women, especially the vast majority who came from southern regions of Italy, faced enormous economic hardship. Many young men and women had to leave school early to begin their work lives because their families needed the money. Very few attended high school in the years before World War I—fewer than 1 percent, according to one scholar. Italian Americans' financial struggles, in conjunction with their strikingly large numbers, made them particular targets of urban and labor reformers. As early as 1904, Gino Speranza, future head of the Society for the Protection of Italian Immigrants, was lamenting "How It Feels to Be a Problem." (See Document 1.)

Their engagement—or lack thereof—in the world of politics also made them targets of reformers. Italian immigrants gained a reputation as a profoundly insular population, disengaged from American political and cultural life. They did cluster together, often identifying themselves in terms of their regions, or even villages of origin, rather than in terms of nationality, but this was not unusual. The development of nationalism and a firm sense of national identity were nineteenth-century phenomena in Europe, and many immigrants from across the European continent arrived in the United States thinking of their place of origin in terms of region rather than country. What was unusual about Italian immigrants was their extremely low rate of naturalization and accompanying low levels of political participation. By 1910, only 25 percent of those eligible for citizenship had naturalized.

Not only did many Italian immigrants not naturalize, they also frequently migrated back and forth between the United States and Italy.

They were not alone; many migrants considered their stay in the United States temporary, and returned home one or more times to reestablish connections or to take advantage of the money they earned abroad. It was Italians in particular, however, who earned a reputation as "birds of passage." Although this reputation was unfair to the extent that it singled out Italian migrants, it was hardly inappropriate. In 1908, the year that Sacco—and the largest number of Italians ever— arrived in the United States, census records show that more Italians actually *left* the country than entered. These records did not take into account multiple moves back and forth between the two countries. Moreover, 1908 was the second year of a deep economic depression in the United States. Nonetheless, the statistic is telling.

Italian immigrants were considered by many a highly suspect population, all the more so in an era when the importance of racial and ethnic identity was being reemphasized in ways that challenged the presence of Southern and Eastern European immigrants generally. Racial identity in the United States has of course been critically important from the very first. For African Americans and for Indians, racial identity underlay issues of freedom or slavery, and even life or death. The 1790 Naturalization Act, in effect until the 1950s, defined membership in the American polity in distinctly racial terms, permitting only whites to become naturalized citizens. During the peak years of immigration in the late nineteenth and early twentieth centuries, sociologists and other scholars defined race in biological terms—in terms of immutable characteristics that determined appearance, intelligence, and general ability to cope and succeed in society. These biologically rooted definitions were not new, and other white immigrants such as the Irish had faced racial challenges as early as the 1820s and 1830s. What was new in these years was that a much broader proportion of the population in the United States was now defined in racial terms in far more systematic and pervasive ways. Although African Americans, American Indians, and Asian Americans continued to face the onus of racial difference as nonwhites, the Irish had been able to lay claim to whiteness and racial respectability in the decades since their arrival. Now, though, Southern and Eastern Europeans also began to face challenges in racial terms. New racial hierarchies, based on supposedly scientific studies, were postulated in which these immigrants were commonly defined as white—historically a necessity for full access to rights and privileges in the United States—but the quality of their whiteness came under intense scrutiny. Scholars such as sociologist Edward Ross split Europeans into "higher quality" Northern and

Western Europeans and "lower quality" Southern and Eastern Europeans, and certain of them warned against "interbreeding" between such distinct European populations as the English and the Italians. (See Document 2.) They warned, further, that the disproportional increases in Southern and Eastern European numbers, through migration and high birth rates, would destroy the moral and social fiber of the United States. Opponents of immigration, drawing on these scholars' arguments, ultimately succeeded in passing immigration restriction acts in 1921 and 1924 that all but ended Southern and Eastern Europeans' immigration into the United States.

Even before these acts passed, these new racially based distinctions were applied forcefully to Italian immigrants. Social scientists who created racial hierarchies routinely ranked Southern Italians in particular just above African Americans and below all other European populations. They even had their invaluable identity as white challenged at times, as when they were referred to as "white niggers" in the South. In another, more pointed example, in a court case in Alabama in 1922, a Sicilian woman charged with miscegenation (sexual relations across racial lines) was acquitted. Although she had been involved with a black man, the court ruled that she was "inconclusively white." Italian immigrants' whiteness was rarely challenged in these ways, but their presence in the United States, and their potential impact on American society, were routinely attacked.[1]

THE ANARCHIST WORLD OF SACCO AND VANZETTI

If this was the situation that Italian immigrants in general faced in the United States, it was all the more true for those immigrants who identified themselves as political radicals. Although there were not enormous numbers of radical Italian immigrants—they probably numbered in the tens of thousands—they spanned a broad range of political and ideological choices. There were socialists who argued that the revolution could be fought, and won, through electoral politics; syndicalists who insisted that militant unions would be the vehicles of social revolution; and antistatist anarchists like Sacco and Vanzetti. Each of these groups of radicals sought, through different means, to overthrow the capitalist system and the oppressive governments that sustained this economic system. While socialists wanted to establish, if temporarily, another form of government run by and for the working class, syndicalists imagined authority organized along industrial lines (that is, industry by industry) and anarchists argued the necessity of eliminating all forms of government.

Political radicals among Italian immigrants tended to affiliate themselves with the American organizations that most closely matched their own ideological inclinations. Although the conservative American Federation of Labor (AFL), which concentrated on organizing skilled native-born white workers, asserted itself as the principal voice of the working class in the United States, it was by no means the only one. Nor was it the best one for Italians and other immigrants. Many AFL leaders lobbied constantly for immigration restriction, both out of fear of job competition and because they regarded Italians and other Southern and Eastern European immigrants as inferiors. The Socialist Party of America, founded in 1901, sought mainly to foment revolution through the ballot box. Although its success was limited, it did manage to elect over 1,200 party members to local, regional, and national offices in 1912 alone. Its perennial presidential candidate, Eugene Debs, won 6 percent of the vote that year. Italian immigrant socialists formed a small organization affiliated with the Socialist party, which was very active in organizing workers in midwestern and northeastern garment and textile factories. The Industrial Workers of the World (IWW), founded in 1905, strived to organize the workers ignored by the AFL, including unskilled and semiskilled immigrants, blacks, and women in general. Its egalitarianism and its overtly revolutionary philosophy appealed to Italian immigrant syndicalists who, like the IWW, wanted to fight for revolution through radical labor unions rather than by voting. These immigrant syndicalists created a national uproar when they worked with the IWW to wage two high-profile strikes among immigrant textile workers in Lawrence, Massachusetts, in 1912 and among silk workers in Paterson, New Jersey, the following year. The IWW itself captured the imagination of a wide range of people in the United States, exciting downtrodden and previously ignored workers and frightening mainstream Americans with its confrontational rhetoric and tactics.

Among the most ardent and, to many, the most frightening, radicals in the United States were Italian immigrant anarchists, who were few in number but absolutely devoted to their cause. Sacco and Vanzetti were followers of anarchist Luigi Galleani, members of the small but very determined group of *Galleanisti* in the United States and Italy. *Galleanisti* sought a society free of oppression, of poverty, and of want, and they were dedicated to fighting for it—through violent means if necessary.

Any understanding of Sacco and Vanzetti's anarchism must begin with Galleani himself. Just as immigrants brought cultural traits and institutions such as music, food, and religion with them to the United States, some also brought ideologies and social philosophies. Neither Sacco nor Vanzetti arrived in the United States as anarchists, but certainly Galleani did. He had come of age politically in a critical moment in the history of the Left in Italy. Just as Galleani began to participate actively in political and labor activism, the battle for control of the Italian Left was coming to a head. Electorally minded socialists clashed with anarchists, who wanted to defeat both capitalism and the state. Support for anarchism enjoyed unusual strength in Italy, but the founding of the Italian Socialist party in 1892 marked a decisive victory for advocates of revolution through the political process.

The anarchist movement in Italy did not disappear, but 1892 marked the culmination of a dramatic transformation. Faced throughout the 1880s with increasing persecution by the Italian government and having lost its battle with the socialists, the movement went underground. It became far more secretive, insular, and even paranoid. In the 1870s, leading anarchists in Italy had been centrally involved in the most dramatic uprisings of the decade. By the end of the 1890s, a new generation of anarchist leaders were advocating dramatic singular acts of violence. This strategy, "propaganda of the deed," built on the assumption that the poor and the working class were ready to revolt and just needed a final push. During the final decade of the nineteenth century and the first decade of the twentieth, several heads of state in Europe were assassinated—most by Italian anarchists. (American President William McKinley was also assassinated by an anarchist, in 1901, although his assassin was Polish rather than Italian.)

Luigi Galleani was one of the leading advocates of individual acts of violence in Italy and, eventually, in the United States. Arrested for his radical activities, in the mid-1890s he was sentenced to *domicilio coatto,* a form of internal exile, and sent to an island off the coast of Italy. When he escaped five years later and fled to the United States, he brought his dreams for another world and his strategies for achieving them with him. He settled first in Paterson, New Jersey, in 1901.

Paterson had a long history of anarchist activity. It was home to one of the leading anarchist journals in the United States, *La questione sociale,* which Galleani would edit briefly. It had also been the home of Gaetano Bresci, another Italian anarchist, until mid-1900. When Bresci left early that summer with all of the newspaper's funds, his fellow anarchists were furious. In July, however, his plans, unknown even to his associates, were realized when he assassinated King Umberto II of Italy.

Galleani wrote admiringly of the deed in its aftermath, and he threw himself into strike activity in Paterson. Wounded in the face during a strike in 1902, he fled an arrest warrant into Canada, and then re-crossed the border surreptitiously and resettled in an enclave of Italian anarchists in Barre, Vermont. There, in 1903, he began publication of *Cronaca sovversiva,* which became arguably the leading Italian anar-chist journal in the world. Although its circulation never exceeded a few thousand, its actual reach was far broader; copies were routinely passed hand to hand and reached every continent. Galleani published the newspaper as a weekly in Barre, and then in Lynn, Massachusetts, until he was deported in 1919.

Galleani preached both a glowing vision of the better world that was possible and a deep and relentless hatred of all institutions of oppression. (See Document 3.) The list of these institutions was exten-sive. Galleani even fought against labor unions, especially against radi-cal labor unions like the IWW, which were presumably fighting the same oppression and injustice that Galleani opposed. He argued that all institutions began to restrict the freedoms of their members sooner or later, and that radical labor unions, in their efforts to dodge this inevitability, were also guilty of hypocrisy. He argued that the only route to a better world was the wholesale destruction of the existing one. To that end, he counseled revolutionary expropriation (theft in the name of revolution), the assassination of heads of state, and the use of dynamite against those who stood in the way of progress. He translated French anarchist Clement Duval's tract on property and theft, which argued that thefts committed to advance the revolution could be justified. This advocacy of violence was not merely rhetori-cal. The pamphlet Galleani circulated titled *La salute è in voi! (The Health Is in You!),* which included errors that he had to correct later in *Cronaca,* was a manual on assembling and detonating bombs. (See Document 4.) When he was arrested and scheduled for deportation because of his earlier outspoken opposition to World War I, Galleani called on his followers to seek revenge. (See Document 5.) Consider-able evidence exists that certain *Galleanisti* heeded his call. In late April 1919, a series of letter bombs were mailed to leading capitalists and government officials. Virtually all of the bombs were discovered prior to detonation—many lacked sufficient postage—but a month later another set of bombs were hand-delivered, again to prominent symbols of American capitalism and reaction. A number of these exploded and caused considerable damage.

While the means Galleani advocated were harsh and disturbing, his vision of the future was, by many accounts, awe-inspiring. An enormously gifted speaker, Galleani evoked praise from a wide range of people; one observer commented, "I have never heard an orator more powerful than Luigi Galleani. . . . He has a marvelous facility with words, accompanied by the faculty . . . of precision and clarity of ideas."[2] One story of his power of persuasion, perhaps apocryphal, is that he managed to convert the wife of his prison warden to his revolutionary ideas while in *domicilio coatto,* and brought her with him to the United States. During his deportation hearings in the United States, even as he spoke remarkably openly about the need for violent opposition to oppression, federal agents were deeply impressed by how deftly and artfully he defended his philosophy. He sought a world defined by freedom and a way for men and women to live their lives with dignity as they worked for that new world. It was instantly understandable to the federal agents who interrogated Galleani why, despite the extremity of what he advocated, he had attracted and maintained a small but deeply loyal following.

Among those followers were Nicola Sacco and Bartolomeo Vanzetti, both of whom had migrated to the United States in 1908, Sacco from a small town in southern Italy, Vanzetti from a town in the north. Each man had been raised in relative comfort in Italy. Sacco (whose name at birth was Ferdinando, and who took the name Nicola to honor an adored older brother who had died) was one of seventeen children; his father owned a vineyard and an olive-oil business. Vanzetti's father, after living briefly in California, returned to Italy where he owned a prosperous farm. Sacco was mechanically minded, vastly preferring working with machines to farming. Vanzetti loved reading, and he might well have become a teacher or even a priest—he was devoutly religious in his youth—had his father not compelled him to learn a trade.

Neither of these men came to the United States to foment revolution. Sacco decided to migrate with an older brother out of a sense of adventure, to seek a "free country," as he put it later. Vanzetti, under his father's strong hand, worked for a few miserable years as an apprentice in a pastry shop in a nearby town in Italy before returning to his family home. His migration to the United States was spurred by the death of his mother when he was nineteen years old, an event that left him devastated and badly in need of a new beginning.

Each man embraced anarchism only after his arrival in the United States. Sacco, eager to find a place for himself in a country he saw as full of opportunities, fared well personally. He was struck, however, by how cruel working conditions could be for his fellow immigrants and for other workers. He felt for, in his words, the "prosecuted and the victim," for "all the legion of the human oppressed," and he began acting on his beliefs.[3] In 1912, he collected money to help feed workers involved in the textile strike in Lawrence, Massachusetts, and for the defense fund to help free two strike leaders who had been unjustly arrested. By 1913, Sacco had joined an anarchist study circle in Milford, Massachusetts, and had begun reading Galleani's *Cronaca sovversiva*.

Vanzetti's turn to anarchism was informed not only by the injustices he witnessed in the United States but also by his own bitter personal experience. He had trouble finding work and endured a period of homelessness upon his arrival. His expectations about the United States dashed, he grew disillusioned. As he wrote later in his autobiography, "Here I saw all the brutalities of life, all the injustice, the corruption in which humanity struggles tragically."[4] Like Sacco—though the two had not met by this point—he lent his support to the 1912 textile strike in Lawrence, in Vanzetti's case as a new member of an anarchist circle in Worcester, Massachusetts. In early 1916, Vanzetti threw his energies into a strike at the Plymouth, Massachusetts, Cordage company where he had previously worked. The company, which manufactured rope, was the largest employer of immigrants in the town. Although Vanzetti felt the dollar raise the strikers eventually accepted constituted a defeat, his involvement drew him closer to the *Galleanisti*. He sent regular reports on the strike to the *Cronaca sovversiva,* and by its end had met Galleani personally. (See Document 6.)

Sacco and Vanzetti defied stereotypical perceptions of both immigrants and radicals. Where Italian immigrants were presumed by their critics to be stumbling clods, Sacco and especially Vanzetti were remarkably thoughtful and articulate. On the surface, Vanzetti embodied much of what was most criticized in Italian immigrants; although trained as a chef, he worked for the most part in unskilled positions, finally buying an old cart and peddling fish so that he could set his own hours and work outdoors. He also was part of a considerable population of working-class autodidacts; he read voluminously when he could, striving to educate himself about philosophy, politics, and culture. Sacco, although not the reader that Vanzetti was, had made the investment in time and money to learn a skill. He took a course from a craftsman to learn how to finish shoes, losing the better part of a year's wages to do so. As a result of his training and his dedication to his work, he was at the time of his arrest a highly skilled and capable worker.

Unlike the frightening images of anarchists that dominated popular perceptions at that time (and still do today), Sacco and Vanzetti in many ways led respectable lives. Sacco was a dedicated family man; by 1920, he was by all accounts very happily married, with a son and another child on the way. He had over $1,500 saved; his employer trusted him with the keys to the shop. His letters from prison revealed an extremely sensitive and caring man. (See Document 7.) Vanzetti, though he led a much less structured life, was adored by his friends and neighbors. Like Sacco, he tended a garden in the backyard of the home he rented, and he would grow extra vegetables to distribute to those who wanted or needed them. He became a mentor for his land-lord's son, who still remembered decades later Vanzetti's admonish-ments to treat other people with respect and to follow his dream of a musical career. Friends and neighbors also recalled both men's gentle natures and their inability to harm other living creatures. Sacco, one acquaintance noted, had to have his wife kill the chickens that they would eat for dinner. Vanzetti, a friend recounted, once spent hours a day over the course of several weeks nursing an injured cat back to health.

These were the images of Sacco and Vanzetti presented to the pub-lic during their trial by their legion of followers, who included not only Leftists but also liberal intellectuals and artists and even conservative members of high society. They were, according to their supporters, "philosophical anarchists," still firmly connected to the land, pacifistic in thought and deed. They were the humble shoemaker and fish ped-dler, who, in the words of John Dos Passos, kept alive in their memo-ries "a faint trace of the vanished brightness of . . . the perfect city, where the strong did not oppress the weak, where every man lived by his own work at peace with his neighbors . . . where man could reach his full height free from the old snarling obsessions of god and master."[5]

The trouble is, Dos Passos was wrong—if not about the nature of the two men, then about the kind of anarchism they advocated. Sacco and Vanzetti embodied both sides of Galleani, the man to whose cause they devoted themselves. They sought a more perfect world and tried to implement it, to the extent they could, in the communities in which they lived. Thus, Sacco and Vanzetti each grew extra produce. Sacco and his wife, Rosina, both participated actively in anarchist entertainment and activities, both acting, for example, in anarchist stage productions performed regularly in their area. Vanzetti's gentle nature, so faithfully resurrected by his friends and neighbors, and so clearly captured in his letters from prison, was no fabrication. (See Document 8.) He took seriously the responsibility to treat people with the respect that they deserved.

But each man also took seriously the responsibility to fight for "The Idea," as they referred to their anarchist beliefs, and each, apparently, took seriously Galleani's calls for vengeance when he was deported. Both Sacco and Vanzetti had gone to Mexico during World War I to avoid the possibility of serving in the armed forces or of deportation for refusing to serve. This is where they got to know each other, although they had lived in neighboring Massachusetts towns for some time. In Mexico, a number of *Galleanisti* united and attempted to live in a communal arrangement, seeking out what work each could find and pooling their resources. They also apparently together dedicated themselves to increasing the level and intensity of their revolutionary activity. Evidence points to the distinct possibility that the people most responsible for the two sets of bombs delivered in 1919 were among those who had been in Mexico together. At least one of the men, Carlo Valdinocci, was positively identified after he was blown to pieces trying to deliver a bomb to the doorstep of the attorney general of the United States.

This, then, was the anarchist world within which Sacco and Vanzetti moved before their arrest. It was a world that could be dignified, gentle, and even nurturing on the one hand, and appallingly dogmatic and violent on the other. It was a world in which the intensity of love these anarchists felt for their fellow human beings was matched, and even exceeded, by the depth of the hatred they felt toward institutions and individuals they believed were responsible for oppressing people.

RADICAL POSSIBILITY AND THE RED SCARE

The year that Sacco and Vanzetti were arrested marked the tail end of a period of world agitation and revolution that had been so volatile—that had been considered so dangerous by advocates of existing systems of capitalism and monarchy—that it was virtually impossible to tell in 1920 that it was drawing to a close. Hoping to build on the success of the Bolshevik Revolution in Russia in late 1917, Vladimir Lenin and Leon Trotsky called on socialists worldwide to join their efforts to overthrow existing states. Socialists—and now, following the lead of the Bolsheviks, Communists—especially throughout Europe seemed poised to do so. In Germany and France, socialist victory seemed to some an inevitability. In Italy, most on the Left began to contemplate when, rather than if, they would assume control. One of the reasons that Sacco, Vanzetti, and the other *Galleanisti* lingered in Mexico for as long as they did was because they were expecting to return to Italy after the revolution there.

Many on the Left in the United States were filled with the same sense of expectation. The Socialist party grew in strength during World War I despite the persecution it faced, and after the war ended labor erupted. In 1919, four million people went out on strike, the largest proportion of the workforce to strike in a single year in American history. Many people were convinced that in the United States revolution was coming. Miners and steelworkers, each essential to maintaining heavy industry in the United States, went on strike by the hundreds of thousands, and a strike of shipyard workers in the then notoriously radical city of Seattle spread into a general strike. In Boston, just miles from where Sacco and Vanzetti would be tried, the police went on strike. They had legitimate complaints, but the specter of a city's police force refusing to work convinced many Americans that the social order was collapsing.

The fears that these strikes provoked and the general tumult in the United States after the war escalated concerns about immigrants and radicals that had already reached a point of frenzy during the war. Immigrants, already perceived as inferiors and as drags on wages, were now seen as potentially dangerous to U.S. security. Many immigrant communities faced considerable turmoil over how best to respond to the war, especially in Leftist circles. This mattered little; conservative and even many moderate Americans claimed to see threats to their well-being from virtually every quarter. The federal government passed the Espionage and Sedition acts in 1917 and 1918, respectively, to eliminate potential disloyalty or radicalism. Anyone speaking out against the war could be imprisoned for ten years or more in federal prison. Authorities used these laws quickly and broadly; hundreds of antiwar and radical immigrants were arrested and deported. Members of the Socialist party, including Eugene Debs, were targeted. The IWW never recovered from the sweeping arrests that imprisoned not only its leaders and most prominent and active members but even many people who had only remote or past affiliations with the organization.

The Red Scare, the response to a pervasive fear of an impending social revolution that defined the postwar years, sustained the momentum of the wartime pursuance of immigrants and radicals. The suppression of free speech continued unabated. Hundreds of Left-wing political prisoners continued to languish in jail cells for having spoken out against the war. This was not just a continuation of wartime suppression, however, it was also a response to the perceived threats posed by the 1919 strike wave, the presence of an enormous number of immigrants, and the participation—often exaggerated—of radicals in labor and political activism. Federal efforts to combat radicals were led by A. Mitchell Palmer, who President Woodrow Wilson appointed attorney general in March 1919. Palmer and the federal government focused especially on two particular targets. One was the Union of Russian Workers (URW), which was immediately associated with the threat posed by the Bolshevik Revolution.

The other target was the *Galleanisti* who, federal agents were increasingly convinced, were the ones responsible for the bombs that had been sent and delivered to prominent capitalists and lawmakers throughout the United States in May and June of 1919. Galleani had drawn considerable attention to himself during World War I with his fierce condemnations of the conflict. The *Cronaca sovversiva* lost its second-class mailing privileges and, during its last months, the paper was hand-delivered by loyal *Galleanisti* who took the newspaper by motorcycle to subscribers throughout the northeast. Galleani was arrested and scheduled for deportation soon after the war ended, and his call for revenge may well have inspired the 1919 mailing of the bombs. These explosives were particularly jarring to Attorney General Palmer—his own house had been a target and his life may well have been spared because the bomber slipped as he went up the steps to the house. Those suspected of being involved in these bombings were pursued relentlessly. Anyone affiliated with the *Cronaca sovversiva* or with Galleani became the object of federal attention, especially after federal agents discovered the newspaper's subscription list hidden in a barn outside Boston.

Palmer also cast his net far wider. In June 1919, he appointed William Flynn, former head of the secret service, as head of the Justice Department's Bureau of Investigation. Soon after, Palmer established an antiradical branch of the bureau, the General Intelligence

Division, and placed a young J. Edgar Hoover at its head. Hoover, who began his career in the Library of Congress, started assembling data on radicals and their organizations. Within a remarkably short time, Hoover and his staff had 200,000 cards containing detailed information on radical institutions and publications and 60,000 cards on radicals he deemed dangerous. He set about infiltrating and disrupting a number of the organizations he was investigating.

Hoover's efforts, as well as those of Flynn and Palmer, culminated in early January 1920 in the infamous Palmer Raids. On January 2 and 6, about ten thousand suspected radicals were arrested in raids in thirty-three cities across twenty-three states. The arrests were marked by the absence of due process and by their brutality. In New England, where Sacco and Vanzetti lived, eight hundred people were arrested. As Louis Post, the assistant secretary of labor, documented, half of them were marched in chains through Boston city streets on their way to Deer Island in Boston Harbor. On the island, in the bitter winter cold, they faced a lack of heat, poor sanitation, and strictly enforced isolation from the outside world. One prisoner leapt five stories to his death, one lost his mind, and two died of pneumonia. (See Document 9.)

The Red Scare as a national phenomenon began to wane soon after Sacco and Vanzetti's arrest in May 1920. Palmer's excesses became an embarrassment to all but the most vehement antiradicals. Wholesale violations of civil rights and individual liberties had characterized his methods, and the vigilante violence carried out against even suspected radicals seemed, by the early 1920s, more dangerous than the problem the government had sought to solve. This was especially true as the possibility of social revolution in the United States, which had created such dread among some Americans, began to seem so unlikely that it soon became difficult to imagine it had ever existed.

THE ARREST AND THE TRIAL

The waning possibility of a revolution did not help Sacco or Vanzetti at the time of their arrests. In May 1920, when they were pulled off a trolley car in Brockton, Massachusetts, the fact that they were immigrant radicals was a matter of consequence both to them and to the people investigating the crime for which they were charged.

No direct evidence tied Sacco and Vanzetti personally to the bombings Galleani had apparently called for. Some circumstantial evidence suggested that they were in the same town at the same time as some of the anarchists who were planning the bombings; nothing was ever proven. Nor were they ever accused of participating in the bombings. They were surely aware of the bombings and that they could be implicated in the attacks. Copies of a leaflet titled "Plain Words" were found near the sites of the bombings, and federal agents worked diligently to discover where they had been printed. When Sacco and Vanzetti's comrades Roberto Elia and Andrea Salsedo were arrested in connection with the production of the pamphlets, the *Galleanisti* knew immediately that it meant trouble. Elia and Salsedo were held incommunicado in a federal building in New York for several weeks, and the *Galleanisti*'s fears deepened. Those living in the Boston area decided to send Vanzetti—who had the least structured work life—to investigate. He returned with the firm admonition from fellow radical Carlo Tresca to remove all incriminating materials from their homes as soon as possible. Days later, Salsedo fell to his death from the building in which he was being held. His comrades were sure he had been killed; in fact, he had leapt to his death, overcome by remorse for having informed on his fellow *Galleanisti* about the bombings. News of Salsedo's death reached Sacco and Vanzetti just the day before they were arrested.

The Arrest and "Consciousness of Guilt"

Sacco and Vanzetti were certain when they were detained that it was connected to federal agents' ongoing pursuit of *Galleanisti*. Michael Stewart, the Bridgewater Police Chief who had launched the trap that sprung, accidentally, on the two anarchists, was little more than a local sheriff, but he had been deeply involved in the effort to round up radicals in his area. Stewart had been cooperating with federal authorities' deportation efforts and had been investigating one of Sacco and Vanzetti's friends, Ferruccio Coacci. Coacci had been assigned for deportation but had pled his wife's illness to postpone his departure. When Stewart arrived at his home, however, he thought that Coacci's wife looked fine (in fact, she had a long-standing illness). Moreover, Coacci now seemed to be in a great hurry to leave the United States. In the aftermath of the South Braintree, Massachusetts, robbery and murders, Stewart's suspicions were raised. Surmising that Coacci and a housemate, Mario Buda (also known as Mike Boda), might have been involved in the robbery and having found out that Buda had a car being repaired at a local shop, Stewart asked the owner of the repair shop to inform him when the anarchist tried to pick up his automobile. The night Buda returned for his car with three fellow *Galleanisti,* the repair-shop owner did as he was asked. The men Stewart's police officers caught, though, did not include Buda; only Sacco and Vanzetti were arrested that night.

The two men did look suspicious when they were arrested. Each was armed, Sacco with a loaded .32 Colt automatic and over twenty loose shells, and Vanzetti with a .38 Harrington & Richardson and three or four shotgun shells in his pockets. Sacco also had a draft of an announcement of an anarchist meeting, written by Vanzetti, in his pocket. When questioned by the police and by local district attorney Frederick Katzmann (who would eventually try their case) the next day, they answered warily and often dishonestly. This became a critical issue during the trial. Their lies at the time of their arrest, the prosecution and the trial judge argued, constituted "consciousness of guilt"—evidence that they had committed the crime in South Braintree. (See Document 10.)

Sacco and Vanzetti were alarmed by their arrests, but there was—and still is—enormous disagreement about why. The prosecution would argue that their lies hid their involvement in the robbery. Their defense attorneys pointed out that few of the questions asked on either the first or the second day had to do with the crime for which they would eventually be executed. Many, if not most, of the questions concerned their political beliefs and affiliations. Vanzetti later claimed in a pamphlet written in prison that they had been preparing to hide anarchist literature when they were arrested. (See Document 11.) If they were attempting to hide something much more incriminating— they may have been trying to move a stash of dynamite to a safe place that night—that would have made them even more cautious about disclosing anything to the police.[6]

Bridgewater and the Plymouth Trial

From the start, prosecutors thought their case against Sacco was much stronger than the one against Vanzetti. For one thing, Vanzetti's handlebar mustache was very distinctive, and the prosecution had difficulty finding witnesses to put him at the scene at the time of the crime. Sacco had few distinguishing characteristics—and, as we will see, could possibly have been confused with someone else by witnesses—and the prosecution had fewer problems putting together a case against him.

Because the case against Vanzetti for the South Braintree robbery was so weak, prosecutors arranged to try him first for a failed robbery in Bridgewater on December 24, 1919. Police officer Michael Stewart was convinced that both crimes had been committed by the same gang—the *Galleanisti* he had been tracking. It was not a very sound theory. The police had had Italian authorities intercept Coacci and search his possessions when he arrived in Italy. Although they found a few samples of leather he had taken from his last place of employment, they found no payroll money. Police and prosecutors had tried, unsuccessfully, to connect other *Galleanisti*—Buda and Riccardo Orciani—to either crime. They could not even connect Sacco to the Bridgewater attempted robbery; he had a time card from his factory for that day.

Nonetheless, Vanzetti was convicted for attempted robbery at Bridgewater in a trial in the summer of 1920 that left open many more questions than it resolved. A number of eyewitnesses identified Vanzetti as one of the men they saw attempting to rob the payroll of a local shoe company. Unbeknownst to the defense, these witnesses' accounts had changed considerably since their questioning by Pinkerton agents just after the crime. These infamous private detectives were usually hired to spy on and harass unionizers, but in this instance they had been hired by the company that insured the payroll simply to collect information about the crime. Despite their certainty in identifying Vanzetti at the trial, none of the witnesses had given the Pinkertons descriptions of the robbers that included an Italian immigrant with a big handlebar mustache. At that time, the prosecution had no requirement for full disclosure of evidence to the defense. Attorneys for Sacco and Vanzetti finally learned of the existence of the Pinkerton reports in June 1927, just months before their executions.

One thing that emerged clearly in the courtroom was contempt for Italian immigrants and Italian culture. One prosecution witness, a fourteen-year-old newspaper boy, actually identified Vanzetti by arguing "the way he ran I could tell he was a foreigner." (See Document 12.) On Christmas Eve Italians traditionally prepared eels for dinner. Because of this, Vanzetti argued, he had had a brisk trade in fish sales the day of the attempted robbery. His attorneys presented over a dozen witnesses who testified that they bought eels from Vanzetti or saw him selling them that day; the young boy with whose family Vanzetti had lived, Beltrando Brini, testified that he helped the accused man sell eels all that day. Virtually all of the witnesses testified in Italian, assisted by a translator, and the prosecutor made much of their inability to communicate in English. To make Brini's account look like a fabrication, the prosecutor also got Beltrando Brini to admit that he had rehearsed his testimony. (See Document 13.) Years later, Brini still bristled at the way his account had been dismissed. (See Document 14.) In the end the prosecutor as well as the jury dismissed the testimony of the Italian immigrant witnesses. As one historian noted, "If eating eels on Christmas Eve had been a Puritan tradition, Vanzetti would have been acquitted."[7]

There was also indisputable evidence that the jury tampered with evidence and even brought into the jury room evidence that had not been considered in open court. One jury member brought a shotgun shell with him into the deliberation room to compare with shells that had been introduced as evidence. Jury members also pried open one of the shotgun shells that the prosecution argued had been found on Vanzetti, to see what type of shot was in it. To sidestep these clear grounds for a new trial, the judge, as bent as Chief Stewart on containing the threat of radicalism, sentenced Vanzetti for attempted robbery rather than attempted murder because the lesser charge did not rely on the tampered evidence. The judge in the case was Webster Thayer, who, much to the chagrin of the defendants, would reappear as presiding judge over Sacco and Vanzetti's trial for the South Braintree robbery and murders. In the Bridgewater case, Thayer sentenced Vanzetti to twelve to fifteen years, an unusually lengthy prison term for attempted robbery, especially for a man who had never before been arrested for a crime.

Central Issues of the Sacco and Vanzetti Trial

Not only was this an unusually heavy sentence, it also accomplished what prosecutors had hoped, paving the way for the trial of Sacco and Vanzetti for robbery and murder at South Braintree. Now, the flimsier evidence against Vanzetti for these crimes notwithstanding, he came to this trial as a convicted felon. Frederick Katzmann, the same prosecutor that had tried Vanzetti for the Bridgewater crime, prosecuted the South Braintree crimes. Even more jarring, Judge Webster Thayer, in a very unusual step, actually requested the opportunity to preside over the Sacco and Vanzetti trial. His request was granted, and the trial began on May 31, 1921.

The mound of evidence the prosecution and the defense presented at the trial is most easily digested if it is broken down into three categories. Each side presented eyewitness testimony, and the prosecution also introduced material evidence and ballistics reports. Each type of evidence as presented at the trial was suspect in its own way.

The eyewitnesses were a source of even greater controversy in this trial than in Vanzetti's first one. Both Sacco and Vanzetti put together credible alibis based on eyewitness testimony. Unlike in the Bridgewater case, Sacco could be charged with this crime because he had not been at work that day. He told the police, and later the jury, that he had gone to Boston to get passports for himself and his family. They had been planning to return to Italy, which was one reason he had been saving money. His father had just died, and that hastened his efforts to make the trip. No doubt the heated pursuit of the *Galleanisti* by the Bureau of Investigation hurried his efforts as well. The defense presented a number of witnesses who put Sacco in Boston that day: early in the morning on the street, in a restaurant twice that day, settling a grocery bill. Even the man at the Italian Consulate who told him his photo was not the right size testified that he remembered seeing Sacco that day. Unfortunately, given the prevailing prejudices of the day, virtually all of the witnesses again were Italian immigrants or nationals. Vanzetti, because he had no regular work schedule, faced a greater challenge differentiating this day from any other. He, too, though, was able to contact several people who had seen him that day, including one man who had had a lengthy conversation with him as he fixed his boat.

Only three witnesses put Vanzetti anywhere near the area where the crime was committed. One man testified that he saw Vanzetti on a train heading into South Braintree the morning of the crime; records showed no ticket was sold that could have put him on the train at that time. Another witness claimed that Vanzetti shouted at him in "unmistakable clear English" as he drove by him after the crime had been committed; the defendant spoke English with a very heavy Italian accent. Only one witness put Vanzetti at the crime scene at the time of the robbery and murders. He said that he saw Vanzetti driving the getaway car; Vanzetti had no driver's license and had never learned how to drive.

The prosecution presented witnesses who put Sacco at the crime scene, but even the testimony of the strongest of them was easily challenged. One woman, Mary Splaine, described Sacco in incredibly precise terms, down to the length of his hairline and the size of his left hand. The trouble was, the man she saw was 60 to 80 feet away, in a moving car that was in her sightline for only about 30 feet. This gave Splaine from 1½ to 3 seconds to observe him. (See Document 15.) Another witness, Louis Pelser, provided both the license-plate number of the getaway car and an exacting description of Sacco. Two of his coworkers testified that Pelser dove under a bench when the shooting started; another testified that Pelser told him that he had not seen anything. Yet another witness, Carlos Goodridge, identified Sacco as the man who pointed a gun at him as he drove by; four other witnesses testified that Goodridge told them he had ducked inside a door and could not identify anyone. Lola Andrews told the court that she had spoken to Sacco as he lay under a car repairing it in South Braintree before the crime occurred. A friend with her at the time testified that Andrews had actually spoken to the man standing next to the car.

These witnesses were alarmingly unreliable in other ways as well. Splaine had first accused a workmate of the crime; her boss told an investigator not to believe a thing she said. Pelser told prosecutors and defense attorneys two different stories before telling yet a third at the trial. Carlos Goodridge was actually Erastus Corning, a man with a lengthy criminal past who at one point committed perjury for a marriage license so that he could commit bigamy. Even more disturbing, Lola Andrews may have been responding to pressure to convict the anarchists. She told a friend that a government agent was "bothering the life out of her" to make her identify Sacco. Once again, certain witnesses—Splaine and the man who claimed he saw Vanzetti driving the getaway car—gave descriptions of the men that varied considerably between the time they spoke to Pinkerton detectives and when they took the witness stand. (See Document 16.)

It was not only the prosecutors who were guilty of pressuring witnesses. Fred Moore, Sacco's first lawyer, had little faith in the justice system and no qualms about doing whatever he could to win the case. He tried to blackmail Andrews, having her estranged son implore her to change her testimony. He tried to have Goodridge indicted for a crime committed under his real name when he refused to cooperate with the defense. He got Pelser drunk and had him sign a deposition renouncing his identification; once Pelser sobered up, he renounced his renunciation. Clearly, both sides committed misdeeds.

The larger issue, especially with two lives at stake, was that the eyewitness testimony simply did not hold up. Such testimony is always shaky, especially across cultural lines, when the witness and the defendant are members of different ethnic or racial groups. In this case, thirty-four witnesses who saw one or more men connected with the crime did not identify either Sacco or Vanzetti. Of the eleven who did—four identified Vanzetti and seven identified Sacco—their testimony was faulty, or manipulated, or both.

The material evidence—the specific concrete objects that could tie either man to the scene of the crime—was largely questionable as well. The strongest piece of material evidence, aside from ballistics, that connected Sacco to the robbery was a cap found at the scene. Prosecutor Katzmann argued that it belonged to the indicted anarchist. Sacco denied the cap was his—even trying it on in the courtroom to prove that it was too small, in a dramatic gesture captured by courtroom artists who sketched his effort. Katzmann insisted that the hole in the back of the cap came from a hook at Sacco's workplace. This argument fell apart, however. The police officer who had had it in his possession admitted he had torn the lining in an effort to find out who owned the cap. Again, as in the Bridgewater case, evidence that had been tampered with affected the outcome of the trial. Although this never came up in the courtroom, newspapers reporting on the crime made it clear that the cap had been found two days after the robbery and shootings. No one in the aftermath of the trial would try to argue that the cap could have stayed untouched for two whole days at a crime scene.

The strongest piece of material evidence presented at the trial tying Vanzetti to the crime scene was the gun he had with him when he was arrested. Again, this evidence was shrouded in controversy. The prosecution argued that Vanzetti, or one of his accomplices, had taken the gun from the guard Berardelli as he lay dying. This was a tough argument to make. Berardelli's wife testified that the two of them had taken his gun to be repaired a few weeks before the robbery. She had no memory of either of them having picked the gun up. The records of the gun repair shop were confusing. The prosecutors could not produce a record of the gun having been picked up, but they argued that because it was not there and no record existed showing it had been sold, it must have been picked up. In other words, Vanzetti was accused of taking a gun from one of the guards, even though the prosecution had difficulty even establishing that the gun had been at the crime scene.

Decades later, the veracity of this piece of evidence would fall apart completely. Massachusetts police records released in the 1970s indicated that the serial number on Vanzetti's gun did not match that on Berardelli's. The guns were not even the same caliber; Berardelli's was a .32, and Vanzetti's was a .38. Even worse, the police records made it clear that Prosecutor Frederick Katzmann knew that Vanzetti's gun did not match Berardelli's and still he argued that the guns were one and the same.

At the time of the trial, the rest of the material evidence was even more flimsy, or nonexistent. The prosecution was never able to connect the money to either Sacco or Vanzetti. Nor was it able to connect them to the Buick found in a remote wooded area and identified as the getaway car. The police took fingerprints from the car and from Sacco and Vanzetti, but no fingerprint evidence was presented at the trial. It is difficult to think of any explanation for the prosecution's neglect of this evidence, except that neither man's fingerprints were found on the car.

The ballistics testimony at the trial was the most damaging evidence: against Sacco, because he was the one accused of killing Berardelli, and, by extension, against Vanzetti, because the men insisted on being tried together. Even here the evidence was scant. The bandits had fired four shots into Berardelli, and two into Parmenter. Of the six bullets, one matched the caliber of Sacco's gun. The doctor who performed the autopsy took the bullets out of Berardelli and numbered them in the order in which he extracted them. Bullet number three was the only one that could have come from Sacco's gun, and it was the focus of enormous attention at the trial. Each side presented two witnesses, each of them with credentials as ballistics experts (although the credibility of every one of them would be seriously challenged years later by proponents of each side).

Here too controversy reigned. Predictably, both defense witnesses argued that the gun found on Sacco had not fired the fatal shot. The two witnesses for the prosecution seemingly argued exactly the opposite. But one of them, Captain William Proctor, the head of the Massachusetts State Police who had originally been in charge of the investigation, later confessed that he had given an intentionally vague answer when asked whether he thought Sacco's weapon had fired the bullet. He had, moreover, arranged with the prosecution what he would be asked and what he would answer, to make it appear that he believed that the anarchist's weapon had been involved. (See Documents 17 and 18.) The second prosecution witness, Charles van Amburgh, worked at the time of the trial as an assistant in the ballistics department at a Remington company in Connecticut. He testified that he was "inclined to believe" that the shot came from Sacco's gun. Despite the imprecision of this claim—what exactly does "inclined to believe" mean?—both the prosecution and, tragically, the defense misread it. Each stated in their closing arguments that van Amburgh had argued that the bullet had come from the Italian anarchist's gun. The debate over the ballistics continues, heatedly, to this day.

On Trial for What?

The controversy about the case is rooted in issues far too broad to reduce to individual pieces of evidence or the testimony of one eyewitness or another. While those who believed that the two men were guilty saw the trial as simply a criminal matter, defenders of Sacco and Vanzetti—and Vanzetti himself, in his prison pamphlet—argued that it was part of a much larger battle being waged against radicals, and especially against anarchists, at the time. (See Document 19.) Concern about his identification as a radical certainly informed Vanzetti's actions during the trial for the attempted Bridgewater robbery. He chose not to take the stand in his own defense, a move that his detractors pointed to as an indication of his guilt. His decision was surely rooted at least in part—if not entirely—in his desire to keep his radical politics out of the trial. Even then, this was difficult to do. Prosecutor Katzmann managed to introduce the issue of Vanzetti's anarchism, albeit subtly, by asking defense witnesses questions about political conversations they might have had with the defendant. Judge Thayer linked the trial to radical political beliefs as well, stating that "the defendant's ideals are cognate with the crime"—that anyone who professed anarchist beliefs would be likely to commit criminal acts as well.

At the South Braintree trial, anarchist politics figured even more prominently. Prosecutors and public officials who believed Sacco and Vanzetti were guilty argued effectively that the defendants introduced the issue themselves. The anarchists and their defenders insisted that they were compelled to discuss their political leanings. If they had not explained that they were moving incriminating anarchist materials the night they were arrested, there would have been no explanation for their disingenuousness with the police. Katzmann exploited prejudices against radicals, veering far from the details of the crime to investigate both men's political beliefs. He lured Sacco into making a lengthy speech in defense of anarchism. (See Documents 20 and 21.) Although it no doubt reflected accurately (as accurately as his mastery of English would allow) his political philosophy, by all accounts it stunned the courtroom—full of a jury and spectators who were hardly sympathetic to anarchism—into silence.

Throughout the trial, a hyperpatriotic atmosphere defined the courtroom. Katzmann began his infamous cross-examination of Sacco by repeatedly asking whether he "loved a free country." He tried to make Sacco define his relationship to the United States and to criticize the country while Katzmann presented it in terms of its highest ideals. This questioning, of course, had nothing to do with whether Sacco had committed robbery and murder. Moreover, it is easy to imagine the impact Sacco's response to this patriotic goading, his defense of anarchism, had on certain members of the jury. The jury foreman made a point of saluting the flag every morning before he took his seat.

That this was as much a trial against anarchists as against suspected criminals was evident from the first days of the police investigation. Captain Proctor, the ballistics expert who was initially in charge of the investigation, became convinced that Sacco and Vanzetti could not have committed the crime. The robbery was, he argued, clearly the work of professional criminals. His opinion was not shared by Chief Michael Stewart, whose assessment was that "this crime was committed by men who knew no god." His eagerness to tie together his anti-radical activities and the investigation of the robbery fit the agenda of the district attorney's office neatly. Despite the fact that he had little or no experience with cases of this magnitude, compared to Proctor, Stewart replaced Proctor as head of the investigation.

The stakes, and the magnitude, of the trial were also heightened by the tension between the man who defended Sacco and Vanzetti and the man who presided over their trial. Fred Moore, the radical labor lawyer who had worked to free two other Italian radical labor leaders years earlier, is justly given enormous credit for making the case an international cause. He immediately saw the case as the persecution of two immigrant radicals because of who they were, rather than because of what they might have done. In this sense, Sacco and Vanzetti's detractors were correct. This lawyer, at least through 1924 when he was fired, had made every effort outside the courtroom to turn the proceedings into a political trial. He worked tirelessly, and at such great expense that he was a constant source of alarm to the defense committee, to create support across the United States and in labor and radical circles worldwide on Sacco and Vanzetti's behalf.

Moore's effectiveness in the courtroom was far less impressive. For example, he left susceptible ballistics testimony offered by prosecution witnesses unchallenged. Because this evidence was critical in convicting both men, Moore's failure here was devastating. Just as important, he alienated and angered Judge Thayer almost from the moment he stepped into the courtroom—not that that took much effort on Moore's part. Even if he hadn't violated the Bostonian sense of propriety with his long hair and by removing his jacket and even his *shoes* in the courtroom, Thayer would have had little good to say about him. As far as Thayer was concerned, Moore was an outsider and a defender of the most dangerous elements in society. The Boston lawyers working with Moore, the reputable McAnarney brothers, grew alarmed even as early as jury selection. They begged William

Nicola Sacco (right) and Bartolomeo Vanzetti speaking to Rosina Sacco, Sacco's wife, during the trial. The two men were sitting in what was known as "the cage," a structure in which defendants were enclosed during trials in Massachusetts at that time.

©Bettmann/ CORBIS.

Thompson, a well-known and respected Boston lawyer, to join the case. He refused at that point (he would later join the defense team), but he sat in on the later stages of the jury selection. Watching Thayer grow increasingly impatient with Moore and stare coldly at the bohemian lawyer whenever he overruled him, Thompson told the McAnarneys that their clients were in trouble. His exact words: "Your goose is cooked."

Judge Thayer was not part of old-world Boston, that nearly impenetrable set of elites who exerted enormous economic and political power in the city. That made him all the more eager to prove to them, and to the world, that he was an able defender of the status quo. His antipathy toward radicals was well established by the time of the trial. Although an anarchist had been acquitted in his court not long before Sacco and Vanzetti's trial, Thayer had berated the jury who declared him not guilty, castigating them for shirking their duty as citizens. As judge in the Sacco and Vanzetti trial, Thayer made constant references to the importance of patriotism and loyalty to one's country, and to the duties of citizenship. He led off his charge to the jury by comparing them to American soldiers in World War I, commenting, "he who is loyal to God, to country, to his state and to his fellowmen, represents the highest and noblest type of true American citizenship, than which there is none grander in the entire world."[8] In a trial in which the defendants were men who challenged the value of faith in a god and in any nation, Thayer's intentions in making this statement were unmistakable. He meant to contrast the religious faith and the patriotism he credited to the jury with the unpopular beliefs of the defendants.

Thayer had done much the same thing during the trial. During District Attorney Katzmann's intense questioning of Sacco about his attitude toward the United States, whether he "loved a free country," Thayer intervened in astonishing ways. Not only did he provide the prosecution with tremendous leeway in conducting this utterly irrelevant line of questioning, but he interrupted the cross-examination over and over, not to rein in Katzmann but to make his point more strongly for him. Thayer tried to insist eight separate times during the cross-examination that the defense was arguing that Sacco and Vanzetti were trying to hide anarchist literature the night they were arrested to protect the best interests of the United States and the American government. It is a confusing argument because it makes so little sense on its face. What Thayer was implying—what he said the defense was arguing—was that the defendants were hiding anarchist literature because its distribution would be harmful to the United States. This was absurd; if they were hiding anarchist literature the night they were arrested it was to protect themselves, not the United States. By repeatedly raising his own foundationless interpretation of their actions, however, Thayer forced the defense to admit eight times that Sacco and Vanzetti were *not* protecting the best interests of the United States that night. (See Document 20.)

Most famously, Judge Thayer attacked the defendants unceasingly outside the courtroom. His gleeful comment to a member of his private club after the judge had rejected several motions for a new trial—"Did you see what I did to those anarchist bastards the other day?"—became a rallying cry for Sacco and Vanzetti's defenders. Thayer also harassed club members with detailed accounts of his handling of the case, and his assurances that he would not let radicals run his courtroom. One club member finally asked an attendant not to sit Thayer near him anymore. Thayer harangued Boston Brahmins who defended the anarchists, and he tried to coerce journalists into reporting that he was running a fair trial. Thayer's actions, inside and outside the courtroom, were profoundly influenced by Sacco and Vanzetti's identity as radicals. Thayer was not alone.

Substantial evidence suggests that the Justice Department not only followed the case very carefully but also cooperated with the prosecution. Why would it matter if the Justice Department was involved? It raised the issue, yet again, of what Sacco and Vanzetti were actually being tried for. The Justice Department had far more interest in the two men as anarchists than as alleged robbers and murderers. It would have had nothing to do with the case if not for their radical beliefs.

It is unclear how much the Justice Department knew about the two men before their arrest and how involved it was in building the case against them. Two things are clear, however. First, regardless of how much the Justice Department knew about Sacco and Vanzetti, the two anarchists certainly knew about the Justice Department and about its efforts to track down *Galleanisti*. Second, regardless of whether they had heard of the two men before their arrest, federal agents definitely knew about them after they were in custody. The Justice Department cooperated with the prosecution in several ways. First, it sought, unsuccessfully, to uncover any anarchist circles in the country that had received inexplicably large infusions of cash after the robbery. Second, it translated several articles from radical newspapers and made them available to Katzmann. Third, it worked with Katzmann to put an informer in the cell next to Sacco in an attempt to learn more about a bomb that exploded on the corners of Broad and Wall streets in New York City in September 1920. (*Galleanista* Mario Buda may have been responsible for the bombing. No evidence ever connected it to Sacco, who was already in jail when it exploded.) Finally, the Justice Department tried to place an informer as a boarder with Rosina Sacco; the logic was that she would be in economic need and might be distraught enough over her husband's imprisonment to provide useful information to a sympathetic boarder. This last plan, however, never materialized.

Beyond this extensive involvement in the case by the Justice Department, Sacco and Vanzetti's defense attorneys made even more audacious claims. They took depositions from two former federal agents who asserted it was a shared assumption in the department that the crime was committed by professionals, not by the defendants. Each agent explained that the department's goal was to get Sacco and Vanzetti out of the way, either through a conviction for the South Braintree crime or by deportation on the basis of evidence the department would work to gather during their trial. (See Document 22.) Katzmann's determined efforts to get Sacco and Vanzetti to speak about their anarchist beliefs may well have been the result of an agreement with the Justice Department.

The Appeals

The lengthy trial ended abruptly. After over seven weeks of testimony, and over 150 witnesses, the jury returned a guilty verdict on July 14, 1921. Much of the evidence, especially the eyewitness testimony, seemed remarkably unreliable even at the time. Other evidence, some of the material evidence and the assessments of the ballistics, was not adequately challenged by the defense. All of this was of little consequence. The jury members hardly seemed to give the trial a second thought. They began their deliberations mid-afternoon on July 14 and reached their verdicts just after dinner on the same day. Given the political climate of the country—and the courtroom—at the time, this was not all that surprising.

After Sacco and Vanzetti were found guilty, their lawyers filed a series of unsuccessful appeals. Moore and the McAnarneys filed the first appeals; William Thompson and Herbert Ehrmann filed the final ones. Thompson took over the case in November 1924; Ehrmann joined him in May 1926. The appeals process was extremely lengthy, stretching over six years. Sacco and Vanzetti languished in prison the entire time. Ironically, Vanzetti, because he had been convicted and sentenced for the attempted robbery in Bridgewater, was allowed among the general prison population. He got yard privileges and a job to keep himself occupied. Sacco, convicted for the South Braintree crimes but not yet sentenced, was largely confined to his cell. This had a terrible impact on him, used as he was to working outdoors in his garden and on various machines that needed fixing. Denied these activities, he lived life hard in prison. In addition, true to his anarchist beliefs, he had little faith that the American judicial system would treat him fairly—that it would do anything but condemn him to death. He waged several hunger strikes; he was on one in the last days of his life. He suffered more than once from emotional and mental break-downs, and he was confined at one point for five months in the Bridgewater State Mental Institution. Unlike Sacco, Vanzetti could work and spend at least some part of every day outside; he could also lose himself in studying English and reading. Also unlike Sacco, Vanzetti had at least some hope that he would be set free. He too suf-fered a breakdown and was confined to Bridgewater State Mental Institution; his collapse came immediately after several appeals were turned down.

Sacco had a much clearer sense of their fate. Due to a quirk in the Massachusetts legal system, which was amended soon after their exe-cutions, Sacco and Vanzetti's appeals could only be heard by the judge who had heard their case. Judge Thayer turned each appeal down—four of them in one day—and gloated about it to his friends.

The first four appeals, filed between November 1921 and Septem-ber 1922, concerned a jury member and prosecution witnesses whose testimony the defense argued had been flawed. Defense attorneys got two key prosecution witnesses, Lola Andrews and Louis Pelser, to sign depositions refuting their testimony, and exposed the identity of another, Carlos Goodridge, as a thief and adulterer who had hidden behind an assumed name for years. Moore used coercive tactics to get the original depositions, however, and the prosecution got the wit-nesses to refute these statements. Judge Thayer, in rejecting the appeals, spent much of his response chastising Moore for his conduct.

The next two appeals, filed in April and November 1923, concerned ballistics testimony; the latter dealt with Captain Proctor's affidavit that he had arranged his testimony with the prosecution in a way designed to mislead the jury. The prosecution responded by attacking Proctor's motives—saying that he was bitter that he had been replaced by Stewart as chief investigator on the case and that he had not been reimbursed for a bill he had submitted for services rendered. Prosecutors dodged his charge of arranged testimony, saying only that they had not "repeatedly" (picking up Proctor's language) discussed it. (See Document 18.) Judge Thayer had actually misinterpreted Proctor's testimony during his charge to the jury, stating that the witness had argued that Sacco's gun had fired the fatal shot. In his rejection of the appeal, however, Thayer argued something new. He now insisted that the implications of Proctor's vagueness on the stand— the carefully arranged language that suggested, but didn't state outright, that Sacco's gun had killed Berardelli—had been obvious to everyone who heard it.

The defense also charged that Judge Thayer had conducted himself improperly. This appeal asserted that Thayer's behavior in the courtroom—his appeals to patriotism, allowances for the prosecution on cross-examination, and faulty charge to the jury—had created an environment that rendered a fair trial impossible. The appeal also supplied depositions from a series of people who testified about Thayer's repeated discussions of the case, and his contempt for the defendants and their lawyers, outside the courtroom. It is legal misconduct for a judge sitting on a case to discuss it outside the courtroom, much less to refer to the defendants as "anarchist bastards." The depositions attesting to this misconduct came from a wide range of respected members of society: Boston journalists, a leader of the Boston Federation of Churches, a former Boston city treasurer (see Document 23), a famous essayist and humorist, and a Dartmouth professor (see Document 24). Despite the overwhelming evidence of Thayer's misconduct, however, this appeal was doomed from the start. Once again, Thayer heard the appeal; he dismissed it.

The final appeal was in many ways the most compelling—it produced what remains one of the greatest complications, and one of the greatest mysteries, involved in the case. On November 16, 1925, a prison trustee handed Sacco a note written by Celestino Madeiros, a fellow inmate. In the note, Madeiros, in jail awaiting a retrial for murder and attempted bank robbery, confessed that he—and not Sacco or Vanzetti—had been involved in the South Braintree crime. Sacco had been approached by Madeiros previously, but, thinking he was just another informer, had ignored his entreaties. Now Sacco believed him. The trustee reported that Sacco, having read the note, began to shake and then to cry. It wasn't much to go on—the word of a long-time criminal like Madeiros—but for Sacco and Vanzetti, and for their defense team, it was new hope.

Nov 16 1925
Dedham
Mass
48 Village ave

Dear Editor
  I here by confess to being in
the shoe company crime at south
Braintree on april 15 1920 and that Sacco
and Vanzetti was not there

            Celestino F Medeiros

Celestino Madeiros, on trial for murder and robbery at the time, passed this note to Sacco in prison in November 1925, confessing to his involvement in the South Braintree crime.

The confession suggested a remarkable alternative scenario for the crime. After repeated, and fruitless, requests to authorities to investigate the confession, attorney Herbert Ehrmann undertook his own investigation. He uncovered what he and many others came to believe were the true events in South Braintree on April 15, 1920. According to Ehrmann, the perpetrators of the crime were not Sacco and Vanzetti or other *Galleanisti* but a professional band of criminals of Italian descent, operating out of Providence, Rhode Island. Following a criminal code of ethics, Madeiros had refused to surrender the names of the men who had invited him to participate in the robbery. His description of them, however, led Ehrmann straight to the Morelli gang, which had committed crimes in the area before, had dire financial needs because some of its members were facing expensive trials, and had experience and weaponry that fit the job. (See Document 25.) The leader of the gang at the time, Joseph Morelli, even resembled Sacco. Several witnesses, having originally identified Sacco, later claimed that Morelli was the man they had seen.

The argument that Ehrmann and Thompson put together for the appeal was not flawless, however. Ehrmann was operating under severe financial and time constraints. Try as he might, he could never get Madeiros to say the names of the Morellis out loud. Nor could he get Joseph Morelli, then in prison on another charge, or any other members of the gang, to confess to anything. Madeiros's description of the crime was far from unimpeachable. He had been eighteen years old at the time; although he was already a practiced thief, the gunfire and the deaths frightened him. He told authorities he got drunk before the crime and spent most of the time in South Braintree on the floor of the car. His description of what transpired from that vantage point was flawless, but of course he missed key landmarks easily visible to someone sitting up in the car. He was, as Ehrmann would argue for the rest of his life, able to describe elements of the crime that had been unknown, and that proved accurate upon further investigation. For example, Madeiros was the first to mention that two cars had been involved in the hold-up. Nonetheless, Thayer rejected this appeal as well, dismissing Madeiros as a liar and a thief. (See Document 26.) Ehrmann ardently believed he had found the true criminals. His anguish over Thayer's rejection of the appeal lasted for decades.

After Judge Thayer turned down all seven appeals, recourse for the defense was limited. Sacco and Vanzetti's lawyers could appeal again, this time to the Massachusetts Supreme Judicial Court, but this strategy held out little hope. Again, because of a peculiarity in the state's legal code at the time, this court could only rule on issues of law, not on issues of fact. That meant that any new evidence the defense might uncover—from faulty witness testimony to another, potentially even more plausible set of suspects for the crime like the Morellis—would have no weight before this court. The only successful appeal would be one that established that the law had been misapplied. On the accusation concerning Judge Thayer's personal bias, the basis for a successful appeal was extremely narrow. The defense would have had to establish the judge's mental or psychological incompetence to convince the court to overturn the convictions. That was highly unlikely. In short, the Massachusetts Supreme Judicial Court turned down all of the appeals by April 5, 1927. Four days later, Judge Webster Thayer sentenced Sacco and Vanzetti to death. Options for the two defendants were running out.

Contemporary Responses: Supporters and Detractors

By the time Judge Thayer sentenced them to death, Sacco and Vanzetti were already household names throughout the United States. Support for them—and opposition to them—had started slowly. Fellow radicals and Italian immigrants rallied to their cause almost immediately, eventually joined by American and international labor organizations, liberals and liberal organizations, and even certain typically apolitical and conservative artists and other public figures. Increasingly, as the appeals dragged on, people convinced of Sacco and Vanzetti's guilt joined the fray, insisting that the commotion over the two anarchists represented a grave danger to American society and the American judicial system. The clamor that partisans on each side raised reached a fever pitch by the last months of Sacco and Vanzetti's lives.

Italian American Leftists were the first to raise concerns about the two arrested anarchists. Carlo Tresca, an iconoclastic radical who spent the last four decades of his life fighting for workers' rights in the United States, recognized the danger that Sacco and Vanzetti were in almost immediately. It had been Tresca from whom Vanzetti had sought advice about how to respond to Andrea Salsedo and Roberto Elia's imprisonment in Federal Bureau of Investigation (FBI) offices. When Sacco and Vanzetti were arrested, Tresca rallied the Italian American Left behind them. (See Document 27.) The first support for Sacco and Vanzetti's legal defense came from this source; fellow Italian immigrant radicals immediately began collecting funds in coins and crumpled dollars.

For the first five years, the greatest number of financial contributions to Sacco and Vanzetti's defense came from Italian American Leftists and from Italian immigrants in general. These immigrants not only made individual contributions but also staged events—picnics, theatrical productions, even wrestling matches—to raise money. This assistance was vital because the trial and the appeals were enormously expensive. By 1925, the Sacco-Vanzetti Defense Committee had collected, and spent, $360,000. The funds Italian immigrants collected had come to just under a third of this total. The fact that they had made the largest number of contributions, but that these had not amounted to the largest dollar total indicated two things: Sacco and Vanzetti had widespread support in Italian immigrant working-class communities and these communities remained relatively poor.

It was essential from the first to build additional support for Sacco and Vanzetti. Once again, Carlo Tresca played a critical role, quickly contacting his American Leftist allies and asking them for help. In 1921, he solicited the help of Elizabeth Gurley Flynn, a former IWW member who would remain a radical presence in the labor movement for decades. She organized a national lecture tour, presenting Sacco and Vanzetti as victims of the Red Scare. Thanks to Tresca and Flynn's efforts, labor and Left leaders and intellectuals soon began to recognize the importance of the case. (See Document 28.) In 1921, for example, Socialist Eugene Debs was freed from the prison where he had been serving his sentence for protesting against World War I. His first act upon his release was to send his prison release money, five dollars, to the Sacco and Vanzetti Defense fund. By 1924, even the conservative American Federation of Labor issued a resolution at its national convention, protesting the injustice of the case. The Sacco-Vanzetti Defense Committee, established soon after their arrest, grew larger over time, coming to include not only *Galleanisti* and other Leftists but also a broad range of American liberals.

Sacco and, especially, Vanzetti were able to earn a very dedicated group of advocates among Boston's liberals, many of them the city's "best citizens." Elizabeth Glendower Evans, a wealthy liberal Brahmin, and several of her friends befriended Vanzetti and became convinced of his and Sacco's innocence. Evans attended the trial every day; sent both men food, reading materials, and flowers; and provided considerable economic support to their defense campaign. (See Document 29.)

Members of the Boston Brahmin community also took it upon themselves to teach the prisoners English. Sacco always struggled with
the language, but nonetheless remained grateful to Cerise Jack, wife
of a Harvard professor and a member of the New England Civil Liberties Committee, for her efforts. (See Document 30.) Vanzetti blos-
somed under the tutelage of Virginia MacMechan, a close friend of
Cerise Jack's who worked on his English with him. Some of Vanzetti's
letters in English, especially those from late in his life, were beauti-
fully written.

Sacco and Vanzetti's last lead attorney, William Thompson, was also
a Brahmin who had originally turned down entreaties to take the case.
After Moore was dismissed, defense committee members again
approached Thompson at the end of 1924. He asked for $25,000 as a
retainer, an enormous amount that he hoped would dissuade them
from pursuing his services. They came up with the money, however,
and, over time, Thompson became convinced of Vanzetti's innocence
and of the strength of his character. After his last meeting with
Vanzetti, Thompson declared, "I went into this case as a Harvard
man . . . to help two poor aliens who had, I thought, been unjustly
treated. I have arrived at a humbler attitude. . . . The Harvard graduate, the man of old American traditions, the established lawyer, is now
quite ready to say that nowhere in his soul is there to be found the
faith, the splendid gentility, which make the man, Bartolomeo
Vanzetti."[9] As with so many who spoke with the anarchist, rich and
poor, radical, liberal and conservative, Thompson considered Vanzetti
too dignified, composed, and intelligent to have committed such a
cold-hearted crime.

Liberal support for Sacco and Vanzetti extended nationwide by the
time their last appeals were turned down. Gardner Jackson, a wealthy
liberal reporter from Colorado, had become secretary of the Sacco-
Vanzetti Defense Committee. American author John Dos Passos published a booklet titled *Facing the Chair* in 1927 to draw attention to the
trial and to build support among fellow liberals. (See Document 31.)
Politically oriented magazines like *The Nation* and the *New Republic*
began to pay increased attention to the trial as well. In 1926, for
example, the editors of *New Republic* ran eleven articles or editorials
related to Sacco and Vanzetti. In 1927, the intensity of its coverage
increased dramatically; by year's end, it had published an additional
fifty articles and editorials.

Sacco and Vanzetti also had enemies and detractors. Most of the

Brahmin community, represented faithfully by the conservative *Boston Evening Transcript,* was outraged that men they regarded as common criminals, as murderers, should be hailed as potential martyrs. They were appalled that the word of two anarchists was taken by so many over those of Judge Thayer and District Attorney Katzmann, who, after all, were only upholding the good name of the Massachusetts judicial system. As far as the *Transcript*'s editors were concerned, not just Sacco and Vanzetti but "The Commonwealth [of Massachusetts] is on trial."

They were not alone. The 1920s was a period of enormous reaction and retrenchment in the United States. Opponents of organized labor and immigration had great success early in the decade. The Immigration Restriction acts passed in 1921 and 1924 severely limited the number of immigrants who could enter the United States. In the same years, an anti-union movement, calling its agenda "the American Plan," grew increasingly powerful. It nearly crippled even conservative unions; the American Federation of Labor lost 1.5 million members in the first half of the 1920s.

New organizations pushed the conservative agenda to an extreme. The American Legion, founded by World War I veterans in 1919, declared itself responsible for protecting the United States against dangerous radicals. Within months, it had hundreds of thousands of members. Although its national leaders denounced vigilante violence, local members nationwide tarred and feathered, beat and even killed those they opposed. A new Ku Klux Klan, established in Georgia in 1915, took root throughout the South and the Midwest. By the middle of the 1920s, its membership numbered in the millions. It fought against what its members saw as the insidious influence of blacks, immigrants (especially Catholics), atheists, and radicals on American society. Fundamentalist religious organizations also enjoyed a rejuvenation in the 1920s, carried especially by charismatic evangelical preachers like Aimee Semple McPherson and Billy Sunday.

The Sacco and Vanzetti case touched core issues for each of these organizations and individuals. As immigrants, labor advocates, atheists, and radicals, Sacco and Vanzetti were the sum total of all that was wrong with the United States in their eyes. Worried conservatives like Frank A. Goodwin, the Massachusetts registrar of motor vehicles, lambasted the anarchists at meetings of civic organizations throughout the state and the country. (See Document 32.) Their vantage point was summed up perfectly by Reverend Billy Sunday's famous condemnation of the two men: "Give em' the juice, burn them if they're guilty, I'm tired of hearing these foreigners, these radicals, coming over here and telling us what to do."[10]

The reaction and retrenchment that infused the opposition to Sacco and Vanzetti in the United States spread far beyond its borders. A battle between forces on the Left and Right politically was being waged throughout Europe and much of the rest of the world in the 1920s. The Right, which would emerge victorious in Germany and Spain in the 1930s, won its first major victory in Italy when Benito Mussolini and his Fascist party assumed power in 1922. Although many would turn from the fascist leader when he signed a pact with Hitler and the Nazis at the onset of World War II, Mussolini was initially extremely popular among Americans and especially among Italian immigrants. After decades of being disrespected and mistreated in their new homes, many of these immigrants regarded Mussolini and the strong new Italy he insisted he was building as inspirations and sources of pride. This makes it all the more remarkable that so many of these immigrants supported Sacco and Vanzetti through financial contributions and demonstrations. Certainly the defendants' anarchism was the antithesis of Mussolini's fascism. Italian immigrant radicals and union leaders, opponents of Mussolini's from the first, supported Sacco and Vanzetti as fellow activists and workers; other Italian immigrants empathized with them simply as maligned fellow nationals.

The 1920s were not characterized solely by right-wing reaction internationally; there were also volatile but nonetheless powerful Leftist organizations that led powerful protests on behalf of Sacco and Vanzetti throughout the world. The Left was in transition internationally by the early 1920s, as the wide spectrum of Leftist parties and organizations—including socialists, syndicalists, and anarchists—narrowed in the wake of the Bolshevik Revolution. By the time Sacco and Vanzetti were on trial, the most visible and influential Leftist parties and individuals were now Communist.

Communist parties around the world, many of them strong and still growing in the early 1920s, made the Sacco and Vanzetti case a rallying point and a symbol of the flaws of American justice under the capitalist system. Both American and European Communists often used it cynically. Katherine Anne Porter, an author who worked on behalf of the prisoners, told of an American Communist who mocked a sympathizer's distress over the increasing likelihood that Sacco and Vanzetti were going to be executed. The Communist argued that the two anarchists were more useful, as symbols of American and capitalist injustice, dead than alive. (See Document 33.) Perhaps this callousness was exaggerated, but Communists, especially in Europe, at times showed little concrete knowledge of the case. For at least some on the Left, Sacco and Vanzetti were indeed more important as symbols than as articulate—and innocent—radicals.

Small wonder that Defense Attorney Fred Moore, who encouraged and relied on this support, fell badly out of favor with the defendants. Nicola and Rosina Sacco had never liked him, not only because they thought he spent too much money, but because they did not believe he had their best interests at heart. In 1924, when Sacco dismissed Moore, Sacco signed the letter to him, "your implacable enemy, now and forever." Moore left the case embittered. Despite his often reckless spending on his clients' behalf, Moore was nearly penniless. He had not defended Sacco and Vanzetti particularly ably in court, making errors of law and judgment. But he had made Sacco and Vanzetti household names.

The Lowell Committee, Worldwide Outrage, and the Executions

By the time Judge Thayer sentenced Sacco and Vanzetti to death in April 1927, protest on behalf of Sacco and Vanzetti was worldwide—and growing. Some of the furor—produced by the least informed of the European Communists, for example—could be easily dismissed by authorities in Massachusetts. The extent of the protests, though, both in the United States and internationally, was indisputable. Even some of Sacco and Vanzetti's former foes had begun to change their minds. Months earlier, in October 1926, just after Judge Thayer had rejected the appeal based on Madeiros's confession, the conservative *Boston Herald* had printed an editorial titled "We Submit." The piece, which won its author a Pulitzer Prize, criticized the defendants' anarchist beliefs but still insisted that a new trial was merited. (See Document 34.) Calls such as these were difficult to ignore.

These protests were augmented by the unexpected involvement of respected Harvard Law Professor Felix Frankfurter. Frankfurter, who later became a Supreme Court justice, wrote an impassioned critique of Judge Thayer and Prosecutor Katzmann's handling of the trial. His criticisms were concise and devastating; he dismantled much of the evidence against Sacco and Vanzetti, and he castigated Thayer for his demeanor and actions during the trial and the appeals process. When Frankfurter's article appeared in the *Atlantic Monthly* in March 1927, it caused an immediate uproar. It was highly unusual for anyone of

Frankfurter's reputation in the legal world to intervene in an ongoing trial. The vehemence of his judgment of Thayer made his work all the more compelling.

Frankfurter's article demanded a response. Two months later, J. H. Wigmore, dean of Northeastern University Law School and one of the foremost legal minds in the United States, confronted Frankfurter in two lengthy letters in the *Boston Evening Transcript*. His attempt to refute Frankfurter failed miserably. The future Supreme Court justice deflected each point raised by Wigmore. A. Lawrence Lowell, president of Harvard University and a staunch conservative, exclaimed in disgust, "Wigmore's ridiculous article looked as if there was nothing serious to be said on the side of the courts."[11]

There was so much pressure on the Massachusetts judicial system that Governor Alvan Fuller decided to get involved. Normally, the Supreme Judicial Court would have been the last resort—except for an appeal to the U.S. Supreme Court. Because of the expansive protests, however, Fuller decided to review the case personally. He also took the extremely unusual step of establishing a review committee to conduct its own investigation. The committee was headed— indisputably, if informally—by A. Lawrence Lowell, the man who had been so dismayed by Wigmore's inept attack on Frankfurter. The Lowell Committee, as it came to be known, also included Samuel Stratton, president of the Massachusetts Institute of Technology, and Robert Grant, a one-time Probate Court judge.

Although some thought the reviews signaled real hope, little came of either of them. Both Governor Fuller and the committee he established reviewed the trial transcripts, and they interviewed both old and new witnesses, members of the jury, the attorneys for both sides, and Judge Thayer. By all appearances, the reviews by the governor and by the committee were thorough and thoughtful; each took longer than the trial itself had. Questions appeared immediately, however. Defense attorneys were troubled by a work published years earlier by Judge Grant that seemed to cast aspersions on Italians. They were left uneasy by the absolute power that Lowell very quickly established over the committee. They also were angered by the fact that they were not allowed to be present at all the sessions at which the committee or the governor questioned various parties. Although these were extra-legal proceedings, outside the bounds of normal legal procedure, Sacco and Vanzetti's lawyers insisted that certain elements of due process had to be maintained.

Defense attorneys were equally disturbed by the indisputable bias revealed by both the committee and the governor. In one very complicated exchange, for example, Lowell tried very obviously to catch a respected member of the Italian immigrant community who had provided an alibi for Sacco in a lie. When it appeared he had succeeded, Lowell was triumphant. However, when the trap fell apart, and it became clear that the man hadn't lied, Lowell not only refused to apologize publicly, he kept the refutation of his accusation out of the public record. Governor Fuller himself assumed an antagonistic attitude toward those whose testimony might benefit the two defendants. He quizzed puzzled witnesses, there solely to share their knowledge of the Morellis, about Sacco and Vanzetti's activities. He got into a shouting match with one Sacco and Vanzetti defender. In the end, many were disappointed, but few were surprised, to learn that Lowell had drafted the committee's report before it even heard the defense's closing argument.

The Lowell Committee's report, issued on July 27, 1927, concluded that Sacco was guilty of the crimes of which he was accused and that Vanzetti was "on the whole" guilty as well. (See Document 35.) The vagueness of this clause, as well as what the defense attorneys judged to be shoddy reasoning, willful misinterpretations, and disregard of trial evidence, would plague them for decades after the executions. Because Governor Fuller had agreed beforehand to abide by the Lowell Committee's decision, little stood between Sacco and Vanzetti and the electric chair. Their executions were now scheduled for August 10.

By that night, Sacco and Vanzetti were prepared to die. They had been moved to cells adjacent to the death chamber and had said their goodbyes. Their impending fate seemed to captivate the entire city. Between 9:50 that night and 7:05 the next morning, not a single crime appeared on Boston's police blotters. Just forty minutes before their executions were to take place, however, word arrived that they had been granted a reprieve. Their execution date was pushed back to midnight, August 23, 1927.

The last two weeks of Sacco and Vanzetti's lives—the clinging to hope, the amazing energies of the vast range of people working on their behalves, the mounting sense of desperation—were captured by a Holyoke English professor named Jeannette Marks in a memoir called *The Thirteen Days*. Protesters clogged the streets of Boston and converged in such large numbers on the prison where the two men were held that in the final days there were over seven hundred police officers stationed around the building. Many of the protesters were the intellectuals, radicals and labor leaders, and workers and immigrants who had followed the case, with increasing despair, for years.

People for whom these sorts of public protests were something brand new were also drawn into the streets of Boston. For example, a number of typically apolitical American poets were drawn into the case. The case inspired dozens of angry poems, some of which appeared in a 1927 collection titled *The Sacco-Vanzetti Anthology of Verse;* one count in the 1940s put the number of protest poems at over 150. These were mostly written by men and women who were activists first and poets second—often a distant second. Their stanzas, filled with revolutionary rhetoric and catchphrases, were perhaps inspiring to the like-minded, but they were rarely very lyrical. However, the plight of the two men also inspired people for whom poetry was a primary, even a singular pursuit. Harlem renaissance poet Countee Cullen published a poem titled "Not Sacco and Vanzetti." (See Document 36.) Dorothy Parker, famous for her acerbic and witty poetry and especially for her drinking escapades as a member of the Algonquin Round Table in New York City in the 1920s, signed petitions and was arrested at mass meetings. Another poet hardly known for her political activism was Edna St. Vincent Millay, whose romantic lyricism made her one of the leading lights in American poetry for decades. She marched, and was arrested, and wrote anguished poems on the two anarchists and their treatment. (See Document 37.)

Support for Sacco and Vanzetti extended well beyond protesters in the Boston area. By the eve of their execution, they had become, in the words of one commentator, the "two most famous prisoners in all the world."[12] A petition with over half a million signatures collected worldwide made its way to Governor Fuller. A wide array of renowned intellectuals and political leaders also raised increasingly angry voices. English author H. G. Wells, French scientist Marie Curie (discoverer of radium), German physicist Albert Einstein, Harvard historian Arthur M. Schlesinger Sr., educational reformer John Dewey, journalist and curmudgeon H. L. Mencken, settlement house founder Jane Addams, all protested the impending execution. So too did several members of the British Parliament, and over one hundred attorneys of the Paris bar. Another appeal came from Alfred Dreyfus, himself among the most famous defendants of the era after his trial for espionage in a profoundly anti-Semitic atmosphere in France in 1894. These politicians and intellectuals were the most prominent protesters, but they were by no means the only ones to speak out. As the day of the execution approached, the magnitude of world opinion on the case became all the more clear.

Never before or since has a trial provoked such worldwide indignation and fury. Protests wracked cities in Europe and the United States. Work stoppages and protests occurred in Boston, of course, as well as a massive demonstration in New York City. Smaller demonstrations took place in towns like Rochester, Indianapolis, Baltimore, Scranton, and Tampa. In the final days, workers held rallies and waged general strikes for the prisoners in London, Paris, Belfast, Moscow, Berlin, Vienna, Budapest, Bucharest, Rome, and Madrid. There were protests in Norway, Sweden, Denmark, Switzerland, Holland, Japan, China, Argentina, Brazil, Chile, Mexico, and Panama, as well as across northern and southern Africa. (See Document 38.) Even Benito Mussolini who, as fascist leader of Italy, opposed anarchism, protested the unfairness of the verdict. (See Document 39.)

As these protests grew and spread, defense attorneys and the defense committee had one last resort—to find a U.S. Supreme Court justice willing, while that court was out of session, to grant a stay of execution. A justice would only do this if he believed there was a realistic chance that the Supreme Court would hear the case and overturn the lower court's decision. There were only two justices with whom Sacco and Vanzetti's defenders felt they had any hope at all. Their best hope, Justice Louis Brandeis, a staunch defender of liberal values, turned out to be their greatest disappointment. Brandeis was very sympathetic, but his wife had immersed herself in defense efforts, even having Rosina Sacco stay at their home for a time, so he argued that he had to recuse himself from the case. Their only remaining hope, the other most liberal justice on the bench, Oliver Wendell Holmes Jr., would not issue a stay. Defense attorneys and defense committee members solicited each Supreme Court justice in turn, then returned to Brandeis and Holmes each again for last-minute pleas. Heartbreakingly, Holmes told them that he was "convinced that these men did not get a square deal," but that as a federal judge he had no jurisdiction over the case.[13]

As hope dimmed, certain protests on behalf of Sacco and Vanzetti turned violent. In several cities in Europe and South America, bombs exploded as their scheduled executions approached. In the United States, bombs sought out very specific targets. A juror's house was blown up, and, by August 1927, several of the leading figures in the prosecution were being guarded around the clock. (As late as 1932, a bomb exploded at Judge Thayer's house; he was convinced that it was the work of people still angry about the case.) Although no one ever tied any *Galleanisti,* or any anarchist at all, to the attacks, the bombs scared many in the United States and, unfortunately, convinced many of how dangerous the prisoners were.

It was all to no avail. A few minutes after midnight, on August 23, 1927, first Sacco, then Vanzetti walked into the death chamber and sat in the electric chair. Sacco, true to himself to the end, said goodbye to his family, declared his undying faith in anarchism, and then, just before the electricity hit him, murmured, "farewell, Mother." Vanzetti shook the warden's hand and thanked him for caring for him, a display of composure that reportedly affected many of the witnesses very deeply. He declared that he wished to forgive "some of the people" who were putting him to death, a compromise that emerged from a lengthy last conversation with Attorney William Thompson, and again he proclaimed his innocence. Both men were preceded, ironically, by Celestino Madeiros, the young Portuguese man who had confessed to the crime for which they were being executed. By 12:30, all three men were dead. The defenders of Sacco and Vanzetti were left weary and heartbroken—and embittered—by the executions. John Dos Passos, who had put together the pamphlet *Facing the Chair* in the early months of 1927, best summed up the attitude of the liberals and intellectuals who had fought for the anarchists. His declaration—"All right we are two nations"—signaled that the trial, so clearly a miscarriage of justice in the eyes of many Americans, and so necessary a defense of American institutions to so many others, had exposed and exacerbated a deep rupture in American society.

THE LEGACY OF SACCO AND VANZETTI

Instant Martyrdom

Sacco and Vanzetti's legacy began even before the appeals did. Both for better and for worse, the two anarchists had become internationally recognized symbols of injustice as they lived out their last years. Liberals expressed their astonishment at the response the trial of the two men had provoked. Oswald Garrison Villard, editor of the liberal journal *The Nation,* declared just before they died, "Talk about the solidarity of the human race! When has there been a more striking example of the solidarity of great masses of people than this?" (See Document 40.) Communists and other Leftists rallied behind the two men, usually deeply concerned for the two men, always aware of the political implications of their imprisonment and impending executions.

After the executions, each year as the anniversary of Sacco and Vanzetti's deaths approached, fellow radicals would hail them as martyrs. Anarchists Emma Goldman and Alexander Berkman, for example, living in Europe after their deportations from the United States, were among those who contributed to efforts to keep Sacco and Vanzetti's names alive after their deaths. (See Document 41.) Their legacy was not built solely by those who abstracted their case and its meaning, however.

The people closest to Sacco and Vanzetti as their deaths approached often saw them in a different light. They argued that what was most impressive about the men was their strength of character. Vanzetti's letters revealed him as a sensitive and articulate man; even most of his enemies acknowledged the artfulness that characterized his writing. Both men faced seven excruciating years in prison with a stoicism and dignity that was little short of amazing.

They met their deaths in much the same way, retaining in their last hours their remarkable composure. While Madeiros, who had eaten himself into a stupor at his last meal, tossed and turned as he tried to sleep, Sacco and Vanzetti wrote last letters to loved ones and spoke calmly to visitors about what faced them. Each had planned carefully what he would say and do in his last minutes, and was able to carry out those plans. Their devotion to their friends and family as their lives ended—Vanzetti's sister arrived from Italy just in time to spend a few hours with her brother—was matched only by their steadfast devotion to anarchism. Vanzetti helped pen a lengthy petition to Governor Fuller requesting a new trial, part of which was an explicit defense of philosophical anarchism. He evoked the names of several anarchist thinkers and practitioners, including Galleani, of course, and, more boldly, Jesus Christ. Sacco refused to sign any document requesting anything from the state, but he read the petition and agreed with it in principle. Certainly he agreed with the defense of anarchy. His long speech documenting his anarchist beliefs when he was cross-examined by Katzmann had no doubt damaged him in the eyes of the jury. Nonetheless, he held these beliefs to his death, shouting "long live anarchy" just before he was electrocuted.

Sacco and Vanzetti's legacy is also rooted firmly in the enduring perception—widely, if not universally, held—that they did not receive a fair trial. This was the basis of the appeals filed by William Thompson and Herbert Ehrmann, especially the one accusing Judge Webster Thayer of bias against the defendants and Fred Moore. They also pointed to the intensely hostile environment in which Sacco and Vanzetti were tried. The widespread fears that the Red Scare evoked contributed to this atmosphere. Every day the two anarchists were marched to and from the courthouse in shackles, and everyone entering the court (including reporters) was searched for weapons. It is now also clear that the police withheld evidence from the defense that could have helped exonerate the two men and manipulated evidence and testimony to convict them.

Despite the enormous number of appeals, despite the professions by their attorneys at certain moments that they had received fair trials, despite the extraordinary review by a committee selected by the governor, Sacco and Vanzetti's defenders argued that they were convicted because of their radical beliefs. Judge Thayer turned down appeals of convictions in his own court; the Supreme Judicial Court was restricted in terms of what it could rule on in appeals. Even the reviews by the governor and the Lowell Committee were, critics suggest, foregone conclusions. Lawyers for Sacco and Vanzetti argued that the committee saw its role as the defender of the state—and the convictions. Defense attorneys Thompson and Ehrmann accused the committee of interrogating defense witnesses, transparently looking for flaws in their testimony. The state's unwillingness to investigate the validity of Madeiros's confession confirmed their suspicion that Sacco and Vanzetti had been targeted.

This perception, that the case was a profound miscarriage of justice, has lingered for decades in broad segments of the Italian American community. To much of this community, the case pointed to the perils of Italian heritage in a profoundly xenophobic era. Among liberal and Leftist Italian Americans (and among many liberals and Leftists generally), the executions represent a stark example of the recurrent injustice of the American judicial system. Who you are and what you believe, they argue, determines how you are judged. One passionate explanation of this vantage point comes from Vera Weisbord, writing in *La parola del popolo,* an Italian American Socialist newspaper when first published in 1908 and a more mainstream liberal-Left journal by 1977, when Weisbord was writing. (See Document 42.)

Exoneration?

The case has reemerged in the political arena in Massachusetts as well, twice more since the executions. In 1959, Alexander Cella, an Italian American state representative from Medford, introduced a bill to exonerate Sacco and Vanzetti. It was a fascinating historical moment for this effort. In 1959, at the height of the Cold War, presumably Cella would have had little chance of success in defending two avowed anarchists. There was a good deal of posturing by their defenders that now makes little sense outside of its historical context. Seeking to distance themselves from the Cold War foe of international communism, they insisted that the two men were anarchists but *not* Communists. (See Document 43.) Although the vast majority of witnesses who testified were sympathetic to the bill for exoneration, it did not pass. Opponents of the bill managed to table it.

Almost twenty years later, Massachusetts Governor Michael S. Dukakis revisited the issue, motivated by the sense that a wrong had been done in that state's past. He also had a more personal connection; in 1959, he had served as a legislative aide to Alexander Cella when he sought the exoneration. In 1977, on the fiftieth anniversary of Sacco and Vanzetti's execution, Dukakis issued a proclamation declaring that because of the atmosphere of hostility against immigrants and those with "unorthodox political views" that prevailed in the 1920s, it had been impossible for the two immigrant anarchists to receive a fair trial. (See Document 44.) Although he carefully avoided passing judgment on the guilt or innocence of Sacco and Vanzetti, still the governor managed to anger a number of people in his state. The State Senate, for example, responded to the proclamation by voting 21–14 to condemn it as illegal. Even fifty years after the trial, it continued to raise hackles in Massachusetts.

Decades later, the question of Sacco and Vanzetti's guilt or innocence remains an open one. There is still little to tie Vanzetti to the crime and still less given recent revelations about his gun. Sacco's situation continues to be more complex. Eyewitness testimony proved an unreliable indicator of his guilt or innocence. Much of the material evidence, including the cap, was shown to be far less than conclusive. But the ballistics evidence continues to confound. Tests on bullets from Sacco's gun run in 1927 and in 1961 (plus an additional test apparently run in 1944) consistently indicated matches with one of the mortal bullets fired into Berardelli. The argument that the bullet—or even the gun—was switched appeared before the trial ended, and it has reemerged several times in the decades following the case. Because evidence that the gun that Vanzetti carried had not belonged to Berardelli was buried, this is not entirely implausible. A 1983 forensic investigation by a specially appointed commission, however, revived the possibility that Sacco's gun was at the crime scene. The commission's evidence was not definitive, but it leaves open the possibility of Sacco's involvement.

Let us assume for the moment, then, that Sacco was guilty. It is important to contemplate, even if this were true, what the implications are for the judicial system in the United States. Regardless of whether Sacco was guilty, it is impossible to argue that he—much less Vanzetti—received a fair trial. One could argue that in the end, Sacco got what he deserved, that he was guilty and was found guilty, and that is what is most important. This supposition presents a compelling irony, however, even a tragedy. Of all the people involved in their defense, including the prisoners themselves, Sacco was the one person most firmly convinced that the state would never let him go. He refused to sign any petitions or to express hope that any of the appeals would work. It was Sacco who most accurately predicted how a capitalist state would act, having captured one of its sworn enemies. He predicted, time and again, that he and Vanzetti would be killed because the state could not afford to free them. Despite a clearly unfair trial and despite a worldwide outburst of indignation and anger, the state did precisely that. It was Sacco, an anarchist and perhaps even a propagandist of the deed, who predicted, more accurately than any American conservative or liberal, how the state would react. It is more controversial but not entirely implausible to argue that Sacco's prediction, aligned perfectly with—and provided a justification for—his commitment to unceasing and even violent opposition to capitalism and the state. In the end, the state of Massachusetts and the United States confirmed for Sacco his most deeply held political beliefs. And it was Sacco who, we are assuming for the moment, actually committed the crime. How could the trial and the executions have done anything but confirm the same thing for Vanzetti?

A NOTE ABOUT THE TEXT

All of Luigi Galleani's documents and Bartolomeo Vanzetti's articles in *Cronaca sovversiva* and *Il martello* (along with Carlo Tresca's comments) were originally written in Italian. All of Nicola Sacco's and Vanzetti's letters, as well as Vanzetti's *Background of the Plymouth Trial,* were written in English. Excerpts from the letters and pamphlet are presented unedited and without attention drawn to grammatical or spelling errors, so that Sacco and Vanzetti's efforts to express themselves in English are kept intact for readers.

NOTES

[1]Matthew Jacobson, *Whiteness of a Different Color: European Immigrants and the Alchemy of Race* (Cambridge, Mass.: Harvard University Press, 1998), and Thomas Guglielmo, *White on Arrival: Italians, Race, Color, and Power in Chicago, 1890–1945* (New York: Oxford University Press, 2003).

[2]Quoted in Paul Avrich, *Sacco and Vanzetti: The Anarchist Background* (Princeton, N.J.: Princeton University Press, 1991), 49.

[3]Quoted in Avrich, *Sacco and Vanzetti,* 26.

[4]Quoted in Roberta Feuerlicht, *Justice Crucified: The Story of Sacco and Vanzetti* (New York: McGraw-Hill, 1977), 23.

[5]John Dos Passos, *Facing the Chair: Story of the Americanization of Two Foreignborn Workmen* (New York: Da Capo Press, 1970 [1927]), 57.

[6]Avrich, *Sacco and Vanzetti,* 149–64.

[7]Feuerlicht, *Justice Crucified,* 181.

[8]*The Sacco-Vanzetti Case: Transcript of the Record of the Trial of Nicola Sacco and Bartolomeo Vanzetti in the Courts of Massachusetts and Subsequent Proceedings, 1920–1927* (Mamaroneck, N.Y.: Paul P. Appel, Publisher, 1969), II, 2239.

[9]Quoted in Edmund M. Morgan and G. Louis Joughin, *The Legacy of Sacco and Vanzetti* (New York: Harcourt, Brace and Company, 1948), 511.

[10]Quoted in Francis Russell, *Tragedy in Dedham: The Story of the Sacco-Vanzetti Case* (New York: McGraw-Hill, 1962), 385.

[11]Quoted in Morgan and Joughin, *Legacy,* 262.

[12]Bruce Biven, "In Dedham Jail," *New Republic,* June 22, 1927.

[13]Quoted in Morgan and Joughin, *Legacy,* 353.

PART TWO

The Documents

Italian America

1

GINO SPERANZA

How It Feels to Be a Problem
May 1904

When Italian immigrants began entering the United States by the millions in the late nineteenth and early twentieth century, part of a massive migration of people worldwide, they provoked a quick and often negative response. Italian immigrants and second-generation Italians were not unaware of assaults on their culture and their identity. One response to these assaults, early in the twentieth century, came from Gino Speranza. Born in Bridgeport, Connecticut, in 1872, and trained as a lawyer, Speranza was acutely aware of widespread negative perceptions of Italian immigrants. A longtime advocate for immigrants' rights and founder of the Society for the Protection of Italian Immigrants in 1907, Speranza addressed a native-born American audience pointedly in his article titled "How It Feels to Be a Problem," excerpted here.

Gino Speranza, "How It Feels to Be a Problem," *Charities,* XII, no. 18 (May 1904): 457, 460, 463.

... Now, considering the large percentage of foreign born in the population of the United States, it is a strange fact how few Americans ever consider how very unpleasant, to say the least, it must be to the foreigners living in their midst to be constantly looked upon either as a national problem or a national peril. And this trying situation is further strained by the tone in which the discussion is carried on as if it applied to utter strangers mile[s] and miles away, instead of to a large number of resident fellow citizens. Perhaps this attitude may be explained by the fact that to the vast majority of Americans "foreigner" is synonymous with the popular conception of the immigrant as a poor, ignorant, and uncouth stranger, seeking for better luck in a new land. But poverty and ignorance and uncouthness, even if they exist as general characteristics of our immigrants, do not necessarily exclude intelligence and sensitiveness. Too often, let it be said, does the American of common schooling interpret differences from his own standard and habits of life, as necessarily signs of inferiority. Foreignness of features or of apparel is for him often the denial of brotherhood. Often, again, the fine brow and aquiline nose of the Latin will seem to the American to betoken a criminal type rather than the impress of a splendid racial struggle.

Then there is another large class of "plain Americans" who justify a trying discussion of the stranger within the gates by the self-satisfying plea that the foreigner should be so glad to be in the "land of the free" that he cannot mind hearing a few "unpleasant truths" about himself.

This is not an attempt to show that the tide of immigration does not carry with it an ebb of squalor and ignorance and undesirable elements. It is rather an endeavor to look at the problem, as it were, *from the inside.* For if America's salvation from this foreign invasion lies in her capacity to assimilate such foreign elements, the first step in the process must be a thorough knowledge of the element that should be absorbed.

Many imagine that the record and strength of the American democracy suffice of themselves to make the foreigner love the new land and engender in him a desire to serve it; that, in other words, assimilation is the natural tendency. Assimilation, however, is a dual process of forces interacting one upon the other. Economically, this country can act like a magnet in drawing the foreigner to these shores, but you cannot rely on its magnetic force to make the foreign an *American.* To bring about assimilation the larger mass should not remain passive. It must attract, *actively attract,* the smaller foreign body.

It is with this in mind that I say that if my countrymen here keep apart, if they herd in great and menacing city colonies, if they do not learn your language, if they know little about your country, the fault is as much yours as theirs. And if you wish to reach us you will have to batter down some of the walls you have yourselves built up to keep us from you. . . .

To feel that we are considered a problem is not calculated to make us sympathize with your efforts in our behalf, and those very efforts are, as a direct result, very likely to be misdirected. My countrymen in America, ignorant though many of them are, and little in touch with Americans, nevertheless feel keenly that they are looked upon by the masses as a problem. It is, in part, because of that feeling that they fail to take an interest in American life or to easily mix with the natives. And though it may seem far-fetched, I believe that the feeling that they are unwelcome begets in them a distrust of those defenses to life, liberty and property which the new country is presumed to put at their disposal. They have no excess of confidence in your courts and it is not surprising, however lamentable, that the more hot-headed sometimes take the law into their own hands. You cannot expect the foreigner of the humbler class to judge beyond his experience—and his experience of American justice may be comprised in what he learns in some of the minor tribunals controlled by politicians, and in what he has heard of the unpunished lynchings of his countrymen in some parts of the new land. What appeal can the doctrine of state supremacy and federal non-interference make to him? Imagine what you would think of Italian justice if the American sailors in Venice, in resisting arrest by the constituted authorities, had been strung up to a telegraph pole by an infuriated Venetian mob, and the government at Rome had said, with the utmost courtesy: "We are very sorry and greatly deplore it, but we can't interfere with the autonomy of the province of Venetia!" . . .

There is one more question that an Italian, speaking for his countrymen here, may urge upon Americans who are interested in the problem of assimilation. It is this: That you should make my countrymen love your country by making them see what is truly good and noble in it. Too many of them, far too many, know of America only what they learn from the corrupt politician, the boss, the "banchiere," and the ofttimes rough policeman. I have been in certain labor camps in the South where my countrymen were forced to work under the surveillance of armed guards. I have spoken to some who had been bound to a mule and whipped back to work like slaves. I have met others who bore the marks of brutal abuses committed by cruel bosses with the consent of their superiors. What conception of American liberty can these foreigners have?

2

EDWARD ROSS

The Old World in the New
1914

Despite the contributions Italian immigrants made in economic and cultural terms, many continued to express alarm over their burgeoning numbers and their obvious differences from native-born Americans. Edward Ross, a leader in the relatively new field of sociology, was among those scholars who wrote increasingly critical analyses of immigrants' dire impact on American society in the years just before and after World War I. This excerpt from The Old World in the New *presents the immigration of Italians into the United States as little short of catastrophic.*

Steerage passengers from a Naples boat show a distressing frequency of low foreheads, open mouths, weak chins, poor features, skew faces, small or knobby crania, and backless heads. Such people lack the power to take rational care of themselves; hence their death-rate in New York is twice the general death-rate and thrice that of the Germans. No other immigrants from Europe, unless it be the Portuguese or the half-African Bravas of the Azores, show so low an earning power as the South Italians. In our cities the head of the household earns on an average $390 a year, as against $449 for the North Italian, $552 for the Bohemian, and $630 for the German. In silk-mill and woolen-mill, in iron-ore mining and the clothing trade, no other nation-

Edward Ross, *The Old World in the New* (New York: The Century Co., 1914), 113–14, 117, 118–19.

ality has so many low-pay workers; nor does this industrial inferiority fade out in the least with the lapse of time.

Their want of mechanical aptitude is often noticed. For example, in a New England mill manned solely by South Italians only one out of fifteen of the extra hands taken on during the "rush" season shows sufficient aptitude to be worth keeping. The operatives require closer supervision than Americans, and each is given only one thing to do, so as to put the least possible strain on his attention.

If it be demurred that the ignorant, superstitious Neapolitan or Sicilian, heir to centuries of Bourbon misgovernment, cannot be expected to prove us his race mettle, there are his children, born in America. What showing do they make? Teachers agree that the children of the South Italians rank below the children of the North Italians. They hate study, make slow progress, and quit school at the first opportunity. While they take to drawing and music, they are poor in spelling and language and very weak in abstract mathematics. In the words of one superintendent, "they lack the conveniences for thinking." More than any other children, they fall behind their grade. They are below even the Portuguese and the Poles, while at the other extremity stand the children of the Scandinavians and the Hebrews. The explanation of the difference is not irregularity of attendance, for among pupils attending three fourths of the time, or more, the percentage of South Italians retarded is fifty-six as against thirty-seven and a half per cent for the Russian-Hebrew children and twenty-nine per cent for the German. Nor is it due to the father's lack of American experience, for of the children of South Italians who have been in this country ten or more years sixty per cent are backward, as against about half that proportion among the Hebrews and the Germans. After allowing for every disturbing factor, it appears that these children, with the dusk of Saracenic or Berber ancestors showing in their cheeks, are twice as apt to drop behind other pupils of their age as are the children of the non-English-speaking immigrants from northern Europe. . . .

Before the boards of inquiry at Ellis Island their emotional instability stands out in the sharpest contrast to the self-control of the Hebrew and the stolidity of the Slav. They gesticulate much, and usually tears stand in their eyes. When two witnesses are being examined, both talk at once, and their hands will be moving all the time. Their glances flit quickly from one questioner to another, and their eyes are the restless, uncomprehending eyes of the desert Bedouin between walls. Yet for all this eager attention, they are slow to catch the meaning of a simple question, and often it must be repeated.

Mindful of these darting eyes and hands, one does not wonder that the Sicilian will stab his best friend in a sudden quarrel over a game of cards. The Slavs are ferocious in their cups, but none is so ready with his knife when sober as the South Italian. In railroad work other nationalities shun camps with many Italians. Contractors are afraid of them because the whole force will impulsively quit work, perhaps flare into riot, if they imagine one of their number has suffered a wrong.

The principal of a school with four hundred Sicilian pupils observes that on the playground they are at once more passionate and more vindictive than other children. Elsewhere, once discipline has been established, "the school will run itself"; but in this school the teacher "has to sit on the lid all the time." Their restlessness keeps the truant officer busy, and their darting, flickering attention denies them concentration and the steady, telling stroke. For all their apparent brightness, when at fourteen they quit school, they are rarely beyond the third or fourth grade.

As grinding rusty iron reveals the bright metal, so American competition brings to light the race stuff in poverty-crushed immigrants. But not all this stuff is of value in a democracy like ours. Only a people endowed with a steady attention, a slow-fuse temper, and a persistent will can organize itself for success in the international rivalries to come. So far as the American people consents [sic] to incorporate with itself great numbers of wavering, excitable, impulsive persons who cannot organize themselves, it must in the end resign itself to lower efficiency, to less democracy, or to both.

3

LUIGI GALLEANI

Anarchy Will Be!
1907

Luigi Galleani, the fearsome and inspiring leader of the anarchist circle with which Sacco and Vanzetti were connected, wrote extensive and eloquent calls for anarchy. This selection, "Anarchy Will Be!", comes from The End of Anarchism?, *written in response to a longtime ally's disavowal of anarchism in 1907.*

... Let us clear up quickly a misunderstanding which has been cleared up many times before, but which arises now and then with the qualms and bigotry of a certain respectable anarchism.

It is the misunderstanding concerning revolutionary expropriation, usually called *theft* by others, although the noun does not fit the deed.

Everyone agrees on one point: in an egalitarian society, where all means of production and exchange are common property and where the products of work have only one purpose—to assure the satisfaction of everyone's needs—theft has no meaning. It is impossible, absurd.

Therefore, among anarchists, no question of principle concerning theft exists.

When it comes to action, or tactics as it is usually called, there was a time when some comrades believed (and some still do) that in order to develop our propaganda, to equip vanguards, to arm them for action, boldly to initiate attacks, or to repel violence by force of arms, financial means would be needed that could not be provided by poor militants with more energy and courage than weapons: so they *expropriated,* as they used to say, with rigorous precision.

Luigi Galleani, *The End of Anarchism?* (Sanday, Orkney, UK: Cienfuegos Press, 1982 [1907]), 58–60, 71.

They took wherever they found it.

What does *expropriation* mean?

It means to take from somebody the goods or real estate that he owns, claiming he has no right to them.

From Saint Clement to Babeuf, Proudhon, Bakunin and the most modest of our comrades, the invalidity of all property titles has never been questioned: expropriation is legitimate unless it ends as its opposite, *appropriation*.[1]

To make myself better understood: if Tom takes Harry's wealth for his own enjoyment, we say that he has appropriated it. The property in question has only changed its titular owner, but as an institution it remains just what it was before. Tom is getting rich, as Harry did in the past, on the shoulders and the labour of harnessed slaves.

Nothing has changed, and there is no reason why we should congratulate Tom for having taken Harry's wealth.

But suppose, as it recently happened, a band of revolutionaries attack a bank; they immobilize the guards, empty the safes and, weapons in hand, defend their retreat. Then, having secured it, they deliver their loot to insurrectionary committees to further the revolutionary movement in their community, to provide the necessary means for attaining victory.

Do you disapprove?

No, you cannot disapprove. There has been expropriation, the very expropriation you have invoked a thousand times as a revolutionary necessity. There has been no appropriation in the sense that the confiscated wealth has been used to re-establish some other private property with all its consequences. Not at all. We are faced exactly with an initial, partial act of revolutionary expropriation. Besides the material advantages for the movement, it initiates, enables and encourages the multitude to proceed to the final expropriation of the ruling class for the benefit of every one. This has been our desire and our aim.

How can we curse, condemn, or reject?

---

[1] Galleani's knowledge of philosophers and radical thinkers was expansive, and he frequently made reference to them in his writings. Here, he mentions Roman Pope St. Clement (d. 100 C.E.); François Babeuf (1760–1797), a participant in the French Revolution; French radical Pierre-Joseph Proudhon (1809–1865), who asserted that "property is theft"; and Russian Mikhail Bakunin (1814–1876), credited by many as one of the founders of anarchism. Each, in his own way, was critical of the concept of private property.

Clement Duval, Vittorio Pini, Ravachol[2] have never taken for themselves a single penny of the loot that they obtained with the constant risk of death or life imprisonment. You may say that they have used that money for questionable propaganda means and action and even conclude that it could have been used in a better way. But you can't condemn. . . .

We do not believe there are useless or harmful acts of rebellion. Every one of them, together with the accidents inseparable from any violent change of the monotonous routine of life, has deep echoes and lasting gains, which compensate abundantly for them.

Let us be understood: we are not being nostalgic for unneeded brutality nor for vulgar coarseness. We too would prefer that every act of rebellion had such sense of proportion that its consequences would correspond perfectly to its causes, not only in measure, but also in timeliness, giving it an irresistible automatic character. Then every act would speak eloquently for itself with no need for glosses or clarifying comments. Furthermore, we would like this unavoidable necessity to assume a highly ethical—and even an aesthetic—attitude. . . .

Unfortunately (and we have at length stated why), the individual act of rebellion, due to intrinsic and extrinsic causes, due to the pressures of the moment, the environment and the subject's own psychology, cannot be different from what it is, no matter what our preference may be.

Then it follows that it would be absurd and ridiculous for us to think of compiling a new calendar of saints, the saints of the social revolution, as it would be to think of condemning them posthumously.

No act of rebellion is useless; no act of rebellion is harmful. . . .

In the field of economics—in contrast to the radical movements which do agree in rejecting private property, in advocating collective ownership of the means of production and exchange, in the remuneration of each according to his aptitude and his labour—libertarian communism—once individual property is abolished, the land and means of production made the communal and indivisible property of all—rejects the theory of remuneration, even if it were to involve the total product of labour; it rejects the principle of compensation as irrational,

---

[2]Clement Duval (1850–1935), Vittorio Pini (d. 1892), and Francois-Claudius Koeningstein (1859–1892), also known as Ravachol, were all active in the French anarchist movement, and were all advocates of revolutionary expropriation—of theft to support revolutionary activity.

unjust and dangerous in so far as it necessarily engenders the authority and the tyranny that make the bourgeois regime infamous; and it proposes, instead, that every member of society, regardless of his aptitudes or work, be entitled to the full satisfaction of his needs, of all his needs. Such satisfaction not only assures the participation of each person in production according to his capacities, but also eliminates the danger of falling once again into a regime of inequality, of authority, of disorder and violence that the social revolution would have abolished.

In the political field, in contrast to the authoritarian goals of the socialists, collectivists, or communists which, because of the foreseeable economic inequalities implicit in their systems, are obliged, even now, to posit a coercive power that contains and appeases their inequities, or, at least, an administration-state which rules and regulates production, distribution and consumption; anarchism proposes, instead, the absolute and irrevocable rejection of government and authority in any form, and in place of the principle of good, fair, brotherly government, it proclaims the *ungovernability* of the individual who possesses within himself the means, the right, and the power for self-government.

4

LUIGI GALLEANI

La salute è in voi!

c. 1905

For Galleani and his followers, anarchism was not simply a philosophical stance — it was a practice. Galleani was an advocate of "propaganda of the deed"; he believed that violent acts could precipitate a revolution. La salute è in voi!, excerpted here, is the infamous manual for making explosives that Galleani published, probably in 1905. This manual was inaccurate, *though; Galleani had to publish corrections in his Italian anarchist journal* Cronaca sovversiva.

Luigi Galleani, *La salute è in voi!* (n.p.: c. 1905).

Explosive Materials

The manufacture of explosives is not difficult, but to be able to make them effectively and without danger it is necessary to follow closely all of the instructions that will follow. Every alteration in the proportions of the substances and the order of the operations can produce a catastrophe or at least a completely failed result.

In general before manufacturing large explosives it is better to first test a quantity 15 or 20 times smaller until one has gained practice and the necessary assurance. Therefore for every explosive we will indicate the amounts for the small tests, and the amounts for the large ones.

Before using an explosive it is best to go into the countryside to test the small quantity.

Before throwing away the liquid acids that remain from the operation, you need to dilute them with water 20 times their volume, or better still, to put them in soda or lime until they stop boiling. This is useful because these liquids won't burn zinc pipes through which they could pass or allow smell to escape that would arouse suspicions.

The materials that are used must be pure enough. They can be obtained from dealers in chemical products or from pharmacists; it is best not to buy everything from the same store so that no one will figure out what you want to make.

The work should be done in a well-ventilated room, with a good chimney and with curtains or some way to prevent anyone outside from knowing what you are doing. You need to be on the top floor because of the odor and smoke that are produced.

The relative forces of the different explosives are as follows: if the blast from a gun has the power of one, an equal quantity of panclastite has a force of 6; of dynamite 7; of dry cotton fulminate 9 (with 50% saltpeter 5); of nitroglycerine 9; of mercury fulminate 10, or 3½; of nitromannite 11.

All of the other explosives that are spoken of often, like MELANITE, etc., are all nitroglycerine based and never surpass the power of NITROGLYCERINE.

Dynamite

Dynamite is a paste made with nitroglycerine and a substance absorbed in powder. It is very easy to make, transport, and store. Because dynamite has become very common, in general it has become much easier to procure it, without having to make the nitroglycerine that is used to make dynamite. In any case it is necessary to study how to handle it and how to use it. It is used in stone and sulfur quarries . . . in road work and in arsenals. It is therefore accessible to miners, soldiers, etc. One good excuse is contraband fishing, which I use, and often in the country, throwing the cartridge with the percussion cap and the lit fuse (covered with tar or wax) where there are fish. Before using dynamite it is always necessary to test it.

Uses of Explosive Materials

We now give some indication of the uses of explosives, but we make note of the fact that though we are not now discussing chemical operations any more, you need to follow STRICTLY the instructions we have given. Now we are discussing the mechanical applications that anyone can vary and multiply according to one's capability and imagination. We repeat the recommendation to first test the explosives that you want to use in the countryside. To do the test you need to be at least 200 meters away from the point of the explosion and if this is lacking you must wait at least a half hour before approaching the load and touching it: in this case it is preferable to put another load near the first one and explode them both.

IMPORTANT OBSERVATION

In all uses of explosives you need to be careful to put the percussion cap outside the load and that the fuse reaches the fulminate of the percussion cap without touching the explosive material, because if it is lit by the fuse before the fulminate, often an explosion won't occur.

Bombs

These are containers full of metal and explosive material, that exploding break into pieces and injure those nearby. They can take any shape, but spherical ones are most effective. To make them explode you need a percussion cap with a fuse that burns quickly enough to just have time to light them and throw them. You can also apply a load or other apparatus all around the fuse holder so that the percussion cap explodes and explodes the load of the bomb. . . .

The bomb is more effective when the metal is more resistant, provided that the load has the force to explode it. Therefore the best metals are iron or steel, rather than copper, brass, or bronze, or cast iron or zinc alone or mixed with tin; lead won't work. THE THICKNESS OF THE WALLS must be at least a ½ centimeter and it is better if they are 1 or 2 centimeters. If you have a container that is too thin, you can adapt it by wrapping around it, very tightly, several rows of wire around nails and other pieces of iron. A bomb with a ½ kilogram of dynamite, with a volume of a half liter, in good conditions, can injure 20 or 30 people. To achieve the same effect with gunpowder you would need a volume of 4 liters; with cotton fulminate ⅖ of a liter would suffice. It is very easy to find containers for bombs, for example: large knobs from beds, metal light bulbs that have a threaded hole; the brass balls that are used on the handles of the printing presses, etc. You can also have manufactured, by a mechanic or a foundryman, with some excuse, hollow balls of iron in one piece or in two pieces that screw together, strong metallic boxes with screw caps, etc. In all cases it is necessary to have a hole for the fuse. . . .

5

LUIGI GALLEANI

Against the War, Against Peace, For Social Revolution
March 18, 1916

This article by Galleani is one of the series of articles he wrote in opposition to World War I. Opposition to the war was widespread in the United States, especially before its official entry into the war in 1917. Few protests were as vociferous as Galleani's, however. His angry denunciations of the war convinced Sacco and Vanzetti, as well as several other Galleanisti, *to cross the border into Mexico to avoid being drafted and to disassociate themselves from the conflict. Galleani's protests eventually also led to the loss of mailing privileges for* Cronaca sovversiva, *and to his arrest and deportation.*

Luigi Galleani, "Against the War, Against Peace, For Social Revolution," *Cronaca sovversiva,* March 18, 1916.

"Truth marches on, and nothing will stop it."   —E. Zola[1]

She climbs, carrying the beacon and palm of victory. But whether merciless or meek, [truth] guards the universal daily experience, and she must climb through Calvary—there is no other way.

Remember! Remember how we warned our confused companions twenty months ago, when the war first started, "If a ray of Truth has kissed you, do not barter that joy with morbid enthusiasms that only turn into disillusionment: do not forsake that joy, at the cost of being left alone while others join the ranks.

It is not weak men that decide the fortunes of the world! Our day will come, do not despair, do not abandon the positions you struggled for, do not betray revolution for war!

War is the fury of pirates, jackals, salesmen, priests, all greedy for gain! Civilization, fatherland, liberty, progress, are nothing but the flag that hides fraud and the necessary tribute in blood."

This is what we wrote nearly two years ago, when the war started!

The Nation

If we mean by "nation" something more universal than that represented by the *ancien régime,* there's no doubt: war is the least national of phenomena. There is no choice: if we refuse that anthropological nonsense of ethnic differentiation, war is stupid and wrong. If we accept racial differences, we must concede that from Punjab to Hungary to . . . Lorraine, etc., all we have is Celts at war, Germanic all in origin, fighting each other with the most fraternal enthusiasm.

The Fatherland

A country—as the citizens within it—claims territorial integrity and the right to self-determination, without foreign intervention and with respect for other countries.

Only this reciprocity is the basis for all countries. If a nation invades the rights of another, its own fundamental rights are contravened.

Italy claims Trente and Trieste from Austria: yet it holds sway over

---

[1]Emile Zola (1840–1902) was the founder of the Naturalist movement in literature. The French author wrote numerous novels and plays, among them *Germinal,* a work on a coal-mining strike that critics described as a call to revolution.

Eritrea, Benadir ... Tripolitania ... it steps upon the rights it claims from Austria, and sends those who returned from fighting a colonial war to fight in the mountains a nationalistic war.

The same may be said of Austria, Germany, England, Russia and France ... not only ethnic motivations ought to be removed from war, but also the *concern for freedom* of the many governments involved.

The reality is very different.

What we call "fatherland" is nothing but a recent flash in the pan of the past century: nobody believes in it any more.

... Through our own well-beloved rebellions of 1848 and 1870, Italy became united and independent.

... But as soon as it was born, the nation became mockery and disillusionment.

The middle class found it too confining, and sought new markets abroad; the proletariat witnessed the reconstitution of old privileges, and went abroad, only to find out that all nations resemble each other—that everywhere there are masters and servants, oppressors and oppressed, rich and poor—and through wandering in a wide world, the proletariat found the ultimate, sole frontier: that between those who work and those who are idle, those who suffer and those who enjoy life: the proletariat's country is the world.

The Alarm

As vanguards, we know that ... the masses slow down after a first success, and that ... the beacon of fire must be brought by us into all bastilles.[2]

At home or in the trench ... the poor of a hundred countries will grow sick of the war: today or tomorrow ... they will rise up and force rapprochements. ... [U]nless we decapitate the central power of each country, mercilessly eliminating all those who could stop the insurrection; unless we feed and arm the revolutionaries ... unless we keep a clear vision of the great task that awaits us ... unless we guarantee to those who lose heart the benefits of a new regime ... unless we have the heroic courage of our convictions ... unless we make justice our cause and triumph our right. ...

Never was revolt so unanimous ... never was the world so united in suffering ... never was hope so alive as it is today ... from the moon-lit

[2]The Bastille was the state prison in Paris; when revolutionaries stormed it on July 14, 1789, it marked the downfall of the French monarchy.

horizon numberless children, elders, workers, weeping and mourning mothers all curse with the same heart and the same disgust the destructive war and a shameful peace, crying out and declaring the alarm, the needed vesper (bells of revolution in medieval Sicily) of liberation.

It is the hour which shall never come again!

Alarm! Alarm! To the vesper that gives us quarter and knows no mercy.

6

BARTOLOMEO VANZETTI

Unbelievable Stuff

July 8, 1916

This article is one of the occasional pieces Vanzetti wrote for Cronaca sovversiva. *It reflects his involvement in the Plymouth Cordage strike concluded a few months earlier, and speaks to the intense rivalry that existed not only between Italian immigrant radicals and conservatives but also among the radicals themselves.*

The panderers of Italian-American socialism throw at me such a barrage of accusations, I would need an entire newspaper column to reply. The only serious accusation . . . I wish to respond to for my dignity . . . and the sake of truth, is that I acted against the workers' interest by denying them the funds received to help them. . . .

The accusation that I distributed money against the will of the donors is absurd . . . those of you who know my conduct during the strike, lie knowing that you lie.

As for my violation of what you call . . . "the workers' assembly," I declare . . . in the face of the policemen you called and paid . . . that I revolted against the clerico-henchmen socialist block, that wanted to lead the strike dictatorially. I did not trust you and do not trust you. I'm not grateful that you didn't alert the authorities . . . and do not

Bartolomeo Vanzetti, "Unbelievable Stuff," *Cronaca sovversiva,* July 8, 1916.

believe you did so to safeguard the good name of the Italians. Where does this frantic desire to defend national honor come from? Internationalists . . . shouldn't even say such things.

You have not gone to the Law simply because—corrupt though the Law is—you would have trembled before it more than the man you accused.

The [Italian] colony doesn't trust me? What colony do you speak of? The workers', or that of the priests, sausage makers, spies, and self-styled high poppies you chummed with during the strike and after? You're not the representatives of the first; if you speak of the second, my hat's off to you: it's the only truth amidst so many lies.

Am I a troublesome element? Of course! All exploiters and profiteers . . . say this. You're in good company.

7

NICOLA SACCO

Letters

1924–1927

Many of their supporters described Sacco and Vanzetti as "philosophical" or as "pastoral" anarchists. As followers of Galleani, however, they were also advocates of fierce and even violent opposition to their perceived enemies. This selection of Sacco's letters from prison speaks to the complexity of his character and to the depth of his ideological commitment. They are to Fred Moore, his (ex) lawyer; to Jessica Henderson, a resident of a Boston suburb who was convinced of Sacco and Vanzetti's innocence; and to his daughter, Ines, and his son, Dante, soon before the execution date.

To Fred Moore, August 18, 1924

SIR:—Saturday I received your letter with enclose the post card that Mrs. M—— R—— sent to me—and the little pamphlet that you use

Marion Denman Frankfurter and Gardner Jackson, eds., *The Letters of Sacco and Vanzetti* (New York: Viking Press, 1928), 21–24.

to send to me it just to insult my soul. Yes, it is true, because you would not forget when you came here two or three times between last month with a groups people—that you know that I did not like to see them any more; but you brought them just seem to make my soul keep just sad as it could be. And I can see how clever and cynic you are, because after all my protest, after I have been chase you and all your philanthropists friends, you are still continue the infamous speculation on the shoulder of Sacco-Vanzetti case. So this morning before these things going any more long, I thought to send you these few lines to advise you and all your philanthropist friends of the "New Trail [Trial] League Committee"[1] to not print any more these letters with my picture and name on, and to be sure to take my name out if they should print any more of these little pamphlets, because you and your philanthropists has been use it from last three years like a instrument of infamous speculation. It is something to carry any man insane or tuberculosis when I think that after all my protest to have my case finish you and all your legione of friends still play the infame game. But, I would like to know if yours all are the boss of my life! I would like to know who his this men that ar abuse to take all the authority to do everything that he does feel like without my responsibility, and carry my case always more long, against all my wish. I would like to know who his this—generous—ma!!! Mr.— Moore—! I am telling you that you goin to stop this dirty game! You hear me? I mean every them word I said here, because I do not want have anything to do any more with "New Trail League Committee," because it does repugnant my coscience.

Many time you have been deluder and abuse on weakness of my comrades good faith, but I want you to stop now and if you please get out of my case, because you know that you are the obstacle of the case; and say! I been told you that from last May 25th—that was the last time you came to see me, and with you came the comrade Felicani and the Profess Guadagni.[2] Do you remember? Well, from that day I told you to get out of my case, and you promised me that you was goin to get out, but my—dear—Mr. Moore! I see that you are still here in my case, and you are still continued to play your famous gam. Of

[1]The New Trial League Committee was established in 1924 after the Sacco-Vanzetti Defense Committee broke with Fred Moore. It existed for only a few months, and several of its members rejoined the Defense Committee.

[2]Aldino Felicani, a printer and fellow *Galleanista,* was the founder of the Sacco-Vanzetti Defense Committee. Felice Gaudagni, a radical professor and editor of the *Gazetta de Massachusetts,* was also a member of the Sacco-Vanzetti Defense Committee.

course it is pretty hard to refuse a such sweet pay that has been come to you right long—in—this big—game. It is no true what I said? If it is not the truth, why did you not finish my case then? Another word, if this was not the truth you would quit this job for long time. It has been past one year last June when you and Mr. Grella[3] from New York came to see me into Bridgewater Hospital and that day between you and I we had another fight—and you will remember when I told this Mr. Moore! I want you to finish my case and I do not want to have anything to do with this politics in my case because it does repugnant my coscience—and your answer to me was this: Nick, if you don't want, Vanzetti does want! Do you remember when you said that? Well, do you think I believe you when you said that to me? No, because I know that you are the one that brings always in these mud in Sacco-Vanzetti case. Otherwise, how I could believe you when you been deluder me many times with your false promise? Well—I anyhow, wherever you do if you do not intent to get out of my case, remember this, that per September I want my case finish. But remember that we are right near September now and I don't see anything and any move yet. So tell me please, why you waiting now for? Do you wait till I hang myself? That's what you wish? Let me tell you right now don't be illuse yourself because I would not be surprise if somebody will find you some morning hang on lamp-post.

Your implacable enemy, now and forever,

NICK SACCO

To Dear Friend Mrs. Henderson, February 9, 1927

Since the day that Mrs. Evans[4] had announced me in one of her good letters, that you were going to come over to see me, I have been waiting every day by day, and the day did come, but that day . . . was too sad! But nevertheless, to have seen you together with the mother and had talk with you were please for me. Yes, because you, like all the great good mothers that just soon their painful soften down, just soon their struggle pass away, they open their hearts to receive the pain of

---

[3]Mr. Grella was presumably another supporter of Sacco and Vanzetti.

[4]Mrs. Evans was Elizabeth Glendower Evans, the wealthy Bostonian who was one of Sacco and Vanzetti's staunchest supporters.

Marion Denman Frankfurter and Gardner Jackson, eds., *The Letters of Sacco and Vanzetti* (New York: Viking Press, 1928), 44–45.

their other brother sufferance. Therefore, that is why your welcome visit brought me pleasure, for you are not only one of those noble good mothers that knows and embraces the sufferance of their oppressed brothers, but you have the strength to preserve yet your sensibility toward your dearest and toward the victims of the oppressed humanity.

Four years ago next month, I remember that my companionship Rosina,[5] she like you were sensitive—so much that everytime I used to describe her my prison life, you could see the tears run throughout her beloved face. But from and since that date, since my hunger strike, I have not told her any more my prison confinement for not to see this beloved brittle soul suffer. . . . By the way, Mrs. Henderson, you remember that I was saying to you how much injustice and cruel persecution is in this free society of today, and specially for the poor people. Yes, it is nice and noble to be rich and be kind and generous towards the poor exploit people, but it is much more noble the sacrifice of those who have none and divide his bread with his own oppressed brothers. Pardon me. Mrs. Henderson, it is not for discredit or to ignore you, Mrs. Evans and other human generosity work, which I sincerely believe that is an noble one and I am respectful; but it is the warm sincere voice of an unrest heart beat and a free soul that loved and lived amongst the workers class all his life. . . .

To My Dear Friends and Comrades, August 4, 1927

From the death cell we are just inform from the defense committee that the governor Fuller he has decided to kill us Aug. the 10th. We are not surprised for this news because we know the capitalist class hard without any mercy the good soldiers of the rivolution. We are proud for death and fall as all the anarchist can fall. It is up to you now, brothers, comrades! as I have tell you yesterday that you only that can save us, because we have never had faith in the governor for we have always know that the gov. Fuller, Thayer and Katzmann are the murder.

My warm fraternal regards to all,

NICOLA SACCO

[5]Rose (Rosina) Sacco was Nicola Sacco's wife; they had married in 1912.

Marion Denman Frankfurter and Gardner Jackson, eds., *The Letters of Sacco and Vanzetti* (New York: Viking Press, 1928), 69.

To My Dear Ines, July 19, 1927

I would like that you should understand what I am going to say to you, and I wish I could write you so plain, for I long so much to have you hear all the heart-beat eagerness of your father, for I love you so much as you are the dearest little beloved one.

It is quite hard indeed to make you understand in your young age, but I am going to try from the bottom of my heart to make you understand how dear you are to your father's soul. If I cannot succeed in doing that, I know that you will save this letter and read it over in future years to come and you will see and feel the same heart-beat affection as your father feels in writing it to you.

I will bring with me your little and so dearest letter and carry it right under my heart to the last day of my life. When I die, it will be buried with your father who loves you so much, as I do also your brother Dante and holy dear mother.

You don't know Ines, how dear and great your letter was to your father. It is the most golden present that you could have given to me or that I could have wished for in these sad days.

It was the greatest treasure and sweetness in my struggling life that I could have lived with you and your brother Dante and your mother in a neat little farm, and learn all your sincere words and tender affection. Then in the summer-time to be sitting with you in the home nest under the oak tree shade — beginning to teach you of life and how to read and write, to see you running, laughing, crying, and singing through the verdent fields picking the wild flowers here and there from one tree to another, and from the clear, vivid stream to your mother's embrace.

The same I have wished to see for other poor girls, and their brothers, happy with their mother and father as I dreamed for us — but it was not so and the nightmare of the lower classes saddened very badly your father's soul.

For the things of beauty and of good in this life, mother nature gave to us all, for the conquest and the joy of liberty. The men of this dying old society, they brutally have pulled me away from the embrace of your brother and your poor mother. But, in spite of all, the free spirit of your father's faith still survives, and I have lived for it and for the dream that some day I would have come back to life, to the embrace

Marion Denman Frankfurter and Gardner Jackson, eds., *The Letters of Sacco and Vanzetti* (New York: Viking Press, 1928), 67–69.

of your dear mother, among our friends and comrades again, but woe is me!

I know that you are good and surely you love your mother, Dante, and all the beloved ones—and I am sure that you love me also a little, for I love you much and then so much. You do not know Ines, how often I think of you every day. You are in my heart, in my vision, in every angle of this sad walled cell, in the sky and everywhere my gaze rests.

Meantime, give my best paternal greetings to all the friends and comrades, and doubly so to our beloved ones. Love and kisses to your brother and mother.

With the most affectionate kiss and ineffable caress from him who loves you so much that he constantly thinks of you. Best warm greetings from Bartolo to you all.

YOUR FATHER

To My Dear Son and Companion, August 18, 1927

Since the day I saw you last I had always the idea to write you this letter, but the length of my hunger strike and the thought I might not be able to explain myself, made me put it off all this time.

The other day, I ended my hunger strike and just as soon as I did that I thought of you to write to you, but I find that I did not have enough strength and I cannot finish it at one time. However, I want to get it down in any way before they take us again to the death-house, because it is my conviction that just as soon as the court refuses a new trial to us they will take us there. And between Friday and Monday, if nothing happens, they will electrocute us right after midnight, on August 22nd. Therefore, here I am, right with you with love and with open heart as ever I was yesterday.

I never thought that our inseparable life could be separated, but the thought of seven dolorous years makes it seem it did come, but then it has not changed really the unrest and the heart-beat of affection. That has remained as it was. More. I say that our ineffable affection reciprocal, is today more than any other time, of course. That is not only a great deal but it is grand because you can see the real brotherly love, not only in joy but also and more in the struggle of suffering. Remem-

Marion Denman Frankfurter and Gardner Jackson, eds., *The Letters of Sacco and Vanzetti* (New York: Viking Press, 1928), 70–74.

ber this, Dante. We have demonstrated this, and modesty apart, we are proud of it.

Much we have suffered during this long Calvary. We protest today as we protested yesterday. We protest always for our freedom.

If I stopped hunger strike the other day, it was because there was no more sign of life in me. Because I protested with my hunger strike yesterday as today I protest for life and not for death.

I sacrificed because I wanted to come back to the embrace of your dear little sister Ines and your mother and all the beloved friends and comrades of life and not death. So Son, today life begins to revive slow and calm, but yet without horizon and always with sadness and visions of death.

Well, my dear boy, after your mother had talked to me so much and I had dreamed of you day and night, how joyful it was to see you at last. To have talked with you like we used to in the days—in those days. Much I told you on that visit and more I wanted to say, but I saw that you will remain the same affectionate boy, faithful to your mother who loves you so much, and I did not want to hurt your sensibilities any longer, because I am sure that you will continue to be the same boy and remember what I have told you. I knew that and what here I am going to tell you will touch your sensibilities, but don't cry Dante, because many tears have been wasted, as your mother's have been wasted for seven years, and never did any good. So, Son, instead of crying, be strong, so as to be able to comfort your mother, and when you want to distract your mother from the discouraging soulness, I will tell you what I used to do. To take her for a long walk in the quiet country, gathering wild flowers here and there, resting under the shade of trees, between the harmony of the vivid stream and the gentle tranquility of the mothernature, and I am sure that she will enjoy this very much, as you surely would be happy for it. But remember always, Dante, in the play of happiness, don't you use all for yourself only, but down yourself just one step, at your side and help the weak ones that cry for help, help the prosecuted and the victim, because that are your better friends; they are the comrades that fight and fall as your father and Bartolo fought and fell yesterday for the conquest of the joy of freedom for all and the poor workers. In this struggle of life you will find more love and you will be loved.

I am sure that from what your mother told me about what you said during these last terrible days when I was lying in the iniquitous death-house—that description gave me happiness because it showed you will be the beloved boy I had always dreamed.

Therefore whatever should happen tomorrow, nobody knows, but if they should kill us, you must not forget to look at your friends and comrades with the smiling gaze of gratitude as you look at your beloved ones, because they love you as they love every one of the fallen persecuted comrades. I tell you, your father that is all the life to you, your father that loved you and saw them, and knows their noble faith (that is mine) their supreme sacrifice that they are still doing for our freedom, for I have fought with them, and they are the ones that still hold the last of our hope that today they can still save us from electrocution, it is the struggle and fight between the rich and the poor for safety and freedom, Son, which you will understand in the future of your years to come, of this unrest and struggle of life's death.

Much I thought of you when I was lying in the death-house—the singing, the kind tender voices of the children from the playground, where there was all the life and the joy of liberty—just one step from the wall which contains the buried agony of three buried souls. It would remind me so often of you and your sister Ines, and I wish I could see you every moment. But I feel better that you did not come to the death-house so that you could not see the horrible picture of three lying in agony waiting to be electrocuted, because I do not know what effect it would have on your young age. But then, in another way if you were not so sensitive it would be very useful to you tomorrow when you could use this horrible memory to hold up to the world the shame of the country in this cruel persecution and unjust death. Yes, Dante, they can crucify our bodies today as they are doing, but they cannot destroy our ideas, that will remain for the youth of the future to come.

Dante, when I said three human lives buried, I meant to say that with us there is another young man by the name of Celestino Maderios that is to be electrocuted at the same time with us. He has been twice before in that horrible death-house, that should be destroyed with the hammers of real progress—that horrible house that will shame forever the future of the citizens of Massachusetts. They should destroy that house and put up a factory or school, to teach many of the hundreds of the poor orphan boys of the world.

Dante, I say once more to love and be nearest to your mother and the beloved ones in these sad days, and I am sure that with your brave heart and kind goodness they will feel less discomfort. And you will also not forget to love me a little for I do—O, Sonny! thinking so much and so often of you.

Best fraternal greetings to all the beloved ones, love and kisses to your little Ines and mother. Most hearty affectionate embrace.

YOUR FATHER AND COMPANION

P.S. Bartolo send you the most affectionate greetings. I hope that your mother will help you to understand this letter because I could have written much better and more simple, if I was feeling good. But I am so weak.

8

BARTOLOMEO VANZETTI

Letters

1925, 1927

These letters written by Vanzetti from prison, like Sacco's, speak both to his character and to his commitment to his political beliefs. One of them is to Alice Stone Blackwell, his most frequent correspondent. Blackwell, whose mother was an early woman's rights advocate, was an accomplished crusader for progressive causes. That Vanzetti addressed her as "comrade" indicated his respect for her; he wrote frequently and frankly to her about ideological and political issues. Vanzetti's other letter, to Sacco's son, Dante, was written just days before the execution.

To Dear Comrade Blackwell, November 13, 1925

Your most welcome letter of Nov. 4th reached me in due time. Its news about your health assured me of your recovering and its arguments rouse many thoughts and sentiments within my being. I am going to answer with an attempt to express myself—and this will be a long random letter.

Marion Denman Frankfurter and Gardner Jackson, eds., *The Letters of Sacco and Vanzetti* (New York: Viking Press, 1928), 179–81.

You blame to me, anarchist, Miss H—— because "she hates politics and never votes." Well, these facts cause me to add my admiration and my gratitude to her; and I don't believe that you have written in the hope that I would have approved your "blaming," for, you should believe that I have changed my ideas, in order to expect it. And I cannot see any reason for such belief. I know that you are doing everything possible to my welfare. Therefore, I think that you have said it purposely to have me thinking of controvertial arguments and forgetting my personal troubles and my environment. Thus, to beneficiate me. Most good of you. But, I will not discuss about yours and my different beliefs about ballot, etc., because I have many other things to tell you and I know that you know quite well the reasons of my disbelief—reasons advocate by men such as Bakounin, Kropotkin, Proudhon, Malatesta, Emerson, Shelley, William Goodwin, Reclus, Galleani, Tolstoy, Spencer, and, it seems, also Christ, are named for the love of my beautiful anarchy, not for vanity or worse than that,—and, forgive me....[1]

To me, my life and my liberty are in the hands of enemies who can do what they please of us, because to give or to deny us a new trial is absolutely arbitrary to them. Which, in the world, and where are the reasons that make it reasonable to expect from them a new trial? All that could have been, or is, favorable to us,—in the sense to compel the enemies to give us, against their own will and wishes, a new trial,—has failed or is failing. So that such hope is contrary to all reason, knowledge, realities, facts, experiences, criteria, and logic. The hope of the doomed. Our enemies know very well that by another trial we would be free, and this is the reason why they will forget it; save that they want to free us. I have hopes—but I hope in me and in others.

Yes, I am disappointed already, without having to wait for further damages and offences. How could I not be disappointed? I should be insane and vanquished, while I have the soul of a winner. People have taken the bread out of their children's mouths to help us. Many have dedicated all their energy to the case; other prisoners were wronged; the same great cause has suffered because of us; we are chained, all

---

[1] These thinkers, with one exception, were all either anarchists or advocates of individualism or individual freedoms. The one exception was Herbert Spencer (1820–1903), a British sociologist whose provocative assertions about how society was, and should be, structured were taken up by thinkers across the political spectrum. Vanzetti's reference to Jesus Christ was not unprecedented; many anarchists and other radicals claimed him as a fellow revolutionary.

our beloved in sorrow; the case is lost. We did not come to be vanquished but to win, to destroy a world of crimes and miseries and to re-build with its freed atoms a new world. I am disappointed, but not crushed. I have not become a rat or a renegade. And I can carry my burden to the last, and only that counts.

To My Dear Dante, August 21, 1927

I still hope, and we will fight until the last moment, to revindicate our right to live and to be free, but all the forces of the State and of the money and reaction are deadly against us because we are libertarians or anarchists.

I write little of this because you are now and yet too young to understand these things and other things of which I would like to reason with you.

But, if you do well, you will grow and understand your father's and my case and your father's and my principles, for which we will soon be put to death.

I tell you now that all that I know of your father, he is not a criminal, but one of the bravest men I ever knew. Some day you will understand what I am about to tell you. That your father has sacrificed everything dear and sacred to the human heart and soul for his fate in liberty and justice for all. That day you will be proud of your father, and if you come brave enough, you will take his place in the struggle between tyranny and liberty and you will vindicate his (our) names and our blood.

If we have to die now, you shall know, when you will be able to understand this tragedy in its fullest, how good and brave your father has been with you, your father and I, during these eight years of struggle, sorrow, passion, anguish, and agony.

Even from now you shall be good, brave with your mother, with Ines, and with Susie—brave, good Susie[2]—and do all you can to console and help them.

I would like you to also remember me as a comrade and friend to your father, your mother and Ines, Susie and you, and I assure you

[2]Susie was a close friend of Rosina Sacco's, and lived with the Sacco family in the last years of the trial.

Marion Denman Frankfurter and Gardner Jackson, eds., *The Letters of Sacco and Vanzetti* (New York: Viking Press, 1928), 321–23.

that neither have I been a criminal, that I have committed no robbery and no murder, but only fought modestly to abolish crimes from among mankind and for the liberty of all.

Remember, Dante, each one who will say otherwise of your father and I, is a liar, insulting innocent dead men who have been brave in their life. Remember and know also, Dante, that if your father and I would have been cowards and hypocrits and rinnegetors[3] of our faith, we would not have been put to death. They would not even have convicted a lebbrous dog; not even executed a deadly poisoned scorpion on such evidence as that they framed against us. They would have given a new trial to a matricide and abitual felon on the evidence we presented for a new trial.

Remember, Dante, remember always these things; we are not criminals; they convicted us on a frame-up; they denied us a new trial; and if we will be executed after seven years, four months and seventeen days of unspeakable tortures and wrong, it is for what I have already told you; because we were for the poor and against the exploitation and oppression of the man by the man.

The documents of our case, which you and other ones will collect and preserve, will prove to you that your father, your mother, Ines, my family, and I have sacrificed by and to a State Reason of the American Plutocratic reaction.

The day will come when you will understand the atrocious cause of the above written words, in all its fullness. Then you will honor us.

Now Dante, be brave and good always. I embrace you.

P.S. I left the copy of *An American Bible* to your mother now, for she will like to read it, and she will give it to you when you will be bigger and able to understand it. Keep it for remembrance. It will also testify to you how good and generous Mrs. Gertrude Winslow[4] has been with us all. Good-bye Dante.

BARTOLOMEO

---

[3] A "rinnegatóre" is a traitor.
[4] Gertrude Winslow, a founder of the social justice committee of the Community Church of Boston, was a supporter and confidante of Sacco and Vanzetti.

Radical Possibility and the Red Scare

9

LOUIS POST

The Deportations Delirium of Nineteen-Twenty

1923

Louis Post was assistant secretary of labor from 1913 to 1921 and wit-nessed the excesses of the Red Scare firsthand. He published what he referred to as "a personal narrative of an historic official experience," titled The Deportations Delirium of Nineteen-Twenty, *just after he left office. This excerpt is Post's account of the mass arrests of suspected radi-cals in New England, the region where Sacco and Vanzetti lived.*

Meeting halls and family homes in twenty New England cities and towns were subjected to that ruthless night-raiding of January, 1920. Fourteen of the twenty were in Massachusetts—Boston, Chelsea, Brockton, Bridgewater, Norwood, Worcester, Springfield, Chicopee Falls, Holyoke, Gardner, Fitchburg, Lowell, Lawrence and Haverhill; the remaining six were in New Hampshire—Nashua, Manchester, Derry, Portsmouth, Claremont and Lincoln.

"Concentration points" had been established in both States, mostly in police stations, at each of which an immigration inspector was in attendance with batches of warrants of arrest. Arrests were made, however, quite regardless of warrants.

Nor were search warrants used, though homes were invaded, trunks broken open, personal papers seized and personal privacies shamefully disturbed. Captives were forced to stand in line against the walls of the public-meeting rooms in which they had been caught, and in this position were searched like victims of a predatory holdup.

Louis Post, *The Deportations Delirium of Nineteen-Twenty: A Personal Narrative of an Historic Official Experience* (New York: Da Capo Press, 1970 [1923]), 96–98, 99–101.

Blank questionnaires were filled out by the captors as they questioned their captives. At a hall in Worcester the entire audience attending a publicly advertised meeting, about 200 in all, were questioned, individual by individual, the citizens being thrust out and the aliens, about a hundred, taken to a jail from which all but sixteen were released in the course of the night.

So many prisoners were released with the same contempt for lawful process which characterized the arrests, that the aggregate of arrests in New England can only be estimated. Responsible estimates, however, place the New England total at from 800 to 1,200. A large proportion were released, as arbitrarily as they had been arrested, after periods of imprisonment ranging from a few hours to two or three days.

Altogether the New England raids were disgraceful legal travesties, riotous lynchings in defiance of law by officers of the law; and they were so characterized by a Federal judge of honorable distinction who saw and heard the testimony of the witnesses on both sides. After describing these and other outrages, which had been proved both directly and circumstantially at a hearing on *habeas corpus* writs before him in the United States Court at Boston, this United States Circuit Judge, George W. Anderson, remarked in the course of a comprehensive, convincing and extremely able argument in support of his decision, that "a mob is a mob, whether made up of Government officials acting under instructions from the Department of Justice, or of criminals and loafers and the vicious classes."

Among the meetings raided in New England was one which had assembled to discuss the organization of a co-operative bakery. It was composed of citizens as well as aliens and in about equal proportions. Yet the entire assemblage of thirty-nine persons was arrested and imprisoned in cells until morning. . . .

Captives to the number of considerably more than 400—being from half to a third of the whole number arrested in this part of New England—were taken to the immigration station at Boston and thence to the Deer Island detention place in Boston Harbor. Bitter complaints concerning the circumstances of the arrests and detentions came to the Department of Labor, and in the temporary absence of the Solicitor, who still had Departmental charge of immigration work, the complaints were referred to me. I ordered an investigation by two competent and trustworthy immigration officers, who upon returning from Boston reported that conditions at Deer Island had been for a few days utterly unfit, but were now greatly improved. In explanation of the original unfitness, they assured me that the fault did not lie with the immigration officials at Boston, for too little time had been given to prepare accommodations for the four hundred prisoners delivered at that station by the Department of Justice. By way of verifying their count, one of the investigators remarked to me that the number of prisoners was so large that when they were unshackled "the chains made a pile *that* high"—indicating with his hand a height of about three feet.

"Pile of chains!" I exclaimed.

"Yes, indeed," replied both investigators in one voice. Then one of them, corroborated by the other, explained: "The Department of Justice marched their prisoners through the streets of Boston to the immigrant station in chains. We know it for we saw photographs of the chained prisoners lined up in a group." One of the investigators added, with a queer glance of the eye, that "nothing was lacking in the way of display but a brass band."

Conditions at Deer Island were at that time still chaotic. There was lack of proper heat for the January weather. There was lack of adequate toilet facilities. Incommunicado exactions were rigidly enforced. One of the captives dashed out his brains in a corridor by plunging headlong from the fifth floor above. He did this in the sight of fellow captives who inferred from their own experiences that he had been crazed by his. Another was committed for insanity. Others were on the verge of insanity from the bewildering circumstances of their captivity.

It was in such bewildering circumstances, terrifying as well as bewildering, that the victims of the raids were given their hearings in deportation proceedings, pursuant to warrants of arrest issued either before or after the raids—some before and some after. Each hearing was conducted by an immigrant inspector authorized by law to conduct such hearings. Each was as a rule held in the presence of a Department of Justice detective who acted both as prosecutor and witness. The accused alien, who in many instances was ignorant even of our language and was not always fairly served by interpreters, was denied the right to have counsel—the temporary rule giving discretion to the inspector having remained in force from less than a week before the raids till nearly four weeks afterwards. But in spite of circumstances so adverse to the prisoners, the immigrant inspectors were obliged to acknowledge their inability to find cause for deportation against a majority. One of the inspectors is on record as testifying in court that out of from 30 to 35 of the Deer Island "red" cases he had disposed of, he was obliged to recommend cancellation of the warrants of arrest in fully 25, finding even as much as bare technical cause for deportation in less than ten.

The Arrest and the Trial

THE ARREST AND "CONSCIOUSNESS OF GUILT"

10

DISTRICT ATTORNEY FREDERICK KATZMANN

Closing Argument to the Dedham Jury

July 13, 1921

The night of their arrest and the following day when they were questioned, Sacco and Vanzetti told several lies about their activities. Whether they were lying to cover up their involvement in the South Braintree crime or because they were trying to hide their identity as radicals became a critical issue in the trial. In this excerpt from the trial transcript, Katzmann offers the prosecution's explanation for the falsehoods.

... Now, I was discussing the explanation, that feature of consciousness of guilt or lack of it as to this very crime on the part of the defendants in relation to the Johnson episode.[1] Would you suppose, gentlemen of the jury, that men like Vanzetti, who had been home a week—he had not been home a week, been back from New York a week, three days of which he spent there in Plymouth where he was to procure the house owner who was going to secrete literature, mak-

---

[1] Simon Johnson owned the garage Sacco and Vanzetti and two other *Galleanisti* visited on May 5, 1920. Ruth Johnson, Simon's wife, was the one who telephoned the police.

The Sacco-Vanzetti Case: Transcript of the Record of the Trial of Nicola Sacco and Bartolomeo Vanzetti in the Courts of Massachusetts and Subsequent Proceedings, 1920–1927 (Mamaroneck, N.Y.: Paul P. Appel, Publisher, 1969), II, 2203–04.

ing no effort to do so, despite this terrible news he brought home from New York, and Sacco, with whom he had been for three days substantially, and a little more, made no effort to get this literature out of his house?

Would you suppose these men who had not gotten the automobile, who had not taken it out of the garage and who did not have a single scrap of Socialistic, Anarchistic or whatever type of literature they were afraid of, or any books of the sort in their physical possession, who were simply men who were on foot out there that night and had not accomplished their primary design of obtaining that automobile? What was there for them to be afraid of?

To use the vernacular, "Nobody had the goods on them then." There was no literature in any automobile in which they were seated. There was no literature in their pockets. They were in the same condition, as far as the literature was concerned, as they are now. Whatever might have been in their minds could not be discerned by the authorities nor apprehended. They had no literature.

But they had arsenals upon them. Vanzetti had a loaded 38 calibre revolver, this man who ran to Mexico because he did not want to shoot a fellow human being in warfare, a loaded 38 calibre revolver, any one of the cartridges instantly death dealing. This tender-hearted man who loved this country and who went down to Mexico because he did not believe in shooting a fellow human being, going down to get a decrepit old automobile, had a 38 calibre loaded gun on him.

And his friend and associate, Nicola Sacco, another lover of peace, another lover of his adopted country who abhorred bloodshed and abhorred it so that he went down to Mexico under the name of Mus-macotelli [*sic*] to avoid bearing arms either for his adopted country, or, if he refused it, being an allied nation then when we were in distress, would have been forced to fight for his native land under the registration, had with him, this lover of peace, 32 death dealing automatic cartridges, 9 of them in the gun ready for action and 22 more of them in his pocket,—carried where the ordinary citizen carries it there? No, gentlemen, carried where those who have occasion to use it quickly and want to ship it out and use it quickly would be prone to carry it, that death-dealing instrument.

But more than that, gentlemen, and ammunition enough to kill 37 men if each shot took effect, they had or Vanzetti had four shells—no weapon in which to fire them at the moment that we found, but you will remember, gentlemen, that sticking out the back of the bandit's car on April 15th was either a rifle or a shot-gun, and in Vanzetti's pocket were four 12-gauge shells loaded with buck shot that they were going out to shoot little birds with, with some friend that had visited them at some time before.

Maybe, gentlemen, you think that is the way men would be armed who were going on an innocent trip, innocent so far as death-dealing matters are concerned at night time after closing hours of the garage and when the men who ran it was in bed, going to make a social trip down to see Pappi, the friend of Vanzetti, and he did not know where he lived, save that it was in East Bridgewater, gentlemen. . . .

11

BARTOLOMEO VANZETTI

Background of the Plymouth Trial

c. 1926

This excerpt from a pamphlet titled "Background of the Plymouth Trial," written by Vanzetti and published by a group of his supporters, offers the two anarchists' explanation for their responses when they were arrested. Vanzetti was tried in Plymouth for the attempted robbery in Bridgewater. In this pamphlet, though, he deals with both this trial and the one in which he and Sacco stand accused of robbery and murder in South Braintree.

. . . When arrested and interrogated we told lies. This was strenuosly [*sic*] used against us by both the District Attorney and the Judge as a proof of our consciousness of guilt. The defense counsel thesis was that our fear was due to our consciousness of guilt as radicals, that we feared punishment for our radical activity, and that we knew of brutalities, heavy sentences, and murders inflicted on many radicals for being such. To destroy this counter thesis, Judge Thayer said to the Jury, "They have lied because they were conscious of guilt, they claim

Bartolomeo Vanzetti, "Background of the Plymouth Trial" (Chelsea, Mass.: Road to Freedom Group, c. 1926), 10–12.

they have been frightened because they are radicals, but as radicals they would only be subject to deportation and they could not have feared it since they intended to go to Italy" (Cited by heart). Here as everywhere and always, Judge Thayer had endeavored to invert, falsify and twist the things in order to send us to the electric chair, and get his promotion. It is time to answer him. It is true that Sacco was prepared to go to Italy, and I intended to go the next winter after a season of fishing. We wanted to go to Italy, yes, but not to be deported. We abhor deportation as a violation of individual right and as an insult to human dignity. We feared it because it would also have deprived us of the possibility of returning to this country, to the making of which we had given the vigor of our youth, the blood of our veins, and to which we are bound by love and friendship. It is a shameless lie that we, as slackers, as anarchists, as revolutionists, when arrested, had only to fear deportation. The very day of our arrest we read in the newspapers that the day before our comrade Salsedo had been thrown out of a window to his death from the 11th floor of the Park Row building in New York, where he had been unlawfully and incomunicado confined by the Federal agents, together with comrade Roberto Elia. We knew of comrade Marucco[1] of Penn., who was deported to Italy but never reached the Italian shore. We knew that the real betrayers of this Nation and the real German spies had all been freed from the American prisons; but we also knew that there were and still are, in the United States prisons, hundreds of socialists, syndicalists, and anarchists, guilty of having been against the greatest highway robbery and slaying of history, the war, and for it they were monstrously sentenced. Eugene Debs, one of the few men of the world, one of the best of America's children, was in the federal prison at Atlanta. We knew the martyrs of Chicago,[2] the Mooney and Billings frameup, the Centralia case, the Ettor-Giovannitti case, and the fate of John Hillstrom. We had reasons to be afraid, personal and historical reasons. We also knew that during the then recent arrests in Mass. for deportation, several victims had been dragged to insanity and suicide by the mistreatment to which they were subjected by the Department of Justice. We knew that high politicians and officers had said, one of them, "The

---

[1] Pietro Marucco was a *Galleanista* who was arrested in Latrobe, Pennsylvania, in 1919 and deported; he died, mysteriously, en route, and was buried at sea.

[2] The martyrs of Chicago were anarchists arrested after a bomb was thrown into a crowd of police at a demonstration in Haymarket Square in Chicago in 1886. Four were hanged on November 11, 1887; one committed suicide; three were given lengthy prison sentences.

radicals should be first shot then tried"; another, "I would like to hang all the radicals at the piazza of my house," and the list could be continued, but these prove that we had reason to be afraid, when arrested, even without our consciousness of being radicals, which means we were more hated by the capitalists, judges, and prosecutors than are the criminals. We were arrested and most brutally mistreated, insulted, and menaced. To give a name, an address, or information, would have meant to cause homes to be raided, finding of libertarian literature and private correspondence, hence terrorized, divided families, arrests, indictments, deportations, and so on. Why should we turn spies? We are not men to betray friends and comrades for self liberation; never. Being coerced to speak and determined to hurt none we were compelled to lie. We are not ashamed of it. It proves only our determination not to be cowards. Our lies are all directed to this, if related to the trial their inconsequence becomes most apparent. And if the Judge and the District Attorney made such a fuss about it, it is because they were conscious of having nothing better against us than to treasure the doubt, to fill the Jury's mind with doubts, to use the doubt against us and get a conviction. . . .

BRIDGEWATER AND THE PLYMOUTH TRIAL

12

ASSISTANT DISTRICT ATTORNEY WILLIAM KANE

Examination of Maynard Freeman Shaw, Preliminary Hearings, Plymouth

June 25, 1920

Evidence against Vanzetti was very weak for the South Braintree robbery and murders. His supporters have argued that this is why he was tried first for another botched robbery. This trial, held in Plymouth, Massachu-

The Sacco-Vanzetti Case: Transcript of the Record of the Trial of Nicola Sacco and Bartolomeo Vanzetti in the Courts of Massachusetts and Subsequent Proceedings, 1920–1927 (Mamaroneck, N.Y.: Paul P. Appel, Publisher, 1969), Supplemental Volume, 128–29.

setts, brought the dire implications of Vanzetti's identity as an Italian immigrant to the forefront. This excerpt from the transcript of the Plymouth trial is from the testimony of Maynard Freeman Shaw, a fourteen-year-old boy whose identification of Vanzetti underscored existing prejudices against "foreigners."

. . . *Q.* Can you describe the man that you saw with the gun? *A.* No hat on and I was just getting a fleeting glance at his face, but the way he ran I could tell he was a foreigner, I could tell by the way he ran.

Q. How tall? *A.* Oh, about five feet—from five feet six to five feet eight or nine, I think.

Q. What else was there about the man that you observed at the time? *A.* He had a large overcoat on, a dark colored.

Q. How long a coat was it? *A.* Why, about to his knees, and if anything a little below.

Q. How far away were you from him at the time? *A.* About a hundred and fifty feet from him. I did not stay still quite long; I moved.

Q. Did you notice whether the overcoat was buttoned or unbuttoned? *A.* I am quite sure it was buttoned.

Q. Did you notice anything about the collar? *A.* He was all bundled up except his head. The collar was up around his neck.

Q. You said he had no hat on? *A.* No.

Q. Did you notice the man's head? *A.* There was not any flowing hair that I could see, but he had hair on it.

Q. Did you notice how much? *A.* Very little.

Q. What? *A.* No, about an inch and a quarter or an inch and a half long, the hair.

Q. Did you notice the color of his hair? *A.* Dark; he had a well-kept moustache.

Q. What kind of a moustache as to color[?] *A.* Oh, it was dark but it was not black.

Q. Can you describe the moustache any further except that it was dark and well kept? *A.* That is about all.

Q. That is about all? *A.* Yes, it was attended to, but I did not stop to study the moustache.

Q. Is that all you noticed of the moustache? *A.* Yes.

Q. Did you notice anything else about his face? *A.* There was a foreign look in it, sort of sallow.

Q. Anything else? *A.* No.

Q. Did you notice anything about his complexion? *A.* When I said foreign, that would describe it.

Q. As to color? *A.* It was not white; it was sort of dark, that is what made me think of foreign.

Q. As to color, his complexion? *A.* The face?

Q. Yes. Do you mean by that as to complexion or color? *A.* The color was not white but was light, it was not negroish but——

Q. Is there anything else about the features that you noticed? *A.* Rather knock-kneed, I should say, when he was running. . . .

13

DISTRICT ATTORNEY FREDERICK KATZMANN

Cross-Examination of Beltrando Brini, Preliminary Hearings, Plymouth

June 26, 1920

This is an excerpt from Frederick Katzmann's cross-examination of Beltrando Brini, the son of Vanzetti's one-time landlord, who argued in court that he had been with the anarchist when the Bridgewater crime was attempted. The prosecutor is obviously trying to undermine Brini's testimony.

. . . *Q.* Have you a good memory? *A.* I don't know as I have.

Q. What? *A.* I don't know; I suppose so.

Q. Pretty good, is it not? *A.* I guess so.

Q. It is very good, is it not? Could you repeat that story word for word if I permitted you to do it that you told Mr. Graham[1] just now? *A.* From the beginning in the night?

---

[1]James Graham, a Boston attorney, assisted John Vahey, Vanzetti's attorney in the Bridgewater trial.

The Sacco-Vanzetti Case: Transcript of the Record of the Trial of Nicola Sacco and Bartolomeo Vanzetti in the Courts of Massachusetts and Subsequent Proceedings, 1920–1927 (Mamaroneck, N.Y.: Paul P. Appel, Publisher, 1969), Supplemental Volume, 264–68.

Q. You just start out and tell us the thing?   *A.* Without stopping?

Q. Yes, without stopping.   *A.* On the 23rd of December Mr. Vanzetti came up to my house and asked me if I could go with him and peddle fish. I said I could——

Q. Everything except what was said.   *A.* And that morning I went with him and I met my father and when I met him it was near Maxwell's drug store a little bit South of it as I explained it before. I brought a bundle of fish into Mr. Ferrari's store and my father was also in the store when I went up to him and told him that I was going to Mr. Vanzetti's. He looked at my feet and said "Go home and get your rubbers." I ran home because I wanted to go with him to his house and went home and hunted for my rubbers and I found my rubbers; I remember that I hunted for them quite a little while and then put them on and went to his boarding house where I saw him preparing his fish in a wheelbarrow and I asked him why he was putting the fish in the wheelbarrow.

Q. Something was said about a horse. That is all I need to know about that.   *A.* He said because I could not get a horse. Then he gave me some bundles and told me to go on Cherry Street for them to be delivered. I did so and I remember I went to 15 Cherry Street and I remember I went to Mrs. Bonjonani's house where I gave her the fish and I did not have the right amount and she came and gave it to Mr. Vanzetti. Then we went up Cherry Street and South Cherry and turned down and went down Cherry Street and Mr. Vanzetti went home and got some fish and he loaded it up in his push cart. We went down Cherry Street and then on to Standish Avenue and there delivered some eels and went to Standish Avenue again and went up Court Street and delivered some eels and I delivered some on Court Street and went home and it was near to two o'clock in the afternoon.

Q. No, go right along.   *A.* The night too, do you want?

Q. Yes, just tell us just the same.   *A.* In the night he was up to the house—I left some out of the 23rd.

Q. Put that in.   *A.* While he was asking me, he said he would get a horse. He didn't stay very long and two men came and brought us half a pig. We brought it down cellar and then came up but Frank and Vanzetti did not stay there very long because he told me he had to go home and put his fish in some packages for the day coming. In the morning I saw him as I told you. In the night he was up at my house and stayed in my house quite late. I played with my sisters and paid no attention to what Mr. Vanzetti was doing because I fiddled and I like it and played with my sisters.

Q. The next day? *A.* The next day I found some presents in my stocking, I found some nuts and peanuts, a big bag, a half dollar, a two dollar bill, some candy[.] I told them "Look at what I got in my stocking." I thanked him very much and showed them the necktie.

Q. That is just the same story, isn't it? *A.* Sure.

Q. How many times did you tell that story? *A.* I told it to Mr. Vahey.[2]

Q. How many times did you tell it to Mr. Vahey? *A.* Twice.

Q. Told it here twice, that is four times. How many other times? *A.* I told it at home.

Q. How many times? *A.* About two or three times.

Q. Wasn't it a little more than that? *A.* Maybe more.

Q. How many times more? You have been standing up a long time and when you get tired out will you not feel at liberty to sit down? *A.* Yes.

Q. Maybe more than three times at home? *A.* Maybe more.

Q. Maybe ten times? *A.* No.

Q. Maybe nine times? *A.* Maybe five.

Q. Perhaps six? *A.* No, I don't think so.

Q. Who did you tell it to at home? *A.* My parents.

Q. Both of them? *A.* Yes, sir.

Q. Five times at home? *A.* No.

Q. You are sure it was not six? *A.* No.

Q. Who else did you tell it to? *A.* Mr. Vahey.

Q. You told it here five, told it to your parents and two times you told it to Mr. Vahey? *A.* Yes to him.

Q. How many times did you tell it to your parents? Did you tell it to your sister? *A.* I told it to my parents and to my sisters.

Q. Did you tell it when Bastoni and Esther were there? *A.* Mr. Bastoni was there.

Q. And Balboni? *A.* No.

Q. Mrs. Fortini? *A.* Yes.

Q. Mr. Fortini?[3] *A.* No.

Q. How about the shoemaker? *A.* He was there too.

Q. He was there the five times you told it? *A.* No, he was there when I told it twice to Mr. Vahey, a Boston lawyer.

---

[2]John Vahey was Vanzetti's attorney in the Bridgewater trial.

[3]Enrico Bastoni, Carlo Balboni, and Mary and Frank Fortini were all neighbors of Vanzetti's, who testified that they saw him or bought eels from him the day of the attempted robbery in Bridgewater.

Q. Mr. Graham? He is a nice young gentleman? *A.* Yes, he is a nice gentleman from Boston.

Q. So Mr. Vahey is a nice gentleman to [*sic*]? *A.* Yes.

Q. And so is Mr. Vanzetti? *A.* Yes.

Q. Who else did you tell it to? You see, son, I want to get how many times you told it to anybody and everybody. *A.* I guess that is all.

Q. How long did it take you to tell it to your parents each time? *A.* Some times I did not tell all of it and some times maybe it took me longer.

Q. Now those times you did not tell all, then your papa would say "you left out something, didn't you"? *A.* He would say the first time, but he knew it afterwards and he did say it.

Q. When you left out something at first would not he tell you there was something you had left out? *A.* Sure, at first.

Q. And then you would go back and say it over again? *A.* Not every time, I would just——

Q. Put that in? *A.* Put that in.

Q. And your papa would say "be sure and put that in"? *A.* Yes sir, sure.

Q. And your mother would say it? *A.* Sure.

Q. And the baker would say "be sure and put that in." *A.* He did not say much.

Q. Did you ever learn anything to recite at school? *A.* Yes.

Q. You learned this in the same way, did you? *A.* I told it to my parents.

Q. You know when you were at school and had a little poem or piece of history to recite? *A.* Yes.

Q. And then the teacher would stand there with a book and would correct you? *A.* She would correct me and she would tell the pupils to say it. When I was at the end of my story or history I would say "any criticism?" and then someone would get up and if the pupil left out anything the teacher would tell me about it.

Q. Now that was just the same way—if you left out anything, your papa would tell you and you would go back and put it in, would you not? *A.* Sometimes I would put it in.

Q. And you would start all over again? *A.* No.

Q. The next time you told the story you would be sure to put that part in? *A.* Yes.

Q. You learned it just like a piece at school? *A.* Sure.

Q. Who was the first person you told it to? *A.* My parents.

Q. Were both of them there, your papa and your mamma?   *A.* I am not positive. I think I told it to my mother first.

Q. When was that, the first time, do you remember?   *A.* Soon after I heard of his arrest.

Q. When was that?   *A.* A few days later.

Q. When was it?   *A.* The date?

Q. Yes.   *A.* I could not say the date.

Q. It seemed a terrible thing to you that Mr. Vanzetti was arrested, did it not?   *A.* Sure.

Q. That made a deep impression on your mind?   *A.* Sure.

Q. You felt very sorry and it made a deep impression on your mind, but you could not tell us the date?   *A.* When I first learned that he was arrested?

Q. Yes. Now that was no part that you ever told in this little piece was it? You never put that in the piece—when he was arrested, did you?   *A.* No.

Q. And you don't know what time it was by the clock that day, do you, when you first heard of it?   *A.* No.

Q. You don't even know what day of the week it was, do you?   *A.* No.

Q. And you don't know what day of the month it was, do you? Between ourselves you don't really know what month it was?   *A.* In April.

Q. In April?   *A.* Yes.

Q. That is fine—about what time in April?   *A.* The beginning of April, the first of it.

Q. You heard he had been arrested perhaps and I suppose that the folks were talking about it and reading about it in the newspaper?   *A.* Yes, sir.

Q. You are sure, are you not that on the night before Christmas Mr. Vanzetti came into your house at half past seven?   *A.* Somewheres around that time or later, maybe. I ain't sure about half past seven.

Q. What were you saying when you told Mr. Graham, this gentleman?   *A.* Later or before, I said.

Q. What did you say?   *A.* Half past seven or around there, sometime later or a little bit before.

Q. I am not asking you what time it was he came to your house the night before Christmas, but I am asking you, before I started with you in Court this morning, what did you say to Mr. Graham the time was that Mr. Vanzetti came to your house. When testifying what did you say?   *A.* Half past seven.

Q. You did not say anything about its being later did you, then?   *A.* I don't know if I did or not.

Q. Can you not remember back a half an hour or three quarters of an hour?   *A.* It seems to be around there.

Q. How is your memory about—can you go back and tell me what you said to Mr. Graham within an hour of this time?   *A.* I told you it was about half past seven.

Q. You didn't say anything about it being later, did you?   *A.* I don't remember that I did.

Q. Were you here yesterday?   *A.* Yes.

Q. Do you remember what Mrs. Fortini said about that yesterday afternoon—about what time he left her house? Has anybody talked with you since you stepped down and took a rest and after every one went out of the Court Room?   *A.* At recess today? No.

Q. Nobody said anything to you about that? Now you told the whole of this story to Mr. Vahey the first time, did you not?   *A.* Yes.

Q. And then you told it to him again, did you not, the whole of it all over again?   *A.* Yes.

Q. Right straight along, told him the whole story?   *A.* Not straight along.

Q. Did he ask you a few questions—do you know Mr. Vernogassi?[4]   *A.* Yes.

Q. How many times did you tell it to him?   *A.* Just as many times as before I told it to him.

Q. You told it to Mr. Vernogassi before you told it to Mr. Vahey, did you not?   *A.* I don't know as I did.

Q. I am asking you, didn't you?   *A.* Told it to Mr. Vernogassi before I told it to Mr. Vahey?

Q. Yes.   *A.* I don't remember that I did.

Q. Can you not remember that?   *A.* No.

Q. Take plenty of time and tell us if you did not tell it to Mr. Vernogassi before you told it to Mr. Vahey.   *A.* I don't remember.

Q. Can't remember that?   *A.* No sir.

Q. How long was it after you heard that Mr. Vanzetti was arrested that you told it to anybody?   *A.* Shortly afterwards.

Q. How long?   *A.* About as soon as I heard it.

Q. The same day?   *A.* No.

Q. The next day?   *A.* Yes.

---

[4] Mr. Vernogassi may have been someone who lived in the Brinis' neighborhood.

Q. Anybody ask you at first to tell about it? A. No, I told it myself.
Some people were telling, talking with my mother she said, "Even
the little boy brought me my fish that day."
Q. You don't remember about this except that some people told you?
A. No, I remembered it.
Q. The day before Christmas? A. Yes. . . .

14

FRANCIS RUSSELL

Interview with Beltrando Brini

1962

*This document is taken from an interview conducted with Beltrando
Brini, by then a grown man, by scholar Francis Russell for his 1962 book
on Sacco and Vanzetti.*

. . . By chance I discovered that Beltrando Brini was living in Wollas-
ton, a twenty-minute drive from my home in Wellesley. When a boy
of thirteen, Brini had testified at Vanzetti's first trial that the two of
them had been delivering eels in Plymouth the day before Christmas,
1919—the day Vanzetti was to be found guilty of attempting a holdup
in Bridgewater. As he grew up, Brini had broken away from the Italian
community. He had graduated from Boston University and was now an
elementary school principal. Community affairs seemed to take up
most of his spare time. Two weeks passed before he could find a free
evening to see me. I found his house easily enough, a decent inconspicuous house in a decent inconspicuous street. He was a small man
in his fifties. Like many of the second generation he still looked Italian, but to a diminished degree. He showed me into his living room.
His wife was standing near the fireplace, a thin fair-haired woman, not

Francis Russell, *Tragedy in Dedham: The Story of the Sacco-Vanzetti Case* (New York:
McGraw-Hill Book Company, 1962), 21–23.

Latin at all. After he had introduced me to her we sat down, taking each other's measure while she went into the kitchen to make coffee.

"You know," he said finally, "I could have been a musician. I really could at one time have gotten into the Boston Symphony Orchestra. But I thought it was safer to be a teacher. That's why I never seem to be home nights—always something they want a school principal to be doing, somewhere they want him to be." He looked at me sharply. "You want to know about Vanzetti. He lived with us a long time. He paid more attention to me than my parents did. He was kind to all children. I remember one Halloween we all had jack-o'-lanterns. The others had theirs lighted but mine didn't have a candle in it. Vanzetti came along and asked me why I didn't get a candle. I said I hadn't any money. He asked me how much candles cost and I said two cents, so he fished in his pocket and gave them to me. When I got to the hardware store I found he'd given me a cent and a dime. So I got my candle and I brought him back the nine cents. I'd never had that much money in my pocket before, but I remember how proud of myself I was that I brought that nine cents back to him.

"I remember the last time I saw him before his arrest. It's a thing I somehow still feel ashamed about. A bunch of us were playing ball in Suosso's Lane and somebody hit one over the fence into a garden. While I was climbing over to get it I trampled on some vegetables and the man who owned the garden came out and started to bawl me out. I answered him back, like any fresh kid. Then Vanzetti came along, took me over by the fence, and talked to me. He wasn't angry, he didn't raise his voice, but what he said made me feel ashamed. I didn't feel like playing ball any more. I've often wished it hadn't been that way, the last time I saw him free.

"You know, of course," he went on, "that I testified I was delivering eels with him the morning he was supposed to have been holding up the pay truck in Bridgewater. That's been the terrible thing for me. I *was* there with him all that morning long, and I couldn't make them believe me. Sometimes I've asked myself, Could I have been wrong, could I have dreamed it all? Was Vanzetti really at Bridgewater? But then I know, I *know* that I was delivering eels with him that morning. It couldn't have been any other day, because that's the one day Italians always eat eels, no matter what they cost. And I remember how I started out that morning to go to Vanzetti's house. It was muddy and I forgot my rubbers. At the corner I met my father and he sent me back for them, so I was late. Vanzetti was waiting for me with the pushcart. We delivered eels until, it must have been, two o'clock. It's funny the things you remember. I remember a two-family house where I made a mistake and went to the wrong door. When we got all through Vanzetti paid me off at the corner of Cherry Lane and Court Street. And I know that it happened that way, that it was the day before Christmas, the same day and the same time they said he was holding up the truck in Bridgewater. When I told my story in court Katzmann complimented me on learning my part so well.

"I was only thirteen then and I was scared. I'd never been in a court before. Katzmann would go at me like a tiger, fire three questions at me at once. Thayer would never help me out. His face was so stern. He never said anything, but you could feel his hostility."

Brini's wife came in with a tray, and Brini took a pile of magazines from the coffee table to make room.

"Tell me," I said, as she joined us. "If you had a friend in trouble you knew was innocent, could you lie to establish an alibi for him?"

He leaned back in his chair for some seconds, frowning slightly, while his wife poured the coffee. "I thought you might ask me something like that," he said finally. "No, I couldn't. I suppose you wanted me to say yes, but I couldn't. I don't know why I couldn't, either."

"Could you?" his wife asked me.

"Yes," I said truthfully, "I could quite easily. Under oath too."

"So could I," she said, looking at her husband as if she thought he was being foolish.

"Well," he said, "I know this, that I didn't want to go to court. Young as I was, I knew what a disadvantage it would be for me to get mixed up in it. I wanted to be a musician, and whatever I might want, once I testified, I knew I'd find the way blocked. And it's shadowed me ever since. They've pointed me out—Brini, the boy who testified for a murderer. In 1927 I told my story to Governor Fuller, and he said he believed me, but he never did anything about it. The day before they were executed I tried to see the governor again, but I couldn't get past his secretary. I shouted at him, 'If I lied, why don't you arrest me for perjury?' All he said was, if I was so brave why wasn't I out picketing on the Common. I told him I'd been there the day before, and I asked to be locked up, but he just turned his back."

He set down his coffee cup. "I don't suppose what I've been telling you helps you much. These are just my feelings. Those others, where we delivered the eels that morning, they didn't want to testify either. They were all good Catholics and Vanzetti was an anarchist. But they'd bought the eels, they'd seen Vanzetti, and my father talked to them. They had respect for him, not fear but respect, so they went."

As we talked the lights of the suburban street began to wink out, and I could see it was time for me to go. "You'll probably think of things you forgot to ask me," he said at the door. "Just telephone me or come down, if there's anything more you want to know. Any time." . . .

CENTRAL ISSUES
OF THE SACCO AND VANZETTI TRIAL

15

ASSISTANT DISTRICT ATTORNEY
HAROLD P. WILLIAMS

Examination of Mary Splaine
June 9, 1921

The evidence in the Sacco and Vanzetti case fell into three main categories: eyewitness testimony, material evidence, and ballistics. Much of the eyewitness testimony against the two anarchists was suspect at best. Mary Splaine, a bookkeeper at Slater and Morrill, asserted during the trial that she saw Sacco at the crime scene. Splaine identified Sacco in remarkably precise terms in this excerpt from her testimony.

. . . *Q.* Perhaps we can get a picture that will illustrate a little better what you mean to say. Take the picture which shows the side of the auto, which I take it was toward you. Can you tell better by that, what you mean by that picture? *A.* This (indicating) would be the way it appeared to me, but this curtain here (indicating) was not buttoned down. It was in this space here where the man's body appeared, right where this curtain is.

The Sacco-Vanzetti Case: Transcript of the Record of the Trial of Nicola Sacco and Bartolomeo Vanzetti in the Courts of Massachusetts and Subsequent Proceedings, 1920–1927 (Mamaroneck, N.Y.: Paul P. Appel, Publisher, 1969), I, 223–24.

Q. Where that first curtain is?   *A.* Yes, sir, the first curtain right there (indicating). That curtain was not buttoned down. In this place was where the man's form appeared.

MR. MOORE. Refer to the Exhibit number.

MR. WILLIAMS. Referring to Exhibit 10.

THE COURT. May I see that, please?

(Mr. Williams hands Exhibit 10 to the Court.)

THE COURT. Mr. Williams, I understand that this is the——

MR. WILLIAMS. She says that where that first curtain was the man,— that was not buttoned down, the man's body appeared here, as I understood you?

THE WITNESS. Yes.

THE COURT. Thank you.

Q. Did you see that man that appeared at that place?   *A.* Yes, sir.

Q. Can you describe him to these gentlemen here?   *A.* Yes, sir. He was a man that I should say was slightly taller than I am. He weighed possibly from 140 to 145 pounds. He was a muscular,— he was an active looking man. I noticed particularly the left hand was a good sized hand, a hand that denoted strength or a shoulder that——

Q. So that the hand you said you saw where?   *A.* The left hand, that was placed on the back of the front seat, on the back of the front seat. He had a gray, what I thought was a shirt,—had a grayish, like navy color, and the face was what we would call clear cut, clear-cut face. Through here (indicating) was a little narrow, just a little narrow. The forehead was high. The hair was brushed back and it was between, I should think, two inches and two and one-half inches in length and had dark eyebrows, but the complexion was a white, peculiar white that looked greenish.

Q. How long was he in your view, do you know?   *A.* Now, the distance that it took him to travel from the middle of the street, from the middle of that distance to that corner.

Q. You say "The middle of the distance." You mean what?   *A.* The middle of the distance between the railroad track and the corner of Pearl and Railroad streets.

Q. That is practically to the cobbling shop that is on the corner of Pearl and Railroad, isn't it?   *A.* Yes.

Q. Did you ever see that man after that?   *A.* Yes.

Q. Where did you see him?   *A.* I saw him in the police station in Brockton.

Q. When was that?   *A.* That was three weeks after the murder. . . .

16

PINKERTON AGENT HENRY HELLYER

Reports

April 19, 1920; May 11, 1920

This report is from Henry Hellyer, a Pinkerton agent acting on behalf of Slater and Morrill's insurance company. Hellyer questioned numerous witnesses, including Mary Splaine, just after the robbery. As this excerpt shows, Hellyer received a much different account from Splaine than the one she presented at the trial. This report was kept secret from the defense team — they did not see it until 1927.

... Next I proceeded to #11 Kame Street and got Miss Mary E. Splaine's story on inside conditions at the Slater Morrell [*sic*] office and her statement on whom several of the oldest employees suspect of being concerned in the murders and robbery. She told a long story covering a period of eighteen years, but the most important part concerned happenings of the past two or three years. She had known Mr. Parmenter for eighteen years. In Sept. 1919, Mr. Parmenter suffered a breakdown from overwork and just about that time, one Lewis C. Darling was hired to take charge of the order department, but dropped into Parmenter's job due to Parmenter's sickness. When Mr. Parmenter returned to work, Darling worried a great deal as he was afraid of losing the good job he had dropped into, but he managed to retain the job, but it had been recently said by Mr. Puffer that a change was to occur in the office. Miss Splaine has a desk close by the telephone booth and the booth being constructed of thin wood, any conversation carried on in the booth can be overheard by Miss Splaine. In this manner, she overheard Darling talking over the phone with one Herman Jesse, a former employee who is now a stockbroker. She says he frequently conversed with Jesse and was extensively trading in stocks, most of the conversation she overheard concerned silvers. Darling also had an affair with a female employee named Natalie

---

Herbert Ehrmann papers, box 14, folder 2, Harvard Law School Library.

Hazeldine and though a married man, used to spend a lot of time with this girl. About three weeks ago, the payroll clerk, Miss Cahil, was discharged by Darling so Miss Mahoney was assigned to payroll work. She resented it and said she was going to ball up the payroll; her remark was reported to Parmenter who took charge of the payroll work and saw that it was done properly. One of Darling's most intimate male friends was one Harold Lewis, who with Carl Knipps, was arrested and convicted in the Quincy Court ten years ago for stealing shoes from the Slater Morrell [*sic*] Co. On their promise to reimburse the Company, for the stolen shoes, they were permitted to return to work and a certain amount was taken from their wages every week. In this way they were to pay back between five and six hundred dollars, the value of the shoes stolen by them. Darling and Lewis had the selling of damaged shoes which they sold to a man named Goldstein. Recently Mr. Edward Frayer caught Goldstein paying money to Lewis and therefore suspected Darling and Lewis of grafting, but they explained his suspicions away. About two weeks ago, Harold Lewis got through and on Friday, April 2nd, Lewis C. Darling's home was searched by Police Officers and stolen shoes found there. By some means or other, Darling must have persuaded Mr. Slater to overlook the stealing as he was retained in the position. Prior to his being suspected of stealing shoes, Miss Splaine heard Darling talking over the phone with regard to the purchase of a house which he has since purchased. She said that the sum he agreed to pay down and the monthly payments mentioned by him were entirely out of his reach if he had only his salary to rely on. She further stated that he spent a great deal of money. She says that Darling keeps informed on what Mr. Slater proposed doing by eavesdropping at the door between his (Darling's) and Mr. Slater's office. She says Darling made a practice of staying in his office during the noon hour when Mr. Slater would be liable to discuss confidential matters, believing the next office to be vacant. When Darling's house was searched and stolen goods found, the news was brought to the office and factory by a Quincy girl who has a brother on the Quincy Police Department. The foregoing is the gist of Miss Splaine's statement on affairs prior to the afternoon of Thursday, April 15th. She added a great deal of detail which I omit.

Last Thursday, the payroll was got ready in the usual manner. Miss Mahoney, Mrs. Mack, and Mr. Parmenter putting it up. After putting it up, Mr. Parmenter said that he would take his pay before leaving the office so Miss Mahoney said that he had better as there might be none to take tomorrow. Parmenter and Beredelli [*sic*] left the office about 3:10 p.m. each carrying a black steel box. They were watched from the office windows by Miss Splaine and Greenlaw and were seen to be the only persons on the street in view of the office windows. When they got abreast the Rice & Hutchins factory, Parmenter turned [and] looked toward the office, then shifted the box from one hand to the other and stooped over and picked something up. A moment later, they were lost to view from the office windows and immediately after shooting was heard and a moment later, a large dark green automobile came up the street at a good speed. There were side curtains on the car, but the driver's seat was uncurtained, so Miss Splaine saw a man clad in light gray clothes leaning over the driver's seat from the rear. This man held a revolver which he was firing. She described the man as follows from the momentary glimpse she got of him: round, rather full pale face, black hair, cut pompadour style, powerful square shoulders and wearing gray clothes, no hat. Greenlaw and Knipps ran out to get the number, but were greeted with a bullet. Knipps retreated, but Greenlaw stayed a moment and says the car carried no registration plate on the rear. After seeing the car go, Miss Splaine ran down Pearl Street and saw Beredelli [*sic*] lying on the sidewalk and Parmenter across the street in the vacant lot. She went to Parmenter and spoke to him. After he was carried into the house, Parmenter gave Miss Splaine the money he had on his person, to give to Mrs. Parmenter. She stayed with Parmenter until he was taken to the hospital and afterward went to the hospital and stayed until after 9 p.m. but did not hear him talk about his assailants. This was the first time Miss Splaine ever saw two men take the payroll and one of the very few times those taking it walked. The usual procedure is to take the payroll down in an automobile and Messrs. Frayer, Knight, Lewis, Parmenter, and Beredelli [*sic*] acted as guards. The employed formerly were paid on Wednesdays but about four weeks ago, pay day was changed to Thursday. Last Thursday, Messrs. Knight and Frayer were busy when Parmenter and Beredelli [*sic*] started on foot, whether they were ordered to go that way by anyone only they could tell. Beredelli the guard has not been on the job a great while and was disliked by the office help who felt that he was not trustworthy. Since the robbery and murders, there has been a good deal of open comment by Mr. Puffer, Mr. Bostock, Mr. Knight, and Miss Splaine about Darling's connection with the robbery and murders; they [have been] saying that Mr. Darling probably hatched the scheme and gave those that actually did the work information that would enable them to accomplish the robbery and murders successfully. . . .

Wednesday, May 11, 1920.
. . . As opportunities occurred, I made discreet inquiries about Mr. Darling, whom Miss Mary Splaine accused of being implicated in the murders and robbery. My inquiries show that there is absolutely no grounds for Miss Splaine's accusation, and that Mr. Darling enjoys Mr. Slater's confidence. Today I took the matter up with Mr. Frayer. He ridiculed the idea of Darling being implicated and further stated that no serious attention can be paid to Miss Splaine's stories, because she is one of the most irresponsible persons he ever came in contact with. . . .

17

CAPTAIN WILLIAM PROCTOR

Affidavit

October 20, 1923

Like the eyewitness testimony, the ballistics evidence was also questionable. Captain Proctor was the head of the Massachusetts State Police and had initially been in charge of investigating the robbery and murders with which Sacco and Vanzetti were charged. In this affidavit he gives his account of why he used the precise language he did in testifying about Sacco's gun.

My name is William H. Proctor. I live in Swampscott, Mass., and I am Captain in the Department of Public Safety, in charge of the Division of State Police. I have been Captain for sixteen years and in the State Police Department for thirty-six years. My office is at the State House

The Sacco-Vanzetti Case: Transcript of the Record of the Trial of Nicola Sacco and Bartolomeo Vanzetti in the Courts of Massachusetts and Subsequent Proceedings, 1920–1927 (Mamaroneck, N.Y.: Paul P. Appel, Publisher, 1969), IV, 3641–43.

in Boston. I am making this affidavit in my own office and at the request of Mr. William G. Thompson, who I understood is now one of the counsel for one of the defendants in the [Sacco and Vanzetti] case.

I was associated with the prosecution of the defendants in this case and I had in my custody for a considerable time the Colt automatic pistol taken from the defendant Sacco at the time of his arrest, the cartridges taken from him at the same time, the so-called Fraher shells picked up on the ground at the time of the murder and some other exhibits in the case not material for the purpose which I understand from Mr. Thompson is the subject matter of this statement.

I also had in my custody and made examination of from time to time, with great care, the bullets said to have been taken from the body of Berardelli, all except one of which were, as I testified at the trial, fired from a pistol which was not a Colt automatic pistol. One of them was, as I then testified and still believe, fired from a Colt automatic pistol of 32 calibre.

During the preparation for the trial, my attention was repeatedly called by the District Attorney and his assistants to the question: whether I could find any evidence which would justify the opinion that the particular bullet taken from the body of Berardelli, which came from a Colt automatic pistol, came from the particular Colt automatic pistol taken from Sacco. I used every means available to me for forming an opinion on this subject. I conducted, with Captain Van Amberg [sic] certain tests at Lowell, about which I testified, consisting in firing certain cartridges through Sacco's pistol. At no time was I able to find any evidence whatever which tended to convince me that the particular model bullet found in Berardelli's body, which came from a Colt automatic pistol, which I think was numbered 3 and had some other exhibit number, came from Sacco's pistol and I so informed the District Attorney and his assistant before the trial. This bullet was what is commonly called a full metalpatch bullet and although I repeatedly talked over with Captain Van Amberg [sic] the scratch or scratches which he claimed tended to identify this bullet as one that must have gone through Sacco's pistol, his statements concerning the identifying marks seemed to me entirely unconvincing.

At the trial, the District Attorney did not ask me whether I had found any evidence that the so-called mortal bullet which I have referred to as number 3 passed through Sacco's pistol, nor was I asked that question on cross-examination. The District Attorney desired to ask me that question, but I had repeatedly told him that if he did I should be obliged to answer in the negative; consequently, he put to me this question: Q. Have you an opinion as to whether bullet number 3 was fired from the Colt automatic which is in evidence? To which I answered, "I have." He then proceeded.   Q. And what is your opinion?   A. My opinion is that it is consistent with being fired by that pistol.

That is still my opinion for the reason that bullet number 3, in my judgment, passed through some Colt automatic pistol, but I do not intend by that answer to imply that I had found any evidence that the so-called mortal bullet had passed through this particular Colt automatic pistol and the District Attorney well knew that I did not so intend and framed his question accordingly. Had I been asked the direct question: whether I had found any affirmative evidence whatever that this so-called mortal bullet had passed through this particular Sacco's pistol, I should have answered then, as I do now without hesitation, in the negative.

18

DISTRICT ATTORNEY FREDERICK KATZMANN

Affidavit

October 31, 1923

This affidavit contains Katzmann's response to Proctor's assertion that he had prearranged the questions and responses in his testimony with the prosecution in an effort to mislead the jury.

I, Frederick G. Katzmann, being first duly sworn, on oath, depose and say, that I have read the affidavit of Capt. William H. Proctor dated October 20, 1923; that the said Captain Proctor examined the four bullet which had been recovered from the body of Berardelli, and the Sacco pistol, in the summer and fall of 1920, and he informed me that

The Sacco-Vanzetti Case: Transcript of the Record of the Trial of Nicola Sacco and Bartolomeo Vanzetti in the Courts of Massachusetts and Subsequent Proceedings, 1920–1927 (Mamaroneck, N.Y.: Paul P. Appel, Publisher, 1969), IV, 3681.

three of the said bullets were, in his opinion, fired from a 32 calibre Savage automatic pistol, and that the fourth of said bullets had been fired from a 32 calibre Colt automatic pistol; that later, and prior to his testifying, Captain Proctor told me that he was prepared to testify that the mortal bullet was consistent with having been fired from the Sacco pistol; that I did not repeatedly ask him whether he had found any evidence that the mortal bullet had passed through the Sacco pistol, nor did he repeatedly tell me that if I did ask him that question he would be obliged to reply in the negative.

ON TRIAL FOR WHAT?

19

BARTOLOMEO VANZETTI

On Reasons for Prosecution

c. 1926

The issue of Sacco and Vanzetti's radical beliefs was never far from the surface during the trial. In this document, taken from the pamphlet written while he was imprisoned, Vanzetti offers his explanation for why he and Sacco were being tried. Although its title referred to the Plymouth trial, Vanzetti discussed both trials in his pamphlet; he called the two trials "two parts of a same thing."

. . . The plutocracy rules effectively the world with the help of a big minority of common people and the acquiescence of the great masses. This general historical truth is most strictly related to our case. It does not need explanation. We were handled by supporters of the plutocracy, and judged by them.

We are Anarchists, Italians, and slackers. As Anarchists, we are the most misunderstood, feared, and hated of individuals by the American

Bartolomeo Vanzetti, "Background of the Plymouth Trial" (Chelsea, Mass.: Road to Freedom Group, c. 1926), 5–6, 7.

ragged and golden mobs. As Italians we belong to one of the most scorned and despised nationalities, as adversaries of the war, as slackers, we deserve the rope [i.e., deserve to die] in the opinion of the vulgar majority of the American people, who tried and judged us.

In our quality of libertarians and workers, we had, before our arrest, fought against the American plutocracy, on the workers' side. Sacco had been very active in the strike of the Milford Foundery workers and in the Ettor and Giovannitti case. In short: Sacco had been very active in every strike, struggle, and agitation that happened during the time of his libertarian militancy. I had participated in the strike of the Plymouth Cordage Co. workers in 1915 [*sic*]. This company is one of the greatest money powers of this Nation. The town of Plymouth is its feudal tenure. Of all the local men who took a prominent part in the strike, I was the only one who did not yield or betray the workers. Towards the end of the strike, the Boston Post, a quasi exclusive creature of the Cordage Company said that "About one hundred Italian Anarchists are keeping the strike on, against the will of all the other strikers." That was an exaggerated half truth. But of all the local men who had taken a big part in the strike, I was the only one who, instead of being compensated, was blacklisted by the company, and subjected to a long, vain, and useless police vigilance. And I wholly realized that the Cordage Company would never forget or forgive me for the little that I had done in behalf of its exploited workers. At this point, I must relate the above with the Plymouth trial.

The greater part of the Italian Colony of Plymouth depends upon the Cordage Company, which has such a well organized espionage service, that it knows all the public and private affairs of the town in general, and of its employees in particular. Now many of its employees were positive of my innocence. It was highly voiced by the whole community; Mr. Brown, the Company manager was undoubtedly informed of my innocence, even before the trial. A single word from such a power, and I would have been freed, whereas, in the conduct of the judge, of the prosecutor, and even of my lawyer, the Plymouth trial has, from its very beginning, assumed the appearance of what it has been: a legal lynching. My elimination by legal means, was the revenge of that great money power. . . .

By abuse of their authority and power, the police, the prosecution, and the plutocracy may, by intimidation, coercion, or corruption, by menacing, punishment, or by promising favors, protection, or promotions, compel or induce some indicted or indictable habitual criminals and others greedy and needy unfortunates to perjure against a defendant, to frame him. This has happened in our case. Moral irresponsibles and mental defectives, harlots and crooks, and venal of all kinds have perjured against us and were believed by two popular juries. It is now irrefutably proven.

The fact that I was a worker, living in a community of Italians and that on the day, hour and moment of the crime I had been among them delivering their previously ordered commission of eels and fish, this fact, I say, was very much against me at the Plymouth trial. Because it brought all Italian witnesses on the stand to testify in my behalf, the American jurors, laden with racial, religious, political, and economic prejudice and hatred against the Italian and the radicals, worked out by a shrewd prosecutor and backed by the judge and helped by the counsel of the defense, could not and did not believe those most truthful witnesses. . . .

20

DISTRICT ATTORNEY FREDERICK KATZMANN

Cross-Examination of Nicola Sacco and Judge Webster Thayer's Intervention

July 7, 1921

When Sacco and Vanzetti's beliefs became an open issue in the courtroom, it raised serious questions about whether the two men were being tried for robbery and murder or for their unpopular ideas. This document is Katzmann's cross-examination (with Judge Thayer's startling interventions) that goaded Sacco into making a speech defending anarchism.

Q. [By Mr. Katzmann.] Did you say yesterday you love a free country?
A. Yes, sir.

The Sacco-Vanzetti Case: Transcript of the Record of the Trial of Nicola Sacco and Bartolomeo Vanzetti in the Courts of Massachusetts and Subsequent Proceedings, 1920–1927 (Mamaroneck, N.Y.: Paul P. Appel, Publisher, 1969), II, 1867–74.

Q. Did you love this country in the month of May, 1917. *A.* I did not say,—I don't want to say I did not love this country.

Q. Did you love this country in the month [*sic*] of 1917? *A.* If you can, Mr. Katzmann, if you give me that,—I could explain——

Q. Do you understand that question *A.* Yes.

Q. Then will you please answer it? *A.* I can't answer in one word.

Q. You can't say whether you loved the United States of America one week before the day you enlisted for the first draft? *A.* I can't say in one word, Mr. Katzmann.

Q. You can't tell this jury whether you loved the country or not?

MR. MOORE. I object to that.

A. I could explain that, yes, if I loved——

Q. What? *A.* I could explain that, yes, if I loved, if you give me a chance.

Q. I ask you first to answer that question. Did you love this United States of America in May, 1917? *A.* I can't answer in one word.

Q. Don't you know whether you did or not?

MR. MOORE. I object, your Honor.

THE COURT. What say?

MR. MOORE. I object to the repetition of this question without giving the young man an opportunity to explain his attitude.

THE COURT. That is not the usual method that prevails. Where the question can be categorically answered by yes or no, it should be answered. The explanation comes later. Then you can make any inquiry to the effect of giving the witness an opportunity of making whatever explanation at that time he sees fit to make, but under cross-examination counsel is entitled to get an answer either yes or no, when the question can be so answered. You may proceed, please.

Q. Did you love this country in the last week of May, 1917? *A.* That is pretty hard for me to say in one word, Mr. Katzmann.

Q. There are two words you can use, Mr. Sacco, yes or no. Which one is it? *A.* Yes.

Q. And in order to show your love for this United States of America when she was about to call upon you to become a soldier you ran away to Mexico?

MR. JEREMIAH MCANARNEY. Wait.

THE COURT. Did you?

Q. Did you run away to Mexico?

THE COURT. He has not said he ran away to Mexico. Did you go?

Q. Did you go to Mexico to avoid being a soldier for this country that you loved? *A.* Yes.

Q. You went under an assumed name?   *A.* No.

Q. Didn't you take the name of Mosmacotelli?   *A.* Yes.

Q. That is not your name, is it?   *A.* No.

Q. How long did you remain under the name of Mosmacotelli? *A.* Until I got a job over to Mr. Kelley's.

Q. When was that?   *A.* The armistice.

Q. After the war was practically over?   *A.* Yes, sir.

Q. Then, for the first time, after May, 1917, did you become known as Sacco again?   *A.* Yes, sir.

Q. Was it for the reason that you desired to avoid service that when you came back in four months you went to Cambridge instead of to Milford?   *A.* For the reason for not to get in the army.

Q. So as to avoid getting in the army.   *A.* Another reason why, I did not want no chance to get arrested and one year in prison.

Q. Did not want to get arrested and spend one year in prison for dodging the draft. It that it?   *A.* Yes.

Q. Did you love your country when you came back from Mexico? *A.* The first time?

THE COURT. Which country did you say? You said——

Q. United States of America, your adopted country?   *A.* I did not say already.

Q. When you came back, I asked you. That was before you went. *A.* I don't think I could change my opinion in three months.

Q. You still loved America, did you?   *A.* I should say yes.

Q. And is that your idea of showing your love for this Country? *A.* [Witness hesitates.]

Q. Is that your idea of showing your love for America?   *A.* Yes.

Q. And would it be your idea of showing your love for your wife that when she needed you you ran away from her?   *A.* I did not run away from her.

MR. MOORE. I object.

THE WITNESS. I was going to come after if I need her.

THE COURT. He may answer. Simply on the question of credibility, that is all.

Q. Would it be your idea of love for your wife that you were to run away from her when she needed you?

MR. JEREMIAH MCANARNEY. Pardon me. I ask for an exception on that.

THE COURT. Excluded. One may not run away. He has not admitted he ran away.

Q. Then I will ask you, didn't you run away from Milford so as to avoid being a soldier for the United States?   *A.* I did not run away.

Q. You mean you walked away? *A.* Yes.

Q. You don't understand me when I say "run away," do you? *A.* That is vulgar.

Q. That is vulgar? *A.* You can say a little intelligent, Mr. Katzmann.

Q. Don't you think going away from your country is a vulgar thing to do when she needs you? *A.* I don't believe in war.

Q. You don't believe in war? *A.* No, sir.

Q. Do you think it is a cowardly thing to do what you did? *A.* No, sir.

Q. Do you think it is a brave thing to do what you did? *A.* Yes, sir.

Q. Do you think it would be a brave thing to go away from your own wife? *A.* No.

Q. When she needed you? *A.* No.

Q. What wages did you first earn in this country? *A.* Wage?

Q. Wages, money, pay? *A.* I used to get before I leave?

Q. When you first came to this country? *A.* $1.15.

Q. Per day? *A.* Yes.

Q. What were you getting at the 3-K factory when you got through? *A.* Sometimes sixty, fifty, seventy, eighty, forty, thirty, twenty-five, thirty-five. Depends on how much work was.

Q. That was within eight years after you first came to this country, isn't it? *A.* After seven years,—no, after twelve years.

Q. 1908. I beg your pardon. That is my mistake, Mr. Sacco. I did not mean that. That is within thirteen years? *A.* Yes, sir.

Q. From the time you came to this country? *A.* Yes.

Q. From $1.15 a day to $5 a day or better? *A.* Yes.

Q. And your child was born in this country, wasn't it? *A.* Yes.

Q. And your marriage took place in this country? *A.* Yes.

Q. Is Italy a free country? Is it a republic? *A.* Republic, yes.

Q. You love free countries, don't you? *A.* I should say yes.

Q. Why didn't you stay down in Mexico? *A.* Well, first thing. I could not get my trade over there. I had to do any other job.

Q. Don't they work with a pick and shovel in Mexico? *A.* Yes.

Q. Haven't you worked with a pick and shovel in this country? *A.* I did.

Q. Why didn't you stay there, down there in that free country, and work with a pick and shovel? *A.* I don't think I did sacrifice to learn a job to go to pick and shovel in Mexico.

Q. Is it because,—is your love for the United States of America commensurate with the amount of money you can get in this country per week? *A.* Better conditions, yes.

Q. Better country to make money, isn't it?   *A.* Yes.

Q. Mr. Sacco, that is the extent of your love for this country, isn't it, measured in dollars and cents?

MR. JEREMIAH MCANARNEY. If your Honor please, I object to this particular question.

THE COURT. You opened up this whole subject.

MR. JEREMIAH MCANARNEY. If your Honor please I object to this question. That is my objection.

THE COURT. The form of it?

MR. JEREMIAH MCANARNEY. To the substance and form.

MR. KATZMANN. I will change the form, if your Honor please.

THE COURT. Better change that.

Q. Is your love for this country measured by the amount of money you can earn here?

MR. JEREMIAH MCANARNEY. To that question I object.

THE COURT. Now, you may answer.   *A.* I never loved money.

MR. JEREMIAH MCANARNEY. Save my exception.

THE COURT. Certainly.

Q. What is the reason then?——

THE COURT. I allow this on the ground that the defendants opened it up.

Q. What is the reason you came back?

MR. JEREMIAH MCANARNEY. My exception lies just the same.

THE COURT. Certainly.

MR. MOORE. Both defendants.

THE COURT. Certainly.

Q. What is the reason you came back from Mexico if you did not love money, then?   *A.* The first reason is all against my nature, is all different food over there, different nature, anyway.

Q. That is the first reason. It is against your nature. The food isn't right.   *A.* Food, and many other things.

Q. You stood it for four months, didn't you?   *A.* Three months.

Q. Three months?   *A.* Yes.

Q. You came back all right physically, didn't you?   *A.* I should say yes.

Q. And you had Italian food there, didn't you?   *A.* Yes, made by ourselves.

Q. You could have had it all the time if you sent for it, couldn't you?   *A.* Not all the time. I don't know.

Q. Did you fail to have it at any time in the three months you were there?   *A.* Yes, sir. Different.

Q. What is the difference about it? *A.* Oh, different food that we did not like.

Q. It was Italian food, wasn't it? *A.* No, sir.

Q. Didn't you say it was? *A.* Sometimes after.

Q. You could have had it all the time if you sent for it, couldn't you? *A.* Could have had beans sometimes and any other vegetable.

MR. KATZMANN. I ask that be stricken out and the witness required to answer the question.

Q. Could you have had it by sending for it? *A.* Could not get it all the time.

Q. Why couldn't you get it in Mexico the same as you get it here? *A.* I suppose Mexico is not very much industries as in this country.

Q. Couldn't you send to Boston to get Italian food sent to Monterey, Mexico? *A.* If I was a D. Rockefeller I will.

Q. Then, I take it, you came back to the United States first to get something to eat. Is that right? Something that you liked? *A.* No, not just for eat.

Q. Didn't you say that was the first reason? *A.* The first reason——

Q. Didn't you say that was the first reason? *A.* Yes.

Q. All right. That wasn't a reason of the heart, was it? *A.* The heart?

Q. Yes. *A.* No.

Q. That was a reason of the stomach, wasn't it? *A.* Not just for the stomach, but any other reason.

Q. I am talking first about the first reason. So, the first reason your love of America is founded upon is pleasing your stomach. Is that right? *A.* I will not say yes.

Q. Haven't you said so? *A.* Not for the stomach. I don't think it is a satisfaction just for the stomach.

Q. What is your second reason? *A.* The second reason is strange for me, the language.

Q. Strange language? *A.* Yes.

Q. Were you in an Italian colony there? *A.* If I got them? I can't get that, Mr. Katzmann.

Q. Pardon me. Were you in a group of Italians there? *A.* Yes.

Q. When you came to America in 1908, did you understand English? *A.* No.

Q. A strange language here, wasn't it? *A.* Yes.

Q. What is the third reason, if there is one? *A.* A third reason, I was far away from my wife and boy.

Q. Couldn't you have sent for your wife and your boy? *A.* I wouldn't send for my wife and boy over there, because it was the idea to come back here.

Q. I know that. You are back here. My question is, couldn't you have sent for Mrs. Sacco and your boy? *A.* Extreme condition, it would be bad. I could not go back in this United States, why I would get my wife and my boy.

Q. Your answer means, does it not, you could have had Mrs. Sacco and the boy come down there to live with you? *A.* Yes.

Q. You preferred to come back to this country? *A.* Yes.

Q. But you preferred to remain under the name of Mosmacotelli until the armistice was signed, didn't you? *A.* Yes.

Q. Now, is there any other besides those three reasons why you loved the United States of America? *A.* Well, I couldn't say. Over here there is more accommodation for the working class, I suppose, than any other people, a chance to be more industrious, and more industry. Can have a chance to get anything he wants.

Q. You mean to earn more money, don't you? *A.* No, no, money, never loved money.

Q. Never loved money? *A.* No, money never satisfaction to me.

Q. Money never a satisfaction to you? *A.* No.

Q. What was the industrial condition that pleased you so much here if it wasn't a chance to earn bigger money? *A.* A man, Mr. Katzmann, has no satisfaction all through the money, for the belly.

Q. For the what? *A.* For the stomach, I mean.

Q. We got away from the stomach. Now, I am talking about money. *A.* There is lots of things.

Q. Well, let us have them all. I want to know why you loved America so that after you got to the haven of Mexico when the United States was at war you came back here? *A.* Yes.

Q. I want all the reasons why you came back? *A.* I think I did tell you already.

Q. Are those all? *A.* Yes. Industry makes lots of things different.

Q. Then there is food, that is one? *A.* Yes.

Q. Foreign language is two? *A.* Yes.

Q. Your wife and child is three? *A.* Yes.

Q. And better industrial conditions? *A.* Yes.

Q. Is that all? *A.* That is all.

Q. Among those four reasons, Mr. Katzmann, then, do you find any one that is called love of country? Have you named that reason?

MR. MOORE. I object to that question. The others are reasons, I take it.

THE COURT. Read it, please.

[The question is read.]

THE COURT. That last remark does not belong in your question.

MR. KATZMANN. "Have you named them?" No, I suppose not.

THE COURT. Leave that off, and you may ask it.

MR. KATZMANN. All right.

Q. Did you find love of country among those four reasons?   A. Yes,

Q. Which one is love of country?   A. All together.

Q. All together?   A. Yes, sir.

Q. Food, wife, language, industry?   A. Yes.

Q. That is love of country, is it?   A. Yes.

Q. Is standing by a country when she needs a soldier evidence of love of country?

MR. JEREMIAH MCANARNEY. That I object to, if your Honor please. And I might state now I want my objection to go to this whole line of interrogation?

THE COURT. I think you opened it up.

MR. JEREMIAH MCANARNEY. No, if your Honor please, I have not.

THE COURT. It seems to me you have. Are you going to claim much of all the collection of the literature and the books was really in the interest of the United States as well as these people and therefore it has opened up the credibility of the defendant when he claims that all that work was done really for the interest of the United States in getting this literature out of the way?

MR. JEREMIAH MCANARNEY. That claim is not presented in anything tantamount to the language just used by the Court, and in view of the record as it stands at this time I object to this line of inquiry.

THE COURT. Is that not your claim, that the defendant, as a reason that he has given for going to the Johnson house, that they wanted the automobile to prevent people from being deported and to get this literature all out of the way? Does he not claim that that was done in the interest of the United States, to prevent violation of the law by the distribution of this literature? I understood that was the——

MR. JEREMIAH MCANARNEY. Are you asking that as a question to me?

THE COURT. Yes.

MR. JEREMIAH MCANARNEY. Absolutely we have taken no such position as that, and the evidence at this time does not warrant the assumption of that question.

THE COURT. Then you are not going to make that claim?

MR. JEREMIAH MCANARNEY. I am going to make whatever claim is legitimate.

THE COURT. I want to know what that is. You are going to claim in argument——

MR. JEREMIAH MCANARNEY. I am going to claim this man and Vanzetti were of that class called Socialists. I am going to claim that riot was running a year ago last April, that men were being deported, that twelve to fifteen hundred were seized in Massachusetts.

THE COURT. Do you mean to say you are going to offer evidence on that?

MR. JEREMIAH MCANARNEY. I am going to claim——

THE COURT. I am asking the claim. You must know when I ask the claim I mean a claim that is founded on fact, evidence introduced in the case, and not upon anything else.

MR. JEREMIAH MCANARNEY. We have not concluded the evidence, if your Honor please.

THE COURT. Do you say you are going to introduce evidence to that effect?

MR. JEREMIAH MCANARNEY. We have witnesses which we may introduce here. I do not know whether we will introduce them or not.

THE COURT. When you address me, I wish you would direct yourself to either evidence introduced or evidence you propose to introduce.

MR. JEREMIAH MCANARNEY. Your Honor now sees——

THE COURT. So I can pass judgment then upon that, and I cannot pass judgment as to the competency of something that may not be introduced and never come before me for consideration.

MR. JEREMIAH MCANARNEY. Your Honor now sees the competency of my remarks, when I said to your Honor that I objected to the question in the present state of the evidence?

THE COURT. Are you going to claim that what the defendant did was in the interest of the United States?

MR. JEREMIAH MCANARNEY. Your Honor please, I now object to your Honor's statement as prejudicial to the rights of the defendants and ask that this statement be withdrawn from the jury.

THE COURT. There is no prejudicial remark made that I know of, and none were intended. I simply asked you, sir, whether you propose to offer evidence as to what you said to me.

MR. JEREMIAH MCANARNEY. If your Honor please, the remarks made with reference to the country and whether the acts that he was doing were for the benefit of the country. I can see no other inference to be drawn from those except prejudicial to the defendants.

THE COURT. Do you intend to make that claim?

MR. JEREMIAH MCANARNEY. What claim, please?

THE COURT. The one that I am suggesting.

MR. JEREMIAH MCANARNEY. When this evidence is closed, if your Honor please, I shall argue what is legitimate in the case.

THE COURT. All I ask is this one question, and it will simplify matters very much. Is it your claim that in the collection of the literature and the books and papers that that was done in the interest of the United States? . . .

MR. JEREMIAH MCANARNEY. No, I make no such broad claim as that.

21

NICOLA SACCO

Statement on Anarchism

July 7, 1921

Sacco delivered this impassioned defense of anarchism at the prosecutor's urging during cross-examination by District Attorney Frederick Katzmann. Although it no doubt reflected Sacco's political beliefs (as well as he could express them in English), he could hardly have had an audience sympathetic to his arguments.

. . . *A*. When I was in Italy, a boy, I was a Republican, so I always thinking Republican has more chance to manage education, develop, to build some day his family, to raise the child and education, if you could. But that was my opinion; so when I came to this country I saw there was not what I was thinking before, but there was all the difference, because I been working in Italy not so hard as I been work in this country. I could live free there just as well. Work in the same condition, but not so hard, about seven or eight hours a day, better food. I mean genuine. Of course, over here is good food, because it is bigger country, to any those who got money to spend, not for the working and laboring class, and in Italy is more opportunity to laborer to eat vegetable, more fresh, and I came in this country. When I been started work here very hard and been work thirteen years, hard worker, I could not been afford much a family the way I did have the idea before. I could not put any money in the bank. I could no push my boy some to go to school and other things. I teach over here men

The Sacco-Vanzetti Case: Transcript of the Record of the Trial of Nicola Sacco and Bartolomeo Vanzetti in the Courts of Massachusetts and Subsequent Proceedings, 1920–1927 (Mamaroneck, N.Y.: Paul P. Appel, Publisher, 1969), II, 1875–77.

who is with me. The free idea gives any man a chance to profess his own idea, not the supreme idea, not to give any person, not to be like Spain in position, yes, about twenty centuries ago, but to give a chance to print and education, literature, free speech, that I see it was all wrong. I could see the best men, intelligent, education, they been arrested and sent to prison and died in prison for years and years without getting them out, and Debs, one of the great men in his country, he is in prison, still away in prison, because he is a Socialist. He wanted the laboring class to have better conditions and better living, more education, give a push his son if he could have a chance some day, but they put him in prison. Why? Because the capitalist class, they know, they are against that, because the capitalist class, they don't want our child to go to high school or to college or Harvard College. There would not be no chance, there would not be no,—they don't want the working class educationed; they want the working class to be a low all the times, be underfoot, and not to be up with the head. So, sometimes, you see, the Rockefellers, Morgans, they give fifty,— mean they give five hundred thousand dollars to Harvard College, they give a million dollars for another school. Everybody say, "Well, D. Rockefeller is a great man, the best in the country." I want to ask him who is going to Harvard College? What benefit the working class they will get by those million dollars they give by Rockefeller, D. Rockefellers. They won't get, the poor class, they won't have no chance to go to Harvard College because men who is getting $21 a week or $30 a week, I don't care if he gets $80 a week, if he gets a family of five children he can't live and send his child and go to Harvard College if he wants to eat anything nature will give him. If he wants to eat like a cow, and that is the best thing, but I want men to live like men. I like men to get everything that nature will give best, because they belong,—we are not the friend of any other place, but we are belong to nations. So that is why my idea has been changed. So that is why I love people who labor and work and see better conditions every day develop, makes no more war. We no want fight by the gun, and we don't want to destroy young men. The mother been suffering for building the young man. Some day need a little more bread, so when the time the mother get some bread or profit out of that boy, the Rockefellers, Morgans, and some of the peoples, high class, they send to war. Why? What is war? The war is not shoots like Abraham Lincoln's and Abe Jefferson,[1] to fight for the free country, for the better education, to give chance to any other peoples, not the white people but the

---

[1] "Abe Jefferson" is a reference to Thomas Jefferson.

black and the others, because they believe and know they are mens like the rest, but they are war for the great millionaire. No war for the civilization of men. They are war for business, million dollars come on the side. What right we have to kill each other? I been work for the Irish, I have been working with the German fellow, with the French, many other peoples. I love them people just as I could love my wife, and my people for that did receive me. Why should I go kill them men? What he done to me? He never done anything, so I don't believe in no war. I want to destroy those guns. All I can say, the Government put the literature, give us educations. I remember in Italy, a long time ago, about sixty years ago, I should say, yes, about sixty years ago, the Government they could not control very much these two, — devilment went on, and robbery, so one of the government in the cabinet he says, "If you want to destroy those devilments, if you want to take off all those criminals, you ought to give a chance to Socialist literature, education of people, emancipation. That is why I destroy governments, boys." That is why my idea I love Socialists. That is why I like people who want education and living, building, who is good, just as much as they could. That is all.

22

FBI AGENTS FRED J. WEYAND AND LAWRENCE LETHERMAN

Affidavits

July 1926

The Justice Department not only followed the Sacco and Vanzetti case very carefully but apparently did what it could to cooperate with the prosecution. Its involvement once again raised the issue of what Sacco and Vanzetti were actually being tried for. It seems clear that the Justice Department would have had nothing to do with the case if not for Sacco and Vanzetti's radical beliefs. These affidavits come from two former mem-

The Sacco-Vanzetti Case: Transcript of the Record of the Trial of Nicola Sacco and Bartolomeo Vanzetti in the Courts of Massachusetts and Subsequent Proceedings, 1920–1927 (Mamaroneck, N.Y.: Paul P. Appel, Publisher, 1969), V, 4500–1, 4503–04, 4505, 4506.

bers of the Federal Bureau of Investigation (FBI), who present what they argue was the FBI's perspective on the trial and on Sacco and Vanzetti.

Agent Fred J. Weyand

My name is Fred J. Weyand. I reside in Portland, Maine. I am a Special Agent of the Attorney General's office of the State of Maine, and have been since I resigned as an agent of the Department of Justice about a year and a half ago.

I became connected with the Department of Justice in the year 1916, and shortly afterwards became a Special Agent with an office first at 24 Milk Street, Boston, later at 45 Milk Street, and later at 7 Water Street, where the Department had offices on the eighth floor, and later at the Post Office Building. My duties as Special Agent were in general to investigate and report upon any and all violations of the penal code which I might be assigned to investigate by my superiors, who were first Frederick Smith, next George E. Kelliher, next John Hanrahan, next Charles Bancroft, and last Lawrence Letherman. These were my superiors while I was working from the Boston office. I occasionally worked in other parts of the country and then came under other superiors temporarily. I was a Special Agent during the entire administration of Mitchell Palmer, Attorney General of the United States, and was concerned in the activities against the so-called Reds or Radicals, including arrests and deportations which were instigated by Mr. Palmer, and which included the wholesale raids made in the month of January, 1920, in some of which I participated.

Some time before the arrest of Sacco and Vanzetti on May 5, 1920—just how long before I do not remember—the names of both of them had got on the files of the Department of Justice as Radicals to be watched. The Boston files of the Department, including correspondence, would show the date when the names of these men were first brought to the attention of the Department. Both these men were listed in the files as followers or associates of an educated Italian editor named Galleani. Galleani was the publisher of an anarchistic paper. He lived in Wrentham and published his paper, I think, in Lynn. Among other persons associated with Galleani were Carlo Tresca, Carlo Valdanoci [*sic*], and David Tedesco. The suspicion entertained by the Department of Justice against Sacco and Vanzetti was that they had violated the Selective Service Act, and also that they were anarchists or held Radical opinions of some sort or other. . . .

The understanding in this case between the agents of the Department of Justice in Boston and the District Attorney followed the usual custom, that the Department of Justice would help the District Attorney to secure a conviction, and that he in turn would help the agents of the Department of Justice to secure information that they might desire. This would include the turning over of any pertinent information by the Department of Justice to the District Attorney. Sacco and Vanzetti were, at least in the opinion of the Boston agents of the Department of Justice not liable to deportation as draft dodgers, but only as anarchists, and could not be deported as anarchists unless it could be shown that they were believers in anarchy, which is always a difficult thing to show. It usually can only be shown by self-incrimination. The Boston agents believed that these men were anarchists, and hoped to be able to secure the necessary evidence against them from their testimony at their trial for murder, to be used in case they were not convicted of murder. There is correspondence between Mr. Katzmann and Mr. [William J.] West on file in the Boston office of the Department. Mr. West furnished Mr. Katzmann information about the Radical activities of Sacco and Vanzetti to be used in their cross-examination. . . .

From my investigation, combined with the investigation made by the other agents of the Department in Boston, I am convinced not only that these men had violated the Selective Service rules and regulations and evaded the draft, but that they were anarchists, and that they ought to have been deported. By calling these men anarchists I do not mean necessarily that they were inclined to violence, nor do I understand all the different meanings that different people would attach to the word "anarchist." What I mean is that I think they did not believe in organized government or in private property. But I am also thoroughly convinced, and always have been, and I believe that is and always has been the opinion of such Boston agents of the Department of Justice as had any knowledge on the subject, that these men had nothing whatever to do with the South Braintree murders, and that their conviction was the result of co-operation between the Boston agents of the Department of Justice and the District Attorney. It was the general opinion of the Boston agents of the Department of Justice having knowledge of the affair that the South Braintree crime was committed by a gang of professional highwaymen.

Agent Lawrence Letherman

My name is Lawrence Letherman. I live in Malden, and am in the employ of the Beacon Trust Company. I was in the Federal service for thirty-six years, first in the railway mail service for nine years; then as Post Office Inspector for twenty-five years; then three years as local agent of the Department of Justice in Boston in charge of the Bureau of Investigation. I began the last named duties in September, 1921.

While I was Post Office Inspector I cooperated to a considerable extent with the agents of the Department of Justice in Boston in matters of joint concern, including the Sacco-Vanzetti case. The man under me in direct charge of matters relating to that case was Mr. William West, who is still attached to the Department of Justice in Boston. I know that Mr. West cooperated with Mr. Katzmann, the District Attorney, during the trial of the case, and later with Mr. Williams. I know that before, during, and after the trial of Sacco and Vanzetti Mr. West had a number of so-called "under cover" men assigned to this case, including one Ruzzamenti and one Carbone. I know that by an arrangement with the Department of Justice, Carbone was placed in a cell next to the cell of Sacco for the purpose of obtaining whatever incriminating information he could obtain from Sacco, after winning his confidence. Nothing, however, was obtained in that way. . . .

Before, during, and after the trial, the Department of Justice had a number of men assigned to watch the activities of the Sacco-Vanzetti Defence Committee. No evidence warranting prosecution of anybody was obtained by these men. They were all "under cover" men, and one or two of them obtained employment by the Committee in some capacity or other. I think one of them was a collector. The Department of Justice in Boston was anxious to get sufficient evidence against Sacco and Vanzetti to deport them, but never succeeded in getting the kind and amount of evidence required for that purpose. It was the opinion of the Department agents here that a conviction of Sacco and Vanzetti for murder would be one way of disposing of these two men. It was also the general opinion of such of the agents in Boston as had any actual knowledge of the Sacco-Vanzetti case, that Sacco and Vanzetti, although anarchists and agitators, were not highway robbers, and had nothing to do with the South Braintree crime. My opinion, and the opinion of most of the older men in the Government service, has always been that the South Braintree crime was the work of professionals.

The Boston agents of the Department of Justice assigned certain men to attend the trial of Sacco and Vanzetti, including Mr. Weyand. Mr. West also attended the trial. There is or was a great deal of correspondence on file in the Boston office between Mr. West and Mr. Katzmann, the District Attorney, and there are also copies of reports sent to Washington about the case. Letters and reports were made in triplicate; two copies were sent to Washington and one retained in Boston. The letters and documents on file in the Boston office would throw a great deal of light upon the preparation of the Sacco-Vanzetti case for trial, and upon the real opinion of the Boston office of the Department of Justice as to the guilt of Sacco and Vanzetti of the particular crime with which they were charged. . . .

THE APPEALS

23

GEORGE CROCKER

Testimony before the Lowell Committee
July 11, 1927

The appeals lasted for six years and, in the minds of Sacco and Vanzetti and their defenders, exposed fatal flaws in the way the trial was conducted. One appeal was based on objections to Judge Thayer's conduct in and especially out of the courtroom. George Crocker, a former city treasurer in Boston and one of its leading citizens, testifies here to comments Judge Thayer repeatedly made to him about Sacco and Vanzetti's trial.

Present: President [A. Lawrence] Lowell, Judge [Robert] Grant, President [Samuel] Stratton, Mr. [Dudley?] Ranney, Mr. Thompson, and Mr. Ehrmann.

Q. (By Mr. Thompson) You have been a lawyer for a great many years, and a citizen of Boston, etc.?　A. Yes.

Q. (By President Lowell) City Treasurer of Boston at one time?

Q. (By Mr. Thompson) I did not get that.　A. (By President Lowell) He was Treasurer of Boston at one time.

The Sacco-Vanzetti Case: Transcript of the Record of the Trial of Nicola Sacco and Bartolomeo Vanzetti in the Courts of Massachusetts and Subsequent Proceedings, 1920–1927 (Mamaroneck, N.Y.: Paul P. Appel, Publisher, 1969), V, 4968–69.

Q. (By Mr. Thompson) Oh, yes. Do you recollect while the trial of the Sacco case was going on, being approached by Judge Thayer in the University Club? *A.* I do.

Q. Now, will you state in your own words what you recollect about that matter? Please state as fully and carefully as you can. *A.* Well, the first time, one evening, this gentleman approached me, called me by name and I didn't recollect having met him before, but he began talking to me and told me how we must protect ourselves against reds, then he began to talk about this Sacco — Sacco and Vanzetti case. I finally realized he was the presiding judge in the case and he talked to me a great deal about it until I got away. He told me a good deal about their being reds and anarchists and how we must protect——

Q. (By President Stratton) What did he say? *A.* I cannot remember exactly the words he used, but to the effect that we must protect ourselves against them, there were so many reds in the country, and he had a couple of them up in the trial at which he was presiding.

Q. (By President Lowell) How far along was the trial? *A.* I don't know. Why perhaps halfways through the trial, I don't know.

(By President Lowell) It lasted seven weeks.

Q. (By Judge Grant) You mean the trial? *A.* It took seven weeks.

(By Mr. Crocker) And he talked to me several times along the same lines. He told me about the evidence somewhat, and I got away from him as soon as I could. One morning at breakfast, it was on the morning when he delivered his charge, he was living at the University Club at that time. He either signalled me to come over to his table, or I was at breakfast and he came and sat down, and he began to talk again about this trial and it went in one ear and out, because I didn't want to have anything to do with him. In part he talked about the counsel for the defense in the argument for the defense, and I don't know what it was. I didn't like to listen to it. Then he pulled out of his pocket a paper which he said was part of his charge and he said "Now Moore said so and so yesterday in his argument to the jury and I want to read you part of the charge I am going to deliver. That will hold him.", etc.

Q. (By President Lowell) It would what "hold him"? *A.* Hold him.

Q. (By President Lowell) Hold him.

Q. (By Judge Grant) Where?

A. It would hold him. It was an answer to his argument, McAnarney's argument and he talked and I was very uncomfortable and I got away as soon as I could, and I avoided in the future all talk with him about the case. In fact, I spoke to the head waiter or stewart [*sic*] at the Club "For Heaven's sake, don't put me with that man." . . .

24

JAMES RICHARDSON

Testimony before the Lowell Committee

July 12, 1927

James Richardson, a Dartmouth professor and an old friend of Judge Thayer's, testifies here about comments Thayer made to him about the trial and the defendants.

Present: President Lowell, President Stratton, Judge Grant, Mr. Ranney, Mr. Thompson, and Mr. Ehrmann.

Q. (By Mr. Thompson) Gentlemen, this is Professor Richardson. You are a lawyer by profession? *A.* Yes, sir.

Q. For a long time lived in Massachusetts? *A.* I did, yes.

Q. You have been acquainted with Judge Thayer for a long time? *A.* Yes.

Q. And various other Massachusetts people also? *A.* Yes, sir.

Q. You were a member of our Convention? *A.* I was.

Q. I think I ran against you in Newton and was defeated by you. Now I would like to ask whether on a certain occasion in November 1923 you met Judge Webster Thayer on some athletic field in Hanover? . . .

Q. (By Mr. Thompson) Now, Professor Richardson, I have asked you whether you remember meeting Judge Webster Thayer on some athletic field in Hanover in the year 1923? *A.* 1924.

Q. What was the date? *A.* Early in November.

The Sacco-Vanzetti Case: Transcript of the Record of the Trial of Nicola Sacco and Bartolomeo Vanzetti in the Courts of Massachusetts and Subsequent Proceedings, 1920–1927 (Mamaroneck, N.Y.: Paul P. Appel, Publisher, 1969), V, 5064–66.

Q. What was the year?   *A.* In 1924.

Q. Tell of his being there and your meeting.   *A.* He was on the athletic field when the reference was made.

Q. You were there watching the same thing?   *A.* Quite so. I was there as usual.

Q. Judge Thayer, I believe is a graduate of Dartmouth?   *A.* He is.

Q. He was appointed by Governor McCall, was he not?   *A.* That is my recollection.

Q. Now, will you kindly state as accurately and carefully as you can what you heard him say? I am afraid I shall have you to give us in his exact words, if you can, however disagreeable, as accurately as you can.

Q. (By Judge Grant) At what stage was the trial at that time?   *A.* (By Mr. Thompson) Motions pending. The last motion had not been filed.

Q. (By Mr. Thompson) I beg pardon. Do you recall Mr. Ehrmann, when Judge Thayer had under consideration the last motion? *A.* (By Mr. Ranney) October 1, 1924, came down on that date. *A.* (By Prof. Richardson) Early in November.

Q. (By Mr. Thompson) The other one had not been made. It would be to my advantage and the advantage of my clients to have the motions heard before an impartial judge.

Q. (By Mr. Thompson) Before I filed these affidavits with the Governor I went to Justice Perley Hall and suggested to him sometime before that I would like future proceedings in this case to be before a judge other than Judge Thayer. I told him any judge except Judge Thayer, and for reasons I thought it was hopeless to ask Judge Thayer to pass on his impartiality. So I filed the affidavits. Will you please go on, Prof. Richardson?   *A.* Judge Thayer met on the field with a group about. He spoke to me by name. He has known me for a long time. He immediately went into the subject of the Sacco-Vanzetti case; he referred at once to the motions which had been pending before him, and which he within a short time disposed of. My recollection is, I don't know, but Mr. Ranney is probably correct, would have been that some of these motions had been decided on shortly before this conversation.

(By Mr. Ranney) That is right, all decided.

A. (By Prof. Richardson) All had been decided, probably a short time before. Judge Thayer said as near as I can remember "Did you see what I did with those anarchistic bastards the other day? I guess that will hold them for a while."

Q. (By Mr. Thompson) Yes?   *A.* "Let them go to the Supreme Court now and see what they can get out of them."

Q. Yes?   *A.* There was more of the same sort.

Q. Yes?   *A.* Well, there was more of the same sort. My recollection is fairly accurate.

Q. Yes, he used a word that is commonly used to describe born out of marriage?   *A.* My recollection is that he did. I think he used the words "sons of bitches."

Q. That is not an uncommon expression of his?   *A.* I don't know.

Q. Did he refer to their political views?   *A.* As I have stated he called them anarchists and commented on the matter as such to the best of my recollection. He said "They wouldn't get very far in my court."

Q. Yes? Got up some feeling against the anarchists or socialists?   *A.* No question about that, sir.

Q. When he was giving his views in a disrespectful way was there anyone around that could hear him?   *A.* Yes, I would say he was heard by others.

Q. Yes? What did you do, Professor Richardson, when he made this remarkable demonstration of impartiality [*sic*]?   *A.* I made no comment to the judge whatever, except to nod or something of that sort. There was nothing that I could.

Q. You have known Judge Thayer for some little time?   *A.* I have.

Q. You have an impression of his ability?   *A.* I have.

Q. His general attitude of mind, his bearing, his judicial capacity and impartiality?   *A.* I have.

Q. Well, I will ask you to state it.   *A.* It has never been high, but I must admit that what he said on that day was a surprise to me and I wouldn't have believed it possible. . . .

25

Celestino Madeiros's Statement

April 8, 1926

On November 16, 1925, a prison trustee handed Sacco a note written by Celestino Madeiros, a fellow inmate. In the note, Madeiros confessed that he—and not Sacco or Vanzetti—had been involved in the South Braintree crime. His assertion formed the basis for Sacco and Vanzetti's final appeal. This document contains Celestino Madeiros's responses to questions from authorities after his confession. It comes from a typewritten copy of his transcribed responses now in the Herbert Ehrmann papers housed at the Harvard Law School Library.

. . . When you left school at fourteen, what did you do?
   Went to work in a mill.

How long did you work there?
   About six months.

Then what did you do?
   I don't know what I did.

What did you do in general for the next few years?
   Didn't do much of anything in general.

How old are you now?
   Twenty-four.

In 1923 you were twenty-one. What did you do previous to that?
   I worked on different jobs. Worked for contractors.

Were you arrested more than once?
   Twice.

You had been stealing on and off from the time you were a child?
   Yes.

Celestino Madeiros's statement, April 8, 1926. Herbert Ehrmann papers, box 25, folder 7, Harvard Law School Library.

Probation officers see you?
  Probation officer took me to Taunton.

When did you begin to have convulsions?
  I don't know what you mean by convulsions.

Fits?
  Oh, since I was a kid.

How long? How old when they started?
  I couldn't say.

How often did you have them?
  Sometimes two or three times a week. Sometimes once.

When did you have the last one?
  About a week ago.

As you grew older, did they become more frequent or less?
  Less.

Did you tell us one time that you hadn't had many convulsions after two years before we saw you?
  No. As I been growing up it seems to be less. Sometimes it comes all at once. I have them right along.

How many have you had here?
  A number.

How many do you think?
  I can't tell.

Ten or two hundred?
  About ten or fifteen, I guess.

Do you lose consciousness?
  Yes.

How do you know you do?
  Take like last week's; had one in the shop. All the boys saw me.

Do you bit [sic] your tongue?
  No, I don't think so.

How long previous to last week since you had a convulsion?
  About a month before. I told the doctor here, but he started to laugh at me.

Most of these have been rather mild, is that right? Last a minute or two?
  Yes.

Not in them for days?
  No. As a child I sometimes had them for days.

How much alcohol did you use [*sic*] to drink?
  I only started drinking lately. Used to drink quite a lot lately. Started when I was 20.

How often did you drink?
  Regularly.

Moonshine?
  Yes.

How many quarts a day?
  Wouldn't drink quarts, but about a pint. Depends how the days were.

How did you figure out to make your living after you gave up garage work?
  After I give up garage work I went south.

When you came back?
  I was going to do business there, but I couldn't get along.

What kind of business?
  Garage business.

What year?
  The end of 1923 and beginning of 1924.

Where were you in the south?
  Texas.

You came back at what time?
  Early, just beginning summer.

1923?
  1924, I guess.

This affair took place in November?
  Yes.

How did you decide to make your living after you came back?
  I was going to try,——I lost my money in the south and I was

going to try to start business. Couldn't find much doing and got offered a job in a road house.

Then you went rum running?
  Yes.

When did you start that?
  After I got the job in the road house.

The Blue Bird Inn?
  Yes.

How much money did you make there?
  Quite a lot.

What was your salary?
  Fifteen dollars and board. I made a lot besides.

Sort of a bouncer?
  Yes.

Special money for special privileges you allowed the guests.
  Yes.

How many guests at a time?
  As high as fifty.

Rather small place?
  Yes, but always crowded.

Who supplied the moonshine to the guests?
  We didn't use moonshine. Regular whiskey.

Who got that?
  We got it from Newport.

How many rooms in that Blue Bird Inn?
  It really wasn't a rooming place, just a dance place.

You had a few rooms?
  Two rooms for guests use.

Why did you leave there?
  I didn't leave it. I did in one way. Me and the fellow running it got in an argument. Had fight. That is how I left.

Did you threaten him?
  No, I didn't threaten him I hit him.

What did he do to you?
　He run in his room, so I cam[e] away.

Did you expect a raid to take place?
　I had been expecting it and I wanted him to close the place.

Did the man running it make money?
　Yes. He was making too much.

You wanted more, is that it?
　He was making too much and wanted to run it wide open. I used to
　know most of the guests. No one would go in unless I would allow
　them. After he got making so much money he wanted everyone to
　go in. Two or three young girls I used to chase them out and make
　them go home, sometimes take them home myself, but he used to
　let everybody come in.

How long after did you go in the rum running business?
　I was in it then.

When did you get mixed up with [Fred] Bedard and [James] Weeks?[1]
　As soon as I got through there. They came down after me and they
　said they had good business in rum running.

How did you meet them?
　At the Blue Bird.

They made a proposition to you to [go] in with them?
　Yes.

Who planned this affair in Wrentham?
　Bedard.

How much interested was the Jew? How much interested was Goldberg?
　Just like I was. Me and him didn't know anything about it. Bedard
　knew about it. Him and Weeks came and told us about it. They
　came and got me and went to Goldberg's house and got him.

How long before that took place? A short while?
　Few days.

---

　[1]James Weeks and Fred Bedard participated in the attempted robbery of the First
National Bank in Wrentham, Massachusetts, on November 1, 1924, at which an elderly
cashier was killed. Weeks and Bedard pleaded guilty and were sentenced to life imprisonment. The State refused to strike a deal with Madeiros.

Were they all armed?
   Yes, they were always armed.

Always carried a gun, every one?
   Yes.

Any occasion to use that gun on anyone before?
   No.

You knew it was against the law to carry a gun?
   Yes.

But everybody did it?
   Yes.

Was it planned you were the man to go into the bank?
   Yes. Bedard planned I was to go.

Who was to go with you?
   Me and the Jewish fellow and Weeks.

But Weeks and you were the only two went in? The Jew didn't go did he?
   Yes. He went.

How have you been treated here since you have been here?
   I don't know. Just like they treat anybody else.

Been imposed on because you are Madeiros?
   No. I don't think so. Only about keeping me locked up. Before they didn't let anyone come to see me. Not even my brother-in-law.

They don't even allow your brother-in-law?
   They do now. I just phoned my lawyer and found out and he said it would be all right he would fix it up. When I had the other trial my brother-in-law came up most every day and he couldn't come in.

Why?
   I don't know.

Any explanation?
   No.

Is that they [*sic*] way they treat everybody?
   No. The other prisoners anybody comes in.

Why do they select you to disallow you to have visitors?
   They seem to have the impression I am some kind of a wild man.

Do you think that was due to the attack you made on the officer?
    No. Before that they wouldn't allow visitors.

You have the reputation around here of being a bad man?
    I suppose so. Only that time, I never done anything else here. I suppose that is the reason why.

Do you work in the shop?
    No. They don't let me out of the cell.

Do you have any work in the cell?
    No. Lay down that is about all. They don't even give me a chair.

Do they give you any work of any kind?
    No.

They don't allow you out at all?
    One hour to walk up and down every day.

Inside?
    Yes. The only thing I can do is lay down and read. When I can get anything to read. Half the time I can't get anything to read.

What would you like to read?
    Newspapers and magazines.

Don't your friends send them to you?
    I ain't got many friends.

You have your sister and your mother.
    They don't read.

They could send you papers and magazines.
    Sure if they had lots of money. My mother aint got anybody working for her.

What about your sister?
    My sister's husband has been out of work for about two months.

You don't have to tell me this. But were you trying to be funny when you wanted to assume the responsibility for Mr. Sacco's case? Wasn't there something in the paper that you had confessed to the murder[?]
    Yes.

Then I am prying into no secret.

Why did you want to make a statement of that kind?
    I rather not talk about it.

You must have had some purpose one way or the other for giving out that information.
Maybe it is true.

Would you want to go further and say may be or that it *is* true?
Yes.

It is true?
Yes.

Why did you keep silent and let these two innocent men be accused?
I never knew they was accused.

You hadn't been reading the papers to learn about the Sacco-Vanzetti trial?
No.

How did you know you were the man who committed the crime?
I knew I was the one who committed the crime in South Braintree.

But you hadn't known it all these years?
No.

No one had ever told you?
No. I never heard about Sacco and Vanzetti until I came here.

What year did that take place?
Quite a while ago. I don't remember just what year. 1918 I think.

When was that in the press?
About 5 or 6 months ago.

After your trial?
Yes.

Who was it you told that to?
I had Mr. Thompson, Sacco's lawyer come down.

You sent for him?
Yes.

You told him the details?
Yes. I gave him a statement.

You remember distinctly the episode at the time you shot this man in South Braintree?
No not distinctly. It was quite a while ago.

Did you get away with some money?
  The others got away. I didn't get any.

How much?
  I never knew. I got double crossed in it.

Do you know who killed this man?
  No. I didn't do no shooting.

I thought you said you did?
  No. I simply said I was there.

Did you tell Mr. Thompson the names of the other parties?
  I told him the names they used.

Did you go there with the intention of that robbery?
  Yes. I went there with the party with the intention of that robbery. I
  didn't know what robbery it was.

You must have known their names?
  I did, but it wasn't their right names.

Had you know them long?
  Not for long. Two or three months.

Was that plan in mind?
  Yes. These men, they had Boston connections. Used to come to
  Boston quite often. Used to hang out at South Boston and Rhode
  Island. Before they went on that job they went to South Boston
  first. Went from Rhode Island to Boston and from Boston to Brain-
  tree.

After all these years you weren't interested to find out whether anyone
was arrested?
  No. I wasn't interested. I couldn't learn much. I got arrested myself
  in a short time.

For what?
  Breaking and entering.

What did they do with you?
  I served five months.

It was simply that your conscience made you feel you ought to make
this statement?
  Yes.

You hadn't been reading the newspapers at all?
    No.

You just developed reading the newspapers since being in jail?
    It aint the desire to have the newspapers to read, if I had something
    else to read. Nothing in cell all day but lay in bed. Got to do some-
    thing.

26

JUDGE WEBSTER THAYER

Ruling on the Madeiros Appeal

October 23, 1926

*This document is excerpted from Judge Thayer's lengthy rejection of the
Madeiros appeal.*

... Madeiros is, without doubt, a crook, a thief, a robber, a liar, a rum-
runner, a "bouncer" in a house of ill-fame, a smuggler, and a man who
has been convicted and sentenced to death for the murder of one Car-
penter, who was cashier of the Wrentham Bank. An affidavit from a
man of this type must be examined and scrutinized with the greatest
possible care, caution, and judgment before the verdict of a jury
approved by the Supreme Judicial Court of this Commonwealth is set
aside. For it must be remembered that the Commonwealth has rights
in these verdicts that equal those of the defendants, and those rights,
under our law, must be as safely and carefully guarded and protected
as those of the defendants. For it must be remembered, as already
stated, that it is the jury that determines the guilt or innocence of defendants; and, this being so, the law requires that the presiding Judge,

*The Sacco-Vanzetti Case: Transcript of the Record of the Trial of Nicola Sacco and Bar-
tolomeo Vanzetti in the Courts of Massachusetts and Subsequent Proceedings, 1920–1927*
(Mamaroneck, N.Y.: Paul P. Appel, Publisher, 1969), V, 4726–7, 4776–77.

before setting aside verdicts of a jury on newly-discovered evidence, must be satisfied of the probable truthfulness of such evidence. . . .

At no time has the Court lost sight of the rights of the defendants and those of the Commonwealth in these verdicts, neither has the Court failed to hear at all times the commanding voice of the law that has told, in clear and unmistakeable terms, its duty before it is justified in setting aside verdicts. That duty, imposed upon the Trial Judge the obligation of finding as a fact the truthfulness or probable truthfulness of the material allegations set forth in this Motion for a New Trial. It is not now a question of the guilt or innocence of these defendants, for that question has been determined by the jury in accordance with the law. The Court has nothing to do, under the law, with the determination of the guilt or innocence of these defendants for that (as has been stated) rests within the sole province of the jury. As far as this Court is concerned, the only question involved is, whether or not the verdicts of the jury, that have been affirmed by the Supreme Judicial Court of this Commonwealth, should be set aside on the Confession of Madeiros. In other words, this Court must find that the defendants have established, by a fair preponderance of the evidence, the truthfulness of the Madeiros Confession. But this Court, if his natural feelings of humanity were stretched to the limit, cannot find as a fact that Madeiros told the truth. This being so, his duty is unmistakeably plain. Therefore, this Court, exercising every authority vested in it by the law of this Commonwealth in the granting of motions for new trials on newly-discovered evidence, denies these motions for new trials that are based upon the Confession of Madeiros and all other affidavits filed in connection therewith. Consequently, both Motions for New Trials in both cases are hereby denied.

27

CARLO TRESCA

Vanzetti's Articles Reprinted
in Il martello with Editor's Comments

September 15, 1921

Sacco and Vanzetti's arrest alarmed fellow Italian American radicals like Carlo Tresca immediately. This document, taken from FBI files on Tresca, features sections of articles written by Vanzetti and published, with commentary, by Tresca in his newspaper Il martello *[The Hammer] in 1921. Already by this point Tresca was publicizing the trial and trying to arouse support for Sacco and Vanzetti.*

From the Bastile

Dearest:

Contrary to the opinion and the hope held by comrades, by friends, and by my very lawyers for a verdict of 'not guilty,' I was pessimistic both before and during my trial.

It was the recent and bitter experience which made me predict what happened. I have been found guilty in the second trial, as I was in the first by preconcerted action.

As I am an Italian and of revolutionary propensities to be judged by twelve 100/100 American citizens, in this period pregnant with hatred and intimidation, one must be really a fool, to be blind to the inexorabilities of things and men plotting not for my perdition, but against our ideas, and I feel proud of not having been wrong in my prediction. Nor shall I attempt to analyze in this letter the different causes of phenomena and factors which rendered unavoidable this injustice, but, if

Carlo Tresca, Vanzetti articles and editor's comments, *Il martello* (1921), from FBI files.

the executioner will allow me and the confinement will not wreck my suffering mental qualities, I intend to write minutely and extensively about them.

This letter is dictated by the affection and gratitude I feel for you and for all the good ones, for all who have done and will do to protect my life and my liberty; for all that my comrades did, do, and will do; and also to tell you that I, defeated but not conquered, exhort you all, from my cell of confinement, to continue the good struggle for the true liberty and the true justice. I send you my cry of encouragement. Do not feel overwhelmed if two of the soldiers fall, and learn the good qualities of our foe. Be constant, implacable, decisive, and active for the good, just as our foe is for the evil.

Best regards to Elizabeth Flynn and all the comrades.

Yours for the cause,
BARTOLOMEO VANZETTI.

We receive with approbation this cry of encouragement and repeat it in this fighting newspaper in order to have it spread in the fields, in the factories, in the huts, wherever there are people with callous hands, suffering, working, hoping, and struggling.

You are proud, Bartolomeo, because you could not be mocked, because you showed no sign of weakness when facing the enemy, although you well knew that the efforts of the working class that feel much affection for you and for your cell-mate, Nicola Sacco, the efforts of your lawyers, and the rights of truth and justice had to be defeated against the Chinese Wall of the political and race prejudice, the hatred of the bosses, which is, as you rightly assert, implacable and ferocious.

[From another letter]

Well, dear Tresca, we have been found guilty. Why, it would be a great wonder if we had been absolved.

I expect nothing more than the bourgeois' justice. The American juries condemn by preconcerted action, in spite of everything. After all, they did not have the satisfaction of seeing us tremble, nor will they ever have.

These two comrades in arms and faith are as strong as an oak, which does not bend in the wind storm. And all of us are proud of you. Sacco and Vanzetti, of you, we are flesh of our flesh, of you who have known how to hold aloft, so pure and so immaculate, the flag of the ideal, in the midst of the enemy's field, where you are kept prisoners.

And we shall go on with this work—we from this battle line, the phalanx of our comrades from the advance line of the vast field of the struggle, for the true liberty, for the true justice, but first of all, for your liberation.

This is a pledge which all of us promise to live up to with all energy.

28

ELIZABETH GURLEY FLYNN

Rebel Girl

1955

Carlo Tresca's efforts to publicize the trial bore fruit quickly, as radical labor organizer Elizabeth Gurley Flynn paid early visits to the impris-oned anarchists—the subject of this document—before embarking on a national tour to draw attention to their situation.

. . . Nothing much was said or done about the arrests of Sacco and Vanzetti by anyone at first. They were very humble and obscure foreign-born workers. A small Italian committee of close associates was set up in Boston. But soon they were to realize that this was a dif-ferent matter—not a political charge but a criminal one. Sacco and Vanzetti were bundled into cars and taken around from one town to another, where they were put on exhibition. Strange people were brought in to look at them while the police queried insistently, "Are these the men?"—and insisted: "Sure, these are the guys all right!" They were told to put on certain caps, to crouch down, which was very confusing to Sacco and Vanzetti. . . .

It was not until after this first trial of Vanzetti that I heard the names of Sacco and Vanzetti. I was then secretary of the Workers

Elizabeth Gurley Flynn, *Rebel Girl: An Autobiography: My First Life (1906–1926)* (New York: International Publishers, 1955), 299–300, 303–4, 305–6.

Defense Union in New York City. A woman in New England who occupied a similar post was Mrs. Marion Emerson of the New England Defense Conference. We were both busy with the struggles growing out of the Palmer raids—raising bail, feeding families, hiring lawyers. I went several times to Boston to speak on behalf of hundreds of deportees herded on Deer Island. Dr. George Galvin, a noted physician, was chairman of a huge meeting there.

Just before I left New York on one of these trips, Carlo said, "Elizabetta, there are two Italian comrades in big trouble in Massachusetts on account of Salsadeo [sic]. You investigate while you are there and maybe get the Americans to help." He gave me the address of A. Felicini [sic] who worked on a local Italian newspaper, Le Notizia, in South Boston. I asked Mrs. Emerson who I learned on this trip was related to Ralph Waldo Emerson, if she knew about them. She had vaguely heard of them through the local press. She agreed to go with me to investigate their plight. We went into the turbulent but colorful, overcrowded slums of old Boston, now a little Italy, with its crooked streets and narrow houses, in search of this unknown man on an obscure paper. We found him, but he spoke so little English we had to wait until he found an interpreter. He was very glad to see us and eager to tell us everything. He called together the Italian committee, and for the first time two Americans heard the story of Sacco and Vanzetti. Thus began my seven years' labors to help save Sacco and Vanzetti....

In October 1920 Mary Heaton Vorse and I visited Nicola Sacco in the Dedham Jail. Fred Moore arranged the interview so that we could give some publicity to their plight. Mary wrote a fine article for *The Nation* which began, "We drove through the sweet New England towns." It was autumn, the pungent smell of burning leaves was in the air. As jails go, it was not a bad place, Mary said—it looked like a library, with its large central rotunda; only men were put away on the shelves, not books. Then a handsome youth, slim, erect, with flashing eyes and a gay smile came rapidly toward us. This was Sacco. He was 30 years old. His blue shirt was clean and neat, open at the throat. He greeted me with enthusiasm. "Elizabetta—I know you. I heard you speak for Lawrence strikers!" he said. Then he greeted Fred Moore and met Mrs. Vorse who spoke a little Italian, which gladdened his heart. We all sat down. He told us of himself and his views—"The Idea," he called it, which to him meant social justice. No government, no police, no judges, no bosses, no authority; autonomous groups of people—the people own everything—work in cooperation—distribute by needs—equality, justice, comradeship—love of each other;

eager words like this flowed in a torrent from his lips. He hated to be idle. He wanted to be able to work—this bothered him.

He said he was ready to die for "The Idea"—for the people. But not for "gunman job." He spoke of how he had worked all his life, his hands were the skilled hands of a shoemaker, they were for work not for killing. "To steal money, to kill a poor man for money! This is insult to me!" he said passionately. He threw back his head and explained: "I am innocent. I no do this thing. I swear it on the head of my newborn child!" This vehement cry, "*Io innocente!* You are killing an innocent man!" were the words he shouted at the craven jury months later. To Sacco, a cold-blooded murder of a factory employee to carry out a mercenary holdup was unthinkable. He was hurt, deeply hurt, to be accused of such a thing.

One hand had remained tightly clasped during our talk. But in his anger he spread his fingers apart and a little piece of metal fell out, a Catholic sacred heart medal. He smiled with embarrassment and explained, "Boss' wife, good Irish lady, she came, she cried, and she said, 'Keep this Nick, it will save you!'" "I no believe," he said, "but I no want to hurt her feelings, so I take." I was well acquainted with this idealistic type of kind and good Italian anarchist, who might kill a king as an act of "social justice"—but not a mouse. I believed Sacco when he said, "Elizabetta, I am innocent." I believe it now, after thirty-four years. So confident was he of his innocence that sunny afternoon that he had no fear. He was sure when he told his story in court he would go free. He did not know that he was approaching the valley of the shadow of death. He feared no evil because the truth was with him. But greed, corruption, prejudice, fear, and hatred of radical foreign-born workingmen were weaving a net around him. . . .

After my return from visiting Sacco and Vanzetti we began, through the Workers Defense Union, to arrange public meetings and to raise money on their behalf. On October 4, 1920, we sent out as complete a factual statement as was possible then—the first in English. We stated prophetically, "If convicted they will be sentenced to electrocution."

29

BARTOLOMEO VANZETTI

Letter to Mrs. Evans

August 4, 1927

Sacco and Vanzetti's supporters did not come solely from the ranks of radical and labor advocates. Certain elite Boston women attended the trial daily, supplied the two prisoners with food and flowers, and taught them English. Elizabeth Glendower Evans was an unquestioned—and quite liberal—member of the Boston elite. This Brahmin woman, who was a member of the New England branch of the American Civil Liberties Union (ACLU), remained a dedicated and generous supporter of Sacco and Vanzetti. Vanzetti's letter to her speaks to the close relationship they established.

Charlestown Prison

DEAR MRS. EVANS:

Last night, after 9:00 p.m. Medieros, Nick, and I were brought from our cells in Cherry Hill into the three cells of the deathhouse. In coming, I got a glance to the nighty, starry sky,—it was so long I did seen it before—and thought it was my last glance to the stars.

This morning Rose came to us and have had to stay beyond the bars of our cells. That is a thing for a wife.

Rose brought us your letters which I read both; your article on the actual phase of our case; and the poem of Brent Dow Allinson.[1]

You ask for the Governor interviews with Nick and I. As for Nick, he spoke alone with the Governor and I didn't heard their conversation. Nick told me something of it,—but I prefer to let him say what he wish about it. I know that he stayed for very short time with the Governor.

---

[1]Brent Dow Allinson was a Boston-area poet; the poem Vanzetti mentioned was originally titled "In Honor of Massachusetts," and eventually changed to "Sacco and Vanzetti—Dead!"

Marion Denman Frankfurter and Gardner Jackson, eds., *The Letters of Sacco and Vanzetti* (New York: Viking Press, 1928), 314–16.

As you know, I spoke with the Governor for about ninety minutes at both his interviews with me.

The impression he gave me at the first interview, he repeated at his second one. It is as I told to Mrs. Codman. Only it seemed to me he inclined to see things in a contrary way to us—in fact he should assert a tremendous effort against himself to overwhelm that which, for thousands reasons, feelings and facts is to him a natural hostile tendency toward us, our persons, our case, our ideas, our environment. We are his opposite all at all and all in all, while our enemies are officers to him in all most everything. Consciously, subconsciously, and unconsciously he cannot escape to be tremendously influenced and predisposed against us. But he gave me the impression to be sincere; had made great efforts to know the truth and was not settled, at least deliberately, against us, before to begin his inquiry.

Of course I may be wrong, but this seems to be the truth to me.

We spoke of allmost all the matters of the case. The Governor was man to tell me what troubles his mind against us. Unfortunately, given to the fact that at both time I have believed to be able to told him all my reasons and thoughts, it happened that I spoke to him more of other matters than the ones he mentioned having in mind to tell him of them at the last. Yet I wrote and dictated on these matters to the Governor.

If he is sending us to death, it does not matter how honestly the Governor can be convinced of our guiltiness, his conviction will not make us guilty—we are and will remain innocent, our execution would be the same as murder, our blood will call for revenge. It is for these reasons, for my duty toward my father, brother, sisters, friends, comrades, and all at large and toward myself that I opened my heart to the Governor and talk to him as clear and forceful as I was able. Then even when agonizing, I wrote and dictate to him everything I can remember. I did all I can.

Not a dog, not a snake, not even a scorpion would have been dealed and be dealed as we have and as it seems we will be—in case like our,—by sane or good men.

Dear Mrs. Evans, you have been most good with us. I bless you for all that you have done to our own and to us.

Be of brave heart.

30

BARTOLOMEO VANZETTI

Letter to Mrs. Jack

October 3, 1923

Cerise Jack, the wife of a Harvard professor, was, like Elizabeth Glendower Evans, a member of the New England Civil Liberties Committee and a staunch defender of the two prisoners.

Charlestown Prison

DEAR MRS. JACK:

Few days ago Nick and I have received a big basket of beautiful and savorous peaches from you; and another basket last evening.

I remember to have received other fruit from you during the first trial. Nick told me of your goodness toward us — (and not he alone).

I was also told, last Spring, by a good friend, the beauty of your fruit orchard in bloom. And now I enjoy what those flowers have ripened; and it is indeed providential since our appetite is not very sharp — and the prison food not very good.

These fruits also remember to me the home's garden. At the time I lived there this kind of peaches was very little known. I remember when my father planted the first tree of this kind, in my garden. I tasted few of its fruit before to left my native place. So, if you will consider that these, your fruits, give me life, remember me the most loved place — and prove to me (in this black hour, second only, in sorrow, to that of my mother's death) the sympathy and friendship of you — you may realize, in a way — how I appreciate your present. But you have sent to many. I still have some of the first basket (though I must confess to have gave some of them to some unfortunate youths).

So, while I pray you to not send any more fruit to me, I also pray you to accept my hearty thanks, wishes, and regards.

Marion Denman Frankfurter and Gardner Jackson, eds., *The Letters of Sacco and Vanzetti* (New York: Viking Press, 1928), 101–2.

31

JOHN DOS PASSOS

Facing the Chair

1927

The renowned writer John Dos Passos was arguably the American liberal most deeply affected by the trial, and eventually by Sacco and Vanzetti's executions. Novelist, essayist, poet, and playwright, he published Facing the Chair, *excerpted here, near the end of the appeals process in an effort both to publicize and to evoke protests against the conduct of their trial.*

But what is this criminal garlic-smelling creed that the people of Massachusetts will not face openly?

For half a century Anarchy has been the bogy of American schoolmasters, policemen, old maids, and small town mayors. About the time of the assassination of McKinley a picture was formed in the public mind of the anarchist; redhanded, unwashed foreigner whom nobody could understand, sticks of dynamite in his pocket and bomb in the paper parcel under his arm, redeyed housewrecker waiting only for the opportunity to bite the hand that fed him. Since the Russian Revolution the picture has merged a little with that of the sneaking, slinking, communist Jew, enviously undermining Prosperity and Decency through secret organizations ruled from Moscow.

Gradually among liberals and intelligent people generally certain phases of anarchism have meanwhile been reluctantly admitted into respectable conversation under the phrase "philosophical anarchist," which means an anarchist who shaves daily, has good manners, and is guaranteed not to act on his beliefs. Certain people of the best society, such as Kropotkin and Tolstoy, princes both, having through their anarchy made themselves important figures in European thought and literature, it was impossible to exclude them longer from the pale of decency.

What is this outlaw creed?

When Christianity flourished in the Mediterranean basin, slave and

John Dos Passos, *Facing the Chair: Story of the Americanization of Two Foreignborn Workmen* (New York: Da Capo Press, 1970 [1927]), 56–58, 126–27.

emperor had the hope of the immediate coming of Christ's kingdom, the golden Jerusalem that would appear on earth to put an end to the tears and aches of the faithful. After the first millennium, the City of God, despaired of on earth, took its permanent place in the cloudy firmament with the Virgin Mary at the apex of the feudal pyramid. With the decay of feudalism and the coming of the kingdoms of this world the church became more and more the instrument of the governing orders. Undermined by the eighteenth century, overthrown by the French revolution, the church was restored by the great reaction as the strongest bulwark of Privilege. But in the tough memories of peasants and fishermen—their sons worked in factories—there remained a faint trace of the vanished brightness of the City of God. All our city-dwelling instinct and culture has been handed down to us from these countless urban generations, Cretans, Greeks, Phoenicians, Latins of the Mediterranean basin, Italians of the hilltowns. It is natural that the dwellers on those scraggy hills in sight of that always blue sea should have kept alight in their hearts the perfect city, where the strong did not oppress the weak, where every man lived by his own work at peace with his neighbors, the white Commune where man could reach his full height free from the old snarling obsessions of god and master.

It is this inner picture that is the core of feeling behind all anarchist theory and doctrine. Many Italians planted the perfect city of their imagination in America. When they came to this country they either killed the perfect city in their hearts and submitted to the system of dawg eat dawg or else they found themselves anarchists. There have been terrorists among them, as in every other oppressed and despised sect since the world began. Good people generally have contended that anarchism and terrorism were the same thing, a silly and usually malicious error much fostered by private detectives and the police bomb-squads.

An anarchist workman who works for the organization of his fellow workmen is a man who costs the factory owners money; thereby he is a bomb-thrower and possible murderer in the minds of the majority of American employers.

In his charge to the jury in the Plymouth trial Judge Thayer definitely said that the crime of highway robbery was consistent with Vanzetti's ideals as a radical.

Yet under the conflict between employer and workman, and the racial misunderstanding, in themselves material enough for the creation of a frameup, might there not be a deeper bitterness? The people of Massachusetts centuries ago suffered and hoped terribly for the City of God. This little white courthouse town of Dedham, neat and exquisite under its elms, is the symbol of a withered hope, mortgaged at six per cent to the kingdoms of this world. It is natural that New Englanders, who feel in themselves a lingering of the passionate barbed desire of perfection of their ancestors, should hate with particular bitterness, anarchists, votaries of the Perfect Commune on earth. The irrational features of this case of attempted communal murder can only be explained by a bitterness so deep that it has been forgotten by the very people it moves most fervidly. . . .

What is going to be done if the Supreme Judicial Court continues to refuse Sacco and Vanzetti a new trial? Are Sacco and Vanzetti going to burn in the Chair?

The conscience of the people of Massachusetts must be awakened. Working people, underdogs, reds know instinctively what is going on. The same thing has happened before. But the average law-admiring, authority-respecting citizen does not know. For the first time, since Judge Thayer's last denial of motions for a new trial, there has been a certain awakening among the influential part of the community, the part of the community respected by the press and the bench and the pulpit. Always there have been notable exceptions, but up to now these good citizens have had no suspicion that anything but justice was being meted out by the courts. Goaded by the *New York World* editorials, by Chief Counsel Thompson's eloquence, by the *Boston Herald*'s courageous change of front, they are getting uneasy. It remains to be seen what will come of this uneasiness. The *Boston Herald* suggests an impartial commission to review the whole case. All that is needed is that the facts of the case be generally known.

Everyone must work to that end, no matter what happens, that the facts of the case may be known so that no one can plead ignorance, so that if these men are killed, everyone in the State, everyone in the country will have the guilt on them. So that no one can say "I would have protested but I didn't know what was being done."

Tell your friends, write to your congressmen, to the political bosses of your district, to the newspapers. Demand the truth about Sacco and Vanzetti. Call meetings, try to line up trade unions, organizations, clubs, put up posters. Demand the truth about Sacco and Vanzetti.

If the truth had been told they would be free men today.

If the truth is not told they will burn in the Chair in Charlestown Jail. If they die what little faith many millions of men have in the chance of Justice in this country will die with them.

Save Sacco and Vanzetti.

32

FRANK GOODWIN

Sacco-Vanzetti and the Red Peril: Speech before the Lawrence, Massachusetts, Kiwanis Club

June 30, 1927

The years during which the Sacco and Vanzetti trial took place were marked by staunch reaction against ideas that seemed dangerous to conservatives afraid that American society was being destroyed from within. Numerous organizations, from the American Legion to the Ku Klux Klan to the less well-known Boston-based Industrial Defense Association, fought to defend their distinct and very narrow visions of what the United States ought to be. Frank Goodwin, the registrar of motor vehicles in Massachusetts and widely respected as a civic-minded citizen, gave a speech at the Kiwanis Club in Lawrence, Massachusetts, that represented conservative Americans' concerns. Immigrant workers — Italians numerous among them — had struck Lawrence textile mills in 1912 and again in 1919. Goodwin addressed many people's fears about the scourge of immigrants and the radicalism that Sacco and Vanzetti represented.

. . . It may be that sometime in the distant future there will be no need for religious doctrines and dogmas, and there will be a universal religion, based on the Golden Rule; when the highest ideal will have been attained; when we shall love our enemies; and when, if we are hit on one cheek, we shall turn the other; but as yet we are far from that state of mind, even in the colleges where they are teaching that there is no God, or in Godless Russia, where they murder their enemies without trial.

Thank God for the fundamentalists, both religious and constitutional. They may not be able to appreciate the idealistic attainments, or the superiority complex, of our distinguished college professors, but they are practical enough to know that it is better to hold fast to

Frank Goodwin, "Sacco-Vanzetti and the Red Peril." Speech before the Lawrence, Massachusetts, Kiwanis Club, June 30, 1927. From a pamphlet published and distributed by the Industrial Defense Association, Boston, Massachusetts.

what we have than attempt new experiments before we are mentally or morally ready for them. . . .

The Sacco-Vanzetti case is a blessing in disguise. It has dragged out into the open the enemies of our country, not only those who openly plot to overthrow it by force, but those who are insidiously tearing down the institutions that have made it possible for us to become the greatest nation in the world.

These two murderers, Sacco and Vanzetti, have been found guilty by a jury of twelve citizens, as prescribed by law, who heard all the witnesses under oath and under cross-examination. They saw these witnesses face to face, and were in a position to judge as to their honesty and the truth of their statements. They heard the arguments of counsel, and the charge of the judge, and decided unanimously that these two men were murderers. The Supreme Court has ruled that the conviction was according to law, and it also ruled that there was sufficient evidence to warrant placing the case before the jury for its decision. . . .

This murder was committed seven years ago by these two men. They were not only aliens and avowed enemies of our form of government, but were actively engaged, during the war and before, in attempting to overthrow it by force. . . .

We must let this gang of Reds and their allies know in no uncertain way that we are satisfied with our institutions and form of government, until we can change them for something better, in the way provided by our constitution, and that we are not ready yet to substitute as our national emblem the red flag of anarchy, for the Red, White, and Blue.

33

KATHERINE ANNE PORTER

The Never-Ending Wrong

June 1977

Katherine Anne Porter, a respected author, was among the countless liberals who threw themselves into defending Sacco and Vanzetti in their last days. The portion of her memoir presented here speaks to her experiences fighting on behalf of the two prisoners and her perceptions of certain of those who were fighting along with her.

... [T]his case of Sacco and Vanzetti which began so obscurely and ended as one of the important turning points in the history of this country; not the cause, but the symptom of a change so deep and so sinister in the whole point of view and direction of this people as a nation that I for one am not competent to analyze it. I only know what happened by what has happened to us since, by remembering what we were, or what many of us believed we were, before. We were most certainly then of a different cast of mind and feeling than we are now, or such a thing as the Sacco-Vanzetti protest could never have been brought about by any means; and I much doubt such a commotion could be roused again for any merciful cause at all among us....

Their minds, each one in its very different way, were ragbags of faded Anarchic doctrine, of "class consciousness," of "proletarian snobbism," yet their warmth of feeling gave breath and fresh meaning to such words as Sacco wrote to Mrs. Leon Henderson: "Pardon me, Mrs. Henderson, it is not to discredit and ignore you, Mrs. Evans and other generosity work, which I sincerely believe is a noble one and I am respectful: But it is the warm sincere voice of an unrest heart and a free soul that lived and loved among the workers class all his life."

This was a state of mind, or point of view, which many of the anxious friends from another class of society found very hard to deal with, not to be met on their own bright, generous terms in this crisis

Katherine Anne Porter, *The Never-Ending Wrong* (Boston: Little, Brown and Company, 1977), 4–5, 10–11, 37–38, 41–42, 58–61.

of life and death; to be saying, in effect, we are all brothers and equal citizens; to receive, in effect, the reserved answer: No, not yet. It is clear now that the condemned men understood and realized their predicament much better than any individual working with any organization devoted to their rescue. Their friends from a more fortunate destiny had confidence in their own power to get what they asked of their society, their government; courts were not sacrosanct, they could be mistaken; it was a civic duty now and then to protest their judgments, persuade them by one means or another to reverse their sentences. The two laboring men, who had managed to survive and scramble up a few steps from nearly the bottom level of life, knew well from the beginning that they had every reason to despair, they did not really trust these strangers from the upper world who furnished the judges and lawyers to the courts, the politicians to the offices, the faculties to the universities, who had all the money and the influence—why should they be turning against their own class to befriend two laborers? Sacco wrote to Gardner Jackson, member of an upper-middle-class family, rich enough and ardent enough to devote his means and his time to the Sacco-Vanzetti Defense Committee: "Although we are one heart, unfortunately we represent two opposite class." What they may not have known—we can only hope they did not know—was that some of the groups apparently working for them, people of their own class in many cases, were using the occasion for Communist propaganda, and hoping only for their deaths as a political argument. I know this because I heard and saw. . . .

I remember small, slender Mrs. Sacco with her fine copper-colored hair and dark brown, soft, dazed eyes moving from face to face but still smiling uncertainly, surrounded in our offices by women pitying and cuddling her, sympathetic with her as if she were a pretty little girl; they spoke to her as if she were five years old or did not understand—this Italian peasant wife who, for seven long years, had shown moral stamina and emotional stability enough to furnish half a dozen women amply. I was humiliated for them, for their apparent insensibility. But I was mistaken in my anxiety—their wish to help, to show her their concern, was real, their feelings were true and lasting, no matter how awkwardly expressed; their love and tenderness and wish to help were from the heart. All through those last days in Boston, those strangely innocent women enlisted their altar societies, their card clubs, their literary round tables, their music circles and their various charities in the campaign to save Sacco and Vanzetti. On their rounds, they came now and then to the office of my outfit in their smart thin frocks, stylish hats, and their indefinable air of eager sweetness and light, bringing money they had collected in the endless, wittily devious ways of women's organizations. They would talk among themselves and to her about how they felt, with tears in their eyes, promising to come again soon with more help. They were known as "sob sisters" by the cynics and the hangers-on of the committee I belonged to who took their money and described their activities as "sentimental orgies," of course with sexual overtones, and they jeered at "bourgeois morality." "Morality" was a word along with "charitable" and "humanitarian" and "liberal," all, at one time, in the odor of sanctity but now despoiled and rotting in the gutter where suddenly it seemed they belonged. I found myself on the side of the women; I resented the nasty things said about them by these self-appointed world reformers. . . .

For an endless dreary time we had stood there, massed in measureless darkness, waiting, watching the light in the tower of the prison. At midnight, this light winked off, winked on and off again, and my blood chills remembering it even now—I do not remember how often, but we were told that the extinction of this light corresponded to the number of charges of electricity sent through the bodies of Sacco and Vanzetti. This was not true, as the newspapers informed us in the morning. It was only one of many senseless rumors and inventions added to the smothering air. It was reported later that Sacco was harder to kill than Vanzetti—two or three shocks for that tough body. Almost at once, in small groups, the orderly, subdued people began to scatter, in a sound of voices that was deep, mournful, vast, and wavering. They walked slowly toward the center of Boston. Life felt very grubby and mean, as if we were all of us soiled and disgraced and would never in this world live it down. I said something like this to the man walking near me, whose name or face I never knew, but I remember his words—"What are you talking about?" he asked bitterly, and answered himself: "There's no such thing as disgrace anymore."

I have, for my own reasons, refused to read any book or any article on the Sacco-Vanzetti trial before I had revised or arranged my notes on this trial. Since I have finished, I have read the book by Herbert B. Ehrmann, the "last surviving lawyer involved in the substance of the case on either side," who, I feel, tells the full story of the case. Also, I have read since I finished my story "The Never-Ending Wrong," the article by Francis Russell in the *National Review,* page 887 of August 17, 1973, which was discovered among my magazines early last year and which I have decided should be the epigraph to this story. Mr. Russell believes that the fact that Dante Sacco, Nicola Sacco's son, kept his superhuman or subhuman silence on the whole history of his father proves that Nicola Sacco was guilty; that he refused to confess and so implicated Vanzetti, who died innocent. Sacco, therefore, proved himself doubly, triply, a murderer, an instinctive killer. Maybe.

Another maybe—Vanzetti's speech at the electric chair was the final word of an honest man. It is proven by testimony that he was innocent of murder. He was selling eels on that day, for Christmas. The Italian tradition of eating eels on Christmas Eve occupied his time all that day. He called on all the families he knew who were his friends, to deliver their orders for eels, and during the trial these people, when questioned, told exactly the same story, even to each housewife remembering the hour he delivered the eels, and some of them even went so far as to say how they had prepared them. Their testimonies were ignored when the real trial was begun. Mr. Russell has, I think, overlooked one point in his argument. Vanzetti was comrade-in-arms and in mind and heart with Sacco. They were Anarchists fore-sworn, committed for life to death, for death was the known fate of all who were brought to trial for the crime, as it was considered. My point is this: Sacco was guilty if you like; some minor points make it reasonable, though barely reasonable, to believe it. Vanzetti knew his will and he believed in the cause which he knew contained death for him unless he was very lucky indeed. Anarchy is a strange belief to die for, but my good friend in Mexico, Felipe Carillo, the Governor of Yucatan, explained to me why the revolutionists in his country who were robbing trains, wrecking haciendas, burning houses, destroying crops and even whole villages of helpless people, were right. In their utter misery, they gathered money with violence, seized the materials built with their blood, to create their idea of a good society. It was right to destroy material evil and to take its loot for their cause.

This is the doctrine of desperation, the last murderous rage before utter despair. They were wrong, but not more wrong than the thing they themselves were trying to destroy. The powerful society they opposed gained its power and grew up on the same methods they were taking. Vanzetti kept a sacred pact, not just with his comrade Sacco but with the whole great solemn oath of his life, to the cause of freedom. He fasted, kept his silence, and went to his death with his fellow, a sacrifice to his faith. As he was being strapped into the electric chair, he said, "I wish to tell you that I am an innocent man. I never committed any crime but sometimes some sin. I wish to forgive some people for what they are now doing to me." They both spoke nobly at the end, they kept faith with their vows for each other. They left a great heritage of love, devotion, faith, and courage—all done with the sure intention that holy Anarchy should be glorified through their sacrifice and that the time would come that no human being should be humiliated or be made abject. Near the end of their ordeal Vanzetti said that if it had not been for "these thing" he might have lived out his life talking at street corners to scorning men. He might have died unmarked, unknown, a failure. "Now, we are not a failure. This is our career and our triumph. Never in our full life could we hope to do such work for tolerance, for justice, for man's understanding of man as now we do by accident. Our words—our lives—our pains—nothing! The taking of our lives—lives of a good shoemaker and a poor fish peddler—all! That last moment belongs to us—that agony is our triumph."

This not new—all the history of our world is pocked with it. It is very grand and noble in words and grand, noble souls have died for it—it is worth weeping for. But it doesn't work out so well. In order to annihilate the criminal State, they have become criminals. The State goes on without end in one form or another, built securely on the base of destruction. Nietzsche said: "The State is the coldest of all cold monsters," and the revolutions which destroy or weaken at least one monster bring to birth and growth another. . . .

34

F. LAURISTON BULLARD

We Submit

October 26, 1926

This editorial, for which its author won a Pulitzer Prize, reflected a change of heart for the conservative Boston Herald. *Having steadfastly defended the prosecution and Judge Thayer, the newspaper declared, in late 1926, that enough doubt had been cast on the conduct of the case to merit a new trial.*

In our opinion Nicola Sacco and Bartolomeo Vanzetti ought not to be executed on the warrant of the verdict returned by a jury on July 14, 1921. We do not know whether these men are guilty or not. We have no sympathy with the half-baked views which they profess. But as months have merged into years and the great debate over this case has continued, our doubts have solidified slowly into convictions, and reluctantly we have found ourselves compelled to reverse our original judgment. We hope the supreme judicial court will grant a new trial on the basis of the new evidence not yet examined in open court. We hope the Governor will grant another reprieve to Celestino Madeiros so that his confession may be canvassed in open court. We hope, in case our supreme bench finds itself unable legally to authorize a new trial, that our Governor will call to his aid a commission of disinterested men of the highest intelligence and character to make an independent investigation in his behalf, and that the Governor himself at first hand will participate in that examination, if, as a last resort, it shall be undertaken.

We have read the full decision in which Judge Webster Thayer, who

---

F. Lauriston Bullard, "We Submit," *Boston Herald,* October 26, 1926.

presided at the original trial, renders his decision against the application for a new trial, and we submit that it carries the tone of the advocate rather than the arbitrator. At the outset he refers to "the verdict of a jury approved by the supreme court of this commonwealth" and later he repeats that sentence. We respectfully submit that the supreme court never approved that verdict. What the court did is stated in its own words thus: "We have examined carefully all the exceptions in so far as argued, and finding no error the verdicts are to stand." The supreme court did not vindicate the verdict. The court certified that, whether the verdict was right or wrong, the trial judge performed his duty under the law in a legal manner. The supreme court overruled a bill of exceptions but expressed no judgment whatever as to the validity of the verdict or the guilt of the defendants. Judge Thayer knows this, yet allows himself to refer to the verdict as "approved by the supreme court."

We submit, also, that Judge Thayer's language contains many innuendos which surely are unfortunate in such a document. The petition for a new trial is based in part on the affidavits of two men, Letherman and Weyand, connected respectively with the United States government for thirty-six years and eight years, and both now holding responsible positions out of the federal service. Judge Thayer says that one of these men "seems, for some reason, to be willing to go the limit in his affidavits against the government of the United States," and he refers to "prejudiced affidavits, which appear to be quite easily obtained nowadays." The changes are rung on certain phrases, also, as "fraudulent conspiracy between these two great governments," meaning the governments of the United States and Massachusetts. The judge asserts a conspiracy charge which was not made by counsel for the defense; he asks "who pumped this curiosity into Madeiros"; he compliments the prosecution and refers slightingly to counsel for the defense.

We submit that evidence, if any, in the files of the department of justice having any bearing on this case ought to be examined in open court, or examined in private by the United States attorney-general and reported upon by him before this case shall finally be decided. We have no idea what the files may contain. Mr. Weyand said in his affidavit: "The conviction was the result of co-operation between the Boston agents of the department of justice and the district attorney." We do not know that this is true, but we know there was co-operation; the department and the attorney joined in placing a spy in the cell next to Sacco's, and the prosecution admitted the fact in court.

Now as to Madeiros: A criminal with a bad record, true, and under sentence of death. But the government relied in part on one of his confessions to convict him of a murder. His evidence was accepted against himself when his own life was at stake. His evidence now is offered in behalf of two other men whose lives also are at stake. We submit that Madeiros should be placed on the stand in open court, facing a jury and a judge, and subjected to examination and cross-examination. He may be lying, but the criterion here is not what a judge may think about it but what a jury might think about it. The question is—Would the new evidence be a real factor with a jury in reaching a decision?

We submit that doubt is cast on the verdict of the jury by the important affidavit made after the trial by Capt. [William] H. Proctor of the state police. On the stand, testifying as an expert, his evidence was understood by the jury and the judge to be that the fatal bullet issued from Sacco's pistol. Careful examination of the record discloses curious facts. Capt. Proctor did not here reply to direct questions. His affidavit states what the record implies, that a device was fixed up in advance for dodging direct answer to a direct question. His replies were understood to mean that he believed the bullet came from that weapon. He allowed that impression to go abroad. But his affidavit contradicts that testimony. Now when the supreme court dealt with that point it expressed no opinion as to whether or not an "ambiguous answer" had been arranged to "obtain a conviction." The court ruled only that the trial judge had decided that no such pre-arrangement had been made, and that the supreme court could not "as matter of law" set aside the ruling of the trial judge.

For these and other reasons we hope that the resources of our laws will prove adequate to obtain a new trial. Let it be remembered that the new trial is asked for on the basis of evidence never before the supreme court previously. The court has ruled on exceptions to the old trial, never on all evidence for a new one. If on a new trial the defendants shall again be found guilty we shall be infinitely better off than if we proceed to execution on the basis of the trial already held; the shadow of doubt, which abides in the minds of large numbers of patient investigators of this whole case, will have been removed. And if on second trial Sacco and Vanzetti should be declared guiltless, everybody would rejoice that no monstrous injustice shall have been done. We submit these views with no reference whatever to the personality of the defendants, and without allusion now to that atmosphere of radicalism of which we heard so much in 1921.

35

Advisory [Lowell] Committee Decision

July 27, 1927

Increasing international protests and expressions of concern about the trial coming even from conservative quarters like the editorial staff of the Boston Herald *led to the establishment of an Advisory Committee. The committee, led by Harvard President A. Lawrence Lowell, conducted an investigation of the trial at the request of Governor Alvan Fuller. This excerpt from its report presents its rationale for defending the verdict and for refusing to recommend a new trial.*

. . . From the statements before the Committee by the Judge and by one of the counsel for the defendants it appears that Judge Thayer suggested, out of the presence of the jury, that the counsel should think seriously before introducing evidence of radicalism which was liable to prejudice the jury; but at that stage of the case the counsel thought the danger of conviction so great that they put Sacco and Vanzetti on the stand to explain that their behavior at and after their arrest was due to fear for themselves or their friends of deportation or prosecution on account of their radical ideas, conduct and associations, and not to consciousness of guilt of the murder at South Braintree. We have already remarked that at the present moment their views on these subjects are well known, but they were not so clear at the time. Save for his association with Vanzetti, and his own word on direct examination, there was, up to the time of his cross-examination, in the case of Sacco no certainty that he entertained any such sentiments. The United States authorities, who were hunting for Reds, had found nothing that would justify deportation or other proceedings against either of these men. Except the call for a meeting found in his pocket, there was no evidence that Sacco had taken a prominent part in public meetings, or belonged to any societies of that character; and although wholesale arrests of Reds—fortunately stopped by the

The Sacco-Vanzetti Case: Transcript of the Record of the Trial of Nicola Sacco and Bartolomeo Vanzetti in the Courts of Massachusetts and Subsequent Proceedings, 1920–1927 (Mamaroneck, N.Y.: Paul P. Appel, Publisher, 1969), V, 5378w–78z.

decision of Judge Anderson of the United States Circuit Court—had recently been made in Southeastern Massachusetts, these men had not been among those arrested. At that time of abnormal fear and credulity on the subject little evidence was required to prove that anyone was a dangerous radical. Harmless professors and students in our colleges were accused of dangerous opinions, and it was almost inevitable that anyone who declared himself a radical, possessed of inflammatory literature, would be instantly believed. For these reasons Mr. Katzmann was justified in subjecting Mr. Sacco to a rigorous cross-examination to determine whether his profession that he and his friends were radicals liable to deportation was true, or was merely assumed for the purpose of the defense. The exceptions taken to his questions were not sustained by the Supreme Court.

It has been said that while the acts and language of the Judge, as they appear in the stenographic report, seem to be correct, yet his attitude and emphasis conveyed a different impression. But the jury do not think so. They state that the Judge tried the case fairly; that they perceived no bias; and indeed some of them went so far as to say that they did not know when they entered the jury room to consider their verdict whether he thought the defendants innocent or guilty. It may be added that the Committee talked with the ten available members of the jury—one, the foreman, being dead, and another out of reach in Florida. To the Committee the jury seemed an unusually intelligent and independent body of men, and withal representative, seven of the twelve appearing to be wage-earners, one a farmer, two engaged in dealing in real estate, a grocer, and a photographer. Each of them felt sure that the fact that the accused were foreigners and radicals had no effect upon his opinion, and that native Americans would have been equally certain to be convicted upon the same evidence.

Affidavits were presented to the Committee and witnesses were heard to the effect that the Judge, during and after the trial, had expressed his opinion of guilt in vigorous terms. Prejudice means an opinion or sentiment before the trial. That a judge should form an opinion as the evidence comes in is inevitable, and not prejudicial if not in any way brought to the notice of the jury, as we are convinced was true in this case. Throughout this report the Committee have refrained from reviewing the evidence in detail and have stated only their conclusions with comments upon points that seemed of special significance. From all that has come to us we are forced to conclude that the Judge was indiscreet in conversation with outsiders during the trial. He ought not to have talked about the case off the bench, and doing so was a grave breach of official decorum. But we do not believe that he used some of the expressions attributed to him, and we think that there is exaggeration in what the persons to whom he spoke remember. Furthermore, we believe that such indiscretions in conversation did not affect his conduct at the trial or the opinions of the jury, who indeed, so stated to the Committee.

In one of the motions for a new trial Mr. Thompson, now counsel for the defense, contended that between the District Attorney and officers of the United States Secret Service engaged in investigating radical movements there had been collusion for the purpose either of deporting these defendants as radicals or of convicting them of murder, and thus of getting them out of the way; that with this object Mr. Katzmann agreed to cross-examine them on the subject of their opinions, and that the files of the Federal Department of Justice contain material tending to show the innocence of Sacco and Vanzetti. In support of these charges he filed affidavits by [John] Ruzzamenti, Weyand, Letherman and [Feri Felix] Weiss[1] which declared that the files of the Federal Department of Justice would show the correspondence that took place in the preparation of the case; but none of these affidavits states or implies that there is anything in those files which would help to show that the defendants are not guilty. For the Government to suppress evidence of innocence would be monstrous, and to make such a charge without evidence to support it is wrong. Mr. Katzmann in answer to a question by Mr. Thompson stated to the Committee that the Federal Department had nothing to do with the preparation of the case, and there is no reason to suppose that the Federal agents knew the evidence he possessed. He stated also that he made no agreement with them about the cross-examination. A spy named Carbone was, indeed, placed in the cell next to that of Sacco, and it was stated in an agreement of subsequent counsel that this was to get from him information relating to the South Braintree murder; but Mr. Katzmann, in answer to a question by Mr. Thompson, informs us that that is a mistake; that the Federal authorities wanted to put a man there with the hope of getting information about the explosion on Wall Street. To this he and the sheriff consented, but no information was in fact obtained. . . .

---

[1]Feri Felix Weiss was a private detective who had worked for the Department of Justice until 1919. Weiss suggested that District Attorney Katzmann contact John Ruzzamenti, one of Weiss's informants, to see if he would be willing to share a cell with Sacco to spy on him.

[T]he Committee are of opinion that Sacco was guilty beyond reasonable doubt of the murder at South Braintree. In reaching this conclusion they are aware that it involves a disbelief in the evidence of his alibi at Boston, but in view of all the evidence they do not believe he was there that day.

The evidence against Vanzetti is somewhat different. His association with Sacco tends to show that he belonged to the same group. His having a pistol resembling the one formerly possessed by Berardelli has some importance, and the fact that no cartridges for it were found in his possession, except those in it, is significant. So also is his having cartridges loaded with buckshot, of which his account sounds improbable, and which might well have been used in the gun some witnesses saw sticking out of the back of the car. His falsehoods and his armed condition have a weight similar to that in the case of Sacco. In one way they are a little stronger because he virtually confirms the statement of officer [Michael] Connolly that he tried to draw his pistol when arrested, for he testified that the officer pointed a revolver at him and said "You don't move, you dirty thing",—an admission that the officer thought he was making a movement towards his pistol. On the other hand, all these actions may be accounted for by consciousness of guilt of the attempted robbery and murder at Bridgewater, of which he has been convicted.

The alibi of Vanzetti is decidedly weak. One of the witnesses, [Joseph] Rosen, seems to the Committee to have been shown by the cross-examination to be lying at the trial; another, Mrs. [Alfonsini] Brini, had sworn to an alibi for him in the Bridgewater case, and two more of the witnesses did not seem certain of the date until they had talked it over. Under these circumstances, if he was with Sacco, or in the bandits' car, or indeed in South Braintree at all that day, he was undoubtedly guilty; for there is no reason why, if he were there for an innocent purpose, he should have sworn that he was in Plymouth all day. Now there are four persons who testified that they had seen him;—[Harry] Dolbeare, who says he saw him in the morning in a car on the main street of South Braintree; [Michael] Levangie, who said he saw him—erroneously at the wheel—as the car crossed the tracks after the shooting; and Austin T. Reed, who says that Vanzetti swore at him from the car at the Matfield railroad crossing. The fourth man was [John] Faulkner, who testified that he was asked a question by Vanzetti in a smoking car on the way from Plymouth to South Braintree on the forenoon of the day of the murder, and that he saw him alight at that station. Faulkner's testimony is impeached on two grounds: First, that he said the car was a combination smoker and baggage car, and that there was no such car on that train, but his description of the interior is exactly that of a full smoking car; and, second, that no ticket that could be so used was sold that morning at any of the stations in or near Plymouth, and that no such cash fare was paid or mileage book punched, but that does not exhaust the possibilities. Otherwise no one claims to have seen him, or any man resembling him who was not Vanzetti. But it must be remembered that his face is much more unusual, and more easily remembered, than that of Sacco. He was evidently not in the foreground. On the whole, we are of opinion that Vanzetti also was guilty beyond reasonable doubt.

It has been urged that a crime of this kind must have been committed by professionals, and it is for well-known criminal gangs that one must look; but to the Committee both this crime and the one at Bridgewater do not seem to bear the marks of professionals, but of men inexpert in such crimes.

36

COUNTEE CULLEN

Not Sacco and Vanzetti

1927

Countee Cullen, an accomplished poet who contributed to the artistic and cultural accomplishments of the Harlem Renaissance, was among the artists and writers deeply affected by the trial.

These men who do not die, but send to death.
These iron men whom mercy cannot bend
Beyond the lettered law; what when their breath
Shall suddenly and naturally end?

Countee Cullen, "Not Sacco and Vanzetti," in *On These I Stand: An Anthology of the Best Poems of Countee Cullen* (New York: Harper and Brothers Publishers, 1947), 103.

What shall their final retribution be,
What bloody silver then shall pay the tolls
Exacted for this legal infamy
When death indicts their stark immortal souls?

The day a slumbering but awful God,
Before Time to Eternity is blown,
Examines with the same unyielding rod
These images of His with hearts of stone,
These men who do not die, but death decree,—
These are the men I should not care to be.

37

EDNA ST. VINCENT MILLAY

Justice Denied in Massachusetts
1927, 1928

Edna St. Vincent Millay, among the United States' most accomplished romantic poets, made a rare foray into the world of politics in protesting on behalf of Sacco and Vanzetti. The documents here are a poem she wrote on behalf of the two men and a letter she wrote to Governor Alvan Fuller, asking him to reconsider his decision not to intervene in the case.

"Justice Denied in Massachusetts," 1928

Let us abandon then our gardens and go home
And sit in the sitting-room.
Shall the larkspur blossom or the corn grow under this cloud?
Sour to the fruitful seed

Edna St. Vincent Millay, "Justice Denied in Massachusetts," in *The Buck in the Sun and Other Poems* (New York: Harper and Brothers Publishers, 1928), 32–33.

Is the cold earth under this cloud,
Fostering quack and weed, we have marched upon but cannot
    conquer;
We have bent the blades of our hoes against the stalks of them.

Let us go home, and sit in the sitting-room.
Not in our day
Shall the cloud go over and the sun rise as before,
Beneficent upon us
Out of the glittering bay,
And the warm winds be blown inward from the sea
Moving the blades of corn
With a peaceful sound.
Forlorn, forlorn,
Stands the blue hay-rack by the empty mow.
And the petals drop to the ground,
Leaving the tree unfruited.
The sun that warmed our stooping backs and withered the weed
    uprooted—
We shall not feel it again.
We shall die in darkness, and be buried in the rain.

What from the splendid dead
We have inherited—
Furrows sweet to the grain, and the weed subdued—
See now the slug and the mildew plunder.
Evil does overwhelm
The larkspur and the corn;
We have seen them go under.

Let us sit here, sit still,
Here in the sitting-room until we die;
At the step of Death on the walk, rise and go;
Leaving to our children's children this beautiful doorway,
And this elm,
And a blighted earth to till
With a broken hoe.

Letter to Governor Alvan T. Fuller, August 22, 1927

Your Excellency:

During my interview with you this afternoon I called to your attention a distressing instance of the miscarriage of justice in a neighboring state. I suggested that, for all your careful weighing of the evidence, for all your courage in the face of threats and violent words, for all your honest conviction that these men are guilty, you, no less than the governor of Maine in my story, who was so tragically mistaken, are but human flesh and spirit, and that it is human to err.

Tonight, with the world in doubt, with this Commonwealth drawing into its lungs with every breath the difficult air of doubt, with the eyes of Europe turned westward upon Massachusetts and upon the whole United States in distress and harrowing doubt—are you still so sure? Does no faintest shadow of question gnaw at your mind? For, indeed, your spirit, however strong, is but the frail spirit of a man. Have you no need, in this hour, of a spirit greater than your own?

Think back. Think back a long time. Which way would He have turned, this Jesus of your faith?—Oh, not the way in which your feet are set!

You promised me, and I believed you truly, that you would think of what I said. I exact of you this promise now. Be for a moment alone with yourself. Look inward upon yourself. Let fall from your harassed mind all, all save this: which way would He have turned, this Jesus of your faith?

I cry to you with a million voices: answer our doubt. Exert the clemency which your high office affords.

There is need in Massachusetts of a great man tonight. It is not yet too late for you to be that man.

EDNA ST. VINCENT MILLAY.

Allan Ross Macdougall, ed., *Letters of Edna St. Vincent Millay* (New York: Harper and Brothers Publishers, 1952), 112.

38

BARTOLOMEO VANZETTI

Letter to Little Comrade [Li Pei Kan]

July 23, 1927

Support for Sacco and Vanzetti extended across the globe. This document is a response from Vanzetti to a letter from Li Pei Kan. Born in Shanghai, this Chinese Leftist wrote numerous pamphlets on the trial to publicize it in China, including one [mis]titled "On the Scaffold."

Charlestown Prison

DEAR LITTLE COMRADE,

Your letter dated July 11th was given to me a few days ago, and it gives me joy each time I read it. I will not try to find words with which to thank you for your little picture you sent me. Youth is the hope of mankind, and my heart exults when I look at your photograph and say to myself "Lo! one of those who will pluck and uphold, highly, the flag of freedom, the flag of our supremely beautiful anarchy, which is now slowly falling down from our weakening hands,"—and a good one, as for that. You need to live for many others years, and hard ones, before to realize and understand what comfort and joy such a thought is to your old and dying Bartolo.

I have read of that—say, incident, and I thought it happened to you. It is less bad if it happened to an elderly one, because the elders are more worried and hardened by the vicissitude and adversities of life, so that they can bear better the hard blows of fate, while the young ones are more tender, and could be bent and split by black adversities. You will surely resist to all, and separate all, I am sure of it.

In regards to what you said of our Ideal in your letter, I fundamentally agree with all of it. My words on this subject, of my antecedent letter, were principally intended to fortify your spirit to better face the tremendous struggle for freedom and prevent future delusions by

Marion Denman Frankfurter and Gardner Jackson, eds., *The Letters of Sacco and Vanzetti* (New York: Viking Press, 1928), 307–10.

weakening fatalism and fortify voluntarism in you, as I do with all our young ones and neophites.

Perhaps you know Proudhon better than I, but if not, I advise you to study him. Read his *Peace and War.* I think he approached truth in many subjects nearer than other more recent great ones.

To my understanding, we are actually certainly dragged, with the rest of mankind, toward tyranny and darkness. Where will we land?

The relatively known history testifies, it is true, that mankind has continuously progressed, slowly, insteadily, with advances and retrocessions, yet, steadily progressed.

But the dead civilizations tell their tale as well and what came and passed before the dawn of our historical knowledge, we cannot know. History, like evolution, as we know of it now, fails far from explaining the request of a deep thinker. Then, what will follow to this age of reversion and tyranny? A false democracy again, which in its turn would inevitably yield to another tide of tyranny? As it is happening from thousands of years?

Anarchy, the anarchists alone, we only can break these deadly circles and set life in such a way that by a natural synchronism, produced by the very nature of the things which create the new order, more exactly, which constitute the new order, history will be streamed toward the infinite sea of freedom, instead to turn in the above said dead, close circle, as, it seems, it did 'til now.

It is a titanic task—but humanly possible, and if we know, we will create the happy kingdom of Freedom when the traviated, misled tralignated[1] working class, and people of all classes will, most instinctively, join us for the greatest emancipation of the history. But even then we will have to be at the brightness of our task, or else, only a new tyranny will be substitute to the present one as corollary of the immense holocaust.

These are the reasons why I tell you, young Comrade, heavy and hard words, just as your juvenile ardor, enthusiasm, and faith bliss me, I hope my old experience will complete and fortify you.

My friends must have forgotten to send you *A Proletarian Life,* or they are running short of the copies. But I hope to provide you with a copy in the near future. It is a poor thing, but you will take it for what it is. It was modified without my knowledge of it, to fit it to the Americans, to whom you can tell everything, and they like everything,

---

[1] *Travière* in Italian means to mislead or to lead stray; *tralignàre* is to degenerate. Vanzetti was saying that the working class misled and degenerated.

except the pure, naked truth. In general, of course, but the exceptions to the rule are desperately few. . . .

And now, dear Li, I embrace you with brotherly and glad heart.

39

BENITO MUSSOLINI

Letter to Governor Fuller

July 23, 1927

The final document in this section is a brief telegram from Benito Mussolini to Marquis A. Ferrante, the Italian consul in Boston, who was to convey to Governor Alvan Fuller the fascist leader's thoughts about the Sacco and Vanzetti trial. Although the dictator was hardly sympathetic to anarchism, he was said to be deeply impressed by the fortitude and the courage of the two men.

My opinion is that the governor could commute the sentence and release our nationals from the terrible circumstance in which they have languished for so many years. While I do not believe that clemency would mean a victory for the subversives, it is certain that the execution of Sacco-Vanzetti would provide the pretext for a vast and continuous subversive agitation throughout the world. The Fascist government, which is strongly authoritarian and does not give quarter to the bolsheviks, very often employs clemency in individual cases. The governor of Massachusetts should not lose the opportunity for a humanitarian act whose repercussions would be especially positive in Italy.

Benito Mussolini to Governor Fuller, July 23, 1927, in Philip Cannistraro, "Mussolini, Sacco-Vanzetti, and the Anarchists: The Transatlantic Context," *The Journal of Modern History,* 68 (March 1996), 57.

The Legacy of Sacco and Vanzetti
INSTANT MARTYRDOM

40

OSWALD GARRISON VILLARD

Justice Underfoot
August 17, 1927

The global outrage Sacco and Vanzetti's trial created assured that they would be remembered long after they died. So too did conscious efforts by liberals and Leftists to construct and maintain their legacy. This process began even before they were executed. In this document, Oswald Garrison Villard, editor of the liberal The Nation *and one of the founders of the National Association for the Advancement of Colored People (NAACP), comments on the worldwide support for the two anarchists in their last days.*

One of the most momentous decisions in the history of American jurisprudence has been rendered — and Sacco and Vanzetti are condemned to death. Around the earth the news has winged its way as fast as light and wherever the tidings have reached millions of workers now believe that justice does not exist in America, that two innocent men are going to their doom in order that a social system may be upheld, a tottering social order may triumph. As we write no one can foretell the consequences of Governor Fuller's astounding decision, but from remote quarters there already comes the news of protest meetings, of protest strikes, of the windows of the American Consulate in Buenos Aires smashed, of a sense of horror-struck outrage in one country after another. Talk about the solidarity of the human race! When has there been a more striking example of the solidarity

Katrina Vanden Heuvel, ed., *The Nation, 1865–1990: Selections from the Independent Magazine of Politics and Culture* (New York: Thunder Mouth Press, 1990), 84–85, 86–87, 89.

of great masses of people than this? Ten years ago people were reading of thirty thousand, forty thousand, fifty thousand men done to death in a single day in the war that statesmen, with horrible sacrilege, had falsely dedicated to democracy and to civilization. Those useless massacres nowhere stirred the neutral world as has the fate of these two Italian workers, who have dared to say that they were anarchists, but innocent of the murder with which they are charged. Wherever the American flag flies in foreign lands today, it has to be guarded; it appears the symbol of a monstrous wrong. Men may yet die by the dozen because of Governor Fuller's decision. Rightly or wrongly, we repeat, uncountable multitudes today believe that in America justice is dead.

For ourselves, we are shaken to the core. We had not believed such a decision possible. We do not retract one word from our praise of the industry Governor Fuller has shown, his painstaking examination of the topography of the scene of the crime, of witnesses and jurors, judge and prisoners. We recognize again his honesty of purpose; we acquit him of any charge of political maneuvering; we admit the superficial ability of his opinion. Yet we cannot for one instant accept this verdict in the face of facts known to us for years as they have been known to multitudes of others. It seems to us that he has missed all the important points in the case and that his decision reveals his complete inability to rise above the point of view of his surroundings, his class, and the setting in which great wealth has placed him. Nor are we convinced by the facile report of the Governor's committee of three eminent and conventional gentlemen, two chosen from the highest Boston social circles, all of one type of mind and not one of them representing the vast groups that have felt from the first that they had a vital stake in the fate of these men. After a brief investigation, partaking of the nature of a star-chamber in hearing Judge Thayer and his attorney without attendance of the defense's counsel, they have upheld the court.

As for Governor Fuller's judgment of the case, it no more closes it than the hanging of John Brown ended the Harper's Ferry raid and condemned him to execration and oblivion. More than half the people of this country refused to consider John Brown a traitor or a murderer, though his guilt was unquestionable and was openly confessed, whereas the masses believe Sacco and Vanzetti legally innocent and entitled to have their innocence determined by law and not by prejudice. The people saw behind John Brown issues of far-reaching moment that soon thereafter tore this country apart and for four long

years drenched it in blood. They knew at once that the questions at
stake were not settled on that Charlestown scaffold and could not be;
that the lives and liberties of millions were involved, and the issue was
whether or not the South should be ruled by a despotic economic
oligarchy, whether poor whites and blacks alike should be masters
of their bodies as well as their souls. Rightly or wrongly, the case of
Sacco and Vanzetti has become identified with efforts to reconstruct
the social order, just as the Dreyfus case came to mean infinitely more
important things for France and the world than the fate of one Jewish
major.

Absurd and unjustified, this interpretation of the Sacco-Vanzetti
case seems to all conservatives. But it is there, and not Massachusetts
alone, but the whole of the United States will have it to reckon with.
Governor Fuller's opinion will never upset this belief. For the fact, the
great and unanswerable fact, stands out that here is an instance of a
headlong collision of certain viewpoints which are and must be hope-
lessly antagonistic. The liberals and the workers who are championing
the cause of these men may also have their blind eyes. The truth
remains that the question of the guilt of these men has been subordi-
nated to the clash of these two vital currents of human thought, and
the world at large knows that Sacco and Vanzetti have been judged
and will have been executed by the representatives of one of these
viewpoints alone. And still another fact, a great and unanswerable fact,
stands out that in its essence the guilt or innocence of these men has
been passed upon by only one judge; that what is forbidden in New
York and is impossible in other States of the Union has come to pass
in Massachusetts: the *evidence*—not the technical legal procedure—
has been ruled upon only by the trial judge, he who, if a tithe of the
charges against him by reputable witnesses is true, ought to be
impeached and disgraced—even the Lowell committee admits what it
kindly calls his "indiscretion." . . .

As for Governor Fuller's opinion, he sweeps away the testimony
as to the bias of Judge Thayer by affirming that the judge had a right
to be biased after the testimony was in, whereas the affidavits of
reputable men and women affirm that that bias was evident from
the earliest stages of the trial. We pass over aghast his tribute to the
"clear-eyed" and "courageous" witnesses—some of whom are of
doubtful reputation, contradicted themselves, and testified to the
impossible. Nor would we stress today the old question of the identifi-
cations or the fact that the deadly bullet was never proved to have
been from Sacco's revolver; nor dwell upon the Governor's describing

in one hundred words the Bridgewater hold-up which had nothing to do with the question of a fair trial in the Braintree case. As for the latter, the Governor is quite satisfied that Judge Thayer was right in denying all the seven motions for a new trial. He is not willing that the men should be given the benefit of a doubt, nor will he appeal to the legislature to start the machinery for a new trial in a different atmosphere under a different judge. Would that have rocked the foundations of Massachusetts justice? It might have inflamed the Back Bay clubs, but it would have meant joy and satisfaction wherever newspapers appear.

And not merely to radicals. It is *not* the radicals alone who fought for Sacco and Vanzetti. Noble souls have given years of their lives and their money to this cause who are neither Reds nor foreign-born Americans; nor have they belonged to those holding the anarchist views of the condemned. If there are finer types of our citizenship, or men and women of older American lineage, we should like to have them pointed out to us. They, too, have read every word of the testimony; they have examined the new witnesses; they, too, have studied the motions for a new trial and perused Judge Thayer's denials of them; they have read the affidavits against the judge and they are as good lawyers as the Governor himself. They are as eager as he for the good repute of Massachusetts and its courts, yet they are unconvinced. To them an incredible tragedy is being finished before their eyes; a judicial murder is being committed. Does not the passionate belief of these unselfish supporters of the right merit consideration, if not assent?

As for Sacco and Vanzetti, sometimes we have asked ourselves whether it was not intended that they should die, and whether it is not best for the cause of human progress that they should perish. In his wonderful address to the court—made to Judge Thayer, who did not once dare to look at the prisoners as he condemned them to the chair—Vanzetti voiced this in amazing exaltation of spirit:

> If it had not been for these thing, I might have live out my life, talking at street corners to scorning men. I might have die, unmarked, unknown, a failure. Now we are not a failure. This is our career and our triumph. Never in our full life can we hope to do such work for tolerance, for joostice, for man's onderstanding of man, as now we do by an accident. Our words—our lives—our pains—nothing! The taking of our lives—lives of a good shoemaker and a poor fish-peddler—all! That last moment belong to us—that agony is our triumph!

This, we believe, will be the verdict of history. Certain it is that if the precedents of history hold true, monuments are likely to be erected to Sacco and Vanzetti and the names of their prosecutors will fade out of history. . . .

Let those who would uphold the present system by force beware lest it look green for a while, yet still prove timber and not a tree. Let them beware lest August 10, 1927, be forever recorded as the day of a great American change.

41

EMMA GOLDMAN AND ALEXANDER BERKMAN

Sacco and Vanzetti

August 1929

In this document, anarchists Emma Goldman and Alexander Berkman commemorate the second anniversary of the executions of Sacco and Vanzetti. Both Goldman and Berkman had been deeply involved in revolutionary activity in the United States since before the turn of the century; they were deported in 1919, and, by 1929, they were living in exile in France.

The names of the "good shoe-maker and poor fish-peddler" have ceased to represent merely two Italian workingmen. Throughout the civilised world Sacco and Vanzetti have become a symbol, the shibboleth of Justice crushed by Might. That is the great historic significance of this twentieth century crucifixion, and truly prophetic, were the words of Vanzetti when he declared, "The last moment belongs to us—that agony is our triumph."

We hear a great deal of progress and by that people usually mean improvements of various kinds, mostly life-saving discoveries and labor-saving inventions, or reforms in the social and political life. These may

Emma Goldman and Alexander Berkman, "Sacco and Vanzetti," *The Road to Freedom,* vol. 5 (August 1929).

or may not represent a real advance because reform is not necessarily progress.

It is an entirely false and vicious conception that civilisation consists of mechanical or political changes. Even the greatest improvements do not, in themselves, indicate real progress: they merely symbolise its results. True civilization, real progress consists in *humanising* mankind, in making the world a decent place to live in. From this viewpoint we are very far from being civilised, in spite of all the reforms and improvements.

True progress is a struggle against the inhumanity of our social existence, against the barbarity of dominant conceptions. In other words, progress is a spiritual struggle, a struggle to free man from his brutish inheritance, from the fear and cruelty of his primitive condition. Breaking the shackles of ignorance and superstition; liberating man from the grip of enslaving ideas and practices; driving darkness out of his mind and terror out of his heart; raising him from his abject posture to man's full stature—that is the mission of progress. Only thus does man, individually and collectively, become truly civilised and our social life more human and worth while.

This struggle marks the real history of progress. Its heroes are not the Napoleons and the Bismarcks, not the generals and politicians. Its path is lined with the unmarked graves of the Saccos and Vanzettis of humanity, dotted with the auto-da-fé, the torture chambers, the gallows, and the electric chair. To those martyrs of justice and liberty we owe what little of real progress and civilization we have today.

The anniversary of our comrades' death is therefore by no means an occasion for mourning. On the contrary, we should rejoice that in this time of debasement and degradation, in the hysteria of conquest and gain, there are still MEN that dare defy the dominant spirit and raise their voices against inhumanity and reaction: That there are still men who keep the spark of reason and liberty alive and have the courage to die, and die triumphantly, for their daring.

For Sacco and Vanzetti died, as the entire world knows today, because they were Anarchists. That is to say, because they believed and preached human brotherhood and freedom. As such, they could expect neither justice nor humanity. For the Masters of Life can forgive any offense or crime but never an attempt to undermine their security on the backs of the masses. Therefore Sacco and Vanzetti had to die, notwithstanding the protests of the entire world.

Yet Vanzetti was right when he declared that his execution was his greatest triumph, for all through history it has been the martyrs of progress that have ultimately triumphed. Where are the Caesars and Torquemadas of yesterday? Who remembers the names of the judges who condemned Giordano Bruno and John Brown? The Parsons and the Ferrers, the Saccos and Vanzettis live eternal and their spirits still march on.

Let no despair enter our hearts over the graves of Sacco and Vanzetti. The duty we owe them for the crime we have committed in permitting their death is to keep their memory green and the banner of their Anarchist ideal high. And let no near-sighted pessimist confuse and confound the true facts of man's history, of his rise to greater manhood and liberty. In the long struggle from darkness to light, in the age-old fight for greater freedom and welfare, it is the rebel, the martyr who has won. Slavery has given way, absolutism is crushed, feudalism and serfdom had to go, thrones have been broken and republics established in their stead. Inevitably, the martyrs and their ideas have triumphed, in spite of gallows and electric chairs. Inevitably, the people, the masses, have been gaining on their masters, till now the very citadels of Might, Capital and the State, are being endangered. Russia has shown the direction of the further progress by its attempt to eliminate both the economic and political master. That initial experiment has failed, as all first great social revaluations require repeated efforts for their realisation. But that magnificent historic failure is like unto the martyrdom of Sacco and Vanzetti—the symbol and guarantee of ultimate triumph. . . .

42

VERA B. WEISBORD

Remember Sacco and Vanzetti

July 1977

Among Italian Americans, and especially among liberals and Leftists in that community, the Sacco and Vanzetti case has remained a vital part of their historical memory. On the fiftieth anniversary of the executions, Vera Weisbord shares her reflections on the case and its implications in a Left-leaning Italian American journal published since 1908.

Vera B. Weisbord, "Remember Sacco and Vanzetti," *La parola del popolo* (July 1977).

While President [Jimmy] Carter preaches human rights, crusading as the leader of the whole world, a more realistic stand is taken by a lesser official, Governor [Michael S.] Dukakis who on July 19 issued a statement that Sacco and Vanzetti did not have a fair trial. Coming fifty years after the event, even this belated acknowledgement must be considered as progressive. . . .

Why do we revive this old story of the two comrades, Sacco and Vanzetti? . . . [I]t is because the same conditions which were responsible for this dreadful case still prevail today. Our jails are still holding and our courts still railroading men and women either victims of race prejudice or those who have dared to fight against oppressive conditions.

Divide and conquer! The old slogan of British imperialism which the rulers of this country have inherited is still applied by keeping the ethnic groups apart with all of them looked down upon by the English majority. Removing from the scene radicals who might give leadership to rebellion is still a favorite practice. Imprisonment or implication in a capital crime they did not commit is still resorted to by those who control the industries and the power. The many-headed monster of capitalism grows more clever in its senility, but the voices of rebellion still ring out.

Capitalism in its growing period was a progressive force, vastly expanding the human intelligence, raising the level of science to a magnificent degree, creating a technology which under a better system of property relations may be able to free mankind from slavery. The time has come now when an international movement of workers can save the world from the destruction which threatens it as we see air, water and land sinking into a morass of pollution while the atom, or neutron, bomb menaces humanity itself.

Sacco and Vanzetti were forerunners. They lived their lives fully to the last measure. They met death bravely, as they had lived, protesting their innocence and their faith in anarchism. They are an inspiration for those who today fight the same cause they died for. Let us keep their memory great.

43

STATE REPRESENTATIVE ALEXANDER J. CELLA

Recommending a Posthumous Pardon
for Nicola Sacco and Bartolomeo Vanzetti

April 2, 1959

The issue of the Sacco and Vanzetti trial remained alive not just in specific ideological or ethnic communities but in the political world as well. In 1959, Alexander Cella, an Italian American state representative from Medford, Massachusetts, introduced a bill to exonerate Sacco and Vanzetti. Although the vast majority of the witnesses who testified were sympathetic to the bill for exoneration, it did not pass. This document is Cella's unsuccessful effort to clear the anarchists' names.

. . . Mr. Chairman, this is indeed an historic day for Massachusetts. Over thirty-one years ago, on August 23, 1927, a long and bitter legal struggle to save the lives of two humble Italian immigrants, a fishpeddler and a shoemaker by occupation, ended in tragic failure and Sacco and Vanzetti were imprisoned, separated from their friends and loved ones, slurred and rejected by an American Society that looked suspiciously upon all foreigners, and more particularly upon foreigners who held radical political and social beliefs which seemed to run counter to the accepted popular currents of American political and social thought.

Mr. Chairman, I say that this is an historic day for Massachusetts because now, after all these years, we in the General Court, you and I and all our colleagues, have an opportunity to correct an historical injustice which has besmirched the reputation and standing of Massachusetts in the eyes of the entire world.

Alexander J. Cella, Address on Sacco and Vanzetti. Record of Public Hearing Before Joint Committee on the Judiciary of the Massachusetts Legislature on the Resolution of Representative Alexander J. Cella Recommending a Posthumous Pardon for Nicola Sacco and Bartolomeo Vanzetti, April 2, 1959, 6, 7.

I believe with all the earnestness at my command that Sacco and Vanzetti were innocent of the crime of murder for which they were executed. I believe with all the earnestness at my command that they did not receive a fair and proper trial, and that the sad but indisputable fact of the matter is that the appellate procedures of the administration of justice in Massachusetts at that time were such as to deny to them an opportunity to get their case reheard in the light of new evidence. I believe further that the hostile atmosphere of the times and the climate of hysteria which prevailed influenced the entire proceedings, at the trial and subsequently, and constituted the indispensable backdrop against which unconscionable appeals to racial and political prejudices could operate within the framework of the judicial system to the detriment of these two defendants.

At the very outset, because much confusion has existed and still exists about the political and social beliefs of Sacco and Vanzetti, a few brief words are in order about the nature of their views of government and society. Sacco and Vanzetti were self-professed, avowed anarchists. In this sense, I suppose, they could be called "radicals" but it should be clearly pointed out and understood, in no sense were they communists. They did not believe in violence. They were men of compassion. They did not belong to an organized conspiracy designed to overthrow the government by means of force and violence. Above all else, they were not blindly enamored of developments in Russia under the Bolsheviks. They did not regard the emergence of Soviet power in the early 1920s as the great, world-wide hope for laboring men and the working classes everywhere. In fact, Vanzetti, who is universally recognized as having possessed by far the keener intellect of the two men, analyzed with great and telling perceptiveness the falseness of the Russian Communist image as early as 1926. . . .

Sacco and Vanzetti were opposed to all forms of totalitarianism because they specifically rejected as a matter of fundamental principle the use of governmental power and legalized coercion to direct the activities of the individual in society. They held tenaciously with unyielding devotion to the conviction that the minimum of governmental regulation of private life is certain to yield the maximum of individual human happiness—that, in short, that government is best which governs least, if indeed not at all.

What are we to say of the basic political and social views of Sacco and Vanzetti? What are we to say of the deep-rooted philosophical anarchism which is at the very heart of their thought and action? If there were those who chose to proclaim themselves "anarchists," but

who betrayed the very essence of the anarchist philosophy as es-
poused and practiced by Sacco and Vanzetti by resorting to the use of
force and violence, are we to condemn all anarchists and the philosophy itself?

Let there be no mistaking where I stand. I am not an anarchist. I
believe that the philosophy of anarchism is based upon a faulty conception of human nature—a conception which exalts man far above his
actual human potentialities. Yet, while I cannot in good conscience sub-
scribe to this point of view, I cannot help but admire and respect the
simple goodness, the heartfelt compassion, the humanitarian impulse
which inspires and motivates those who honestly and sincerely believe
that the conditions of their fellow men in society could be vastly improved if only the restrictive power of government could somehow, in
some vague way, be forever eliminated from their social lives.

44

GOVERNOR MICHAEL S. DUKAKIS

Proclamation on the Sacco-Vanzetti Trial

July 19, 1977

*Almost twenty years after Alexander Cella's failed attempt, Massachusetts
Governor Michael S. Dukakis, a former legislative aide to Cella, revisited the issue, motivated by the sense that a wrong had been done in the
state's past. On the fiftieth anniversary of their executions, he issued a
controversial proclamation, excerpted here, that Sacco and Vanzetti had
not received a fair trial.*

Governor Michael S. Dukakis Proclamation, July 19, 1977.

The Commonwealth of Massachusetts

By His Excellency
MICHAEL S. DUKAKIS
Governor
A PROCLAMATION

1977

WHEREAS: A half century ago next month, Nicola Sacco and Bartolomeo Vanzetti were executed by the Commonwealth of Massachusetts after being indicted, tried, and found guilty of murdering Alessandro Berardelli and Frederick A. Parmenter; and

WHEREAS: Nicola Sacco and Bartolomeo Vanzetti were Italian immigrants who lived and worked in Massachusetts while openly professing their beliefs in the doctrines of anarchism; and

WHEREAS: The atmosphere of their trial and appeals was permeated by prejudice against foreigners and hostility toward unorthodox political views; and

WHEREAS: The conduct of many of the officials involved in the case shed serious doubt on their willingness and ability to conduct the prosecution and trial of Sacco and Vanzetti fairly and impartially; and

WHEREAS: The limited scope of appellate review then in effect did not allow a new trial to be ordered based on the prejudicial effect of the proceedings as a whole; and

WHEREAS: This situation was later rectified as a direct result of their case by the adoption of Chapter 341 of the Acts of 1939, which permitted the Massachusetts Supreme Judicial Court to order a new trial not merely because the verdict was contrary to the law, but also if it was against the weight of the evidence, contradicted by newly discovered evidence, or "for any other reason that justice may require"; and

WHEREAS: The people of Massachusetts today take pride in the strength and vitality of their governmental institutions, particularly in the high quality of their legal system; and

WHEREAS: They recognize that all human institutions are imperfect, that the possibility of injustice is ever-present, and that the acknowledgement of fault, combined with a resolve to do better, are signs of strength in a free society; and

WHEREAS: The trial and execution of Sacco and Vanzetti should serve to remind all civilized people of the constant need to guard against our susceptibility to prejudice, our intolerance of unorthodox ideas, and our failure to defend the rights of persons who are looked upon as strangers in our midst; and

WHEREAS: Simple decency and compassion, as well as respect for truth and an enduring commitment to our nation's highest ideals, require that the fate of Nicola Sacco and Bartolomeo Vanzetti be pondered by all who cherish tolerance, justice, and human understanding; and

WHEREAS: Tuesday, August 23, 1977, will mark the fiftieth anniversary of the execution of Nicola Sacco and Bartolomeo Vanzetti by the Commonwealth of Massachusetts;

NOW, THEREFORE, I, Michael S. Dukakis, Governor of the Commonwealth of Massachusetts, by virtue of the authority conferred upon me as Supreme Executive Magistrate by the Constitution of the Commonwealth of Massachusetts, and by all other authority vested in me, do hereby proclaim Tuesday, August 23, 1977, "NICOLA SACCO AND BARTOLOMEO VANZETTI MEMORIAL DAY"; and declare, further, that any stigma and disgrace should be forever removed from the names of Nicola Sacco and Bartolomeo Vanzetti, from the names of their families and descendants, and so, from the name of the Commonwealth of Massachusetts; and I hereby call upon all the people of Massachusetts to pause in their daily endeavors to reflect upon these tragic events, and draw from their historic lessons the resolve to prevent the forces of intolerance, fear, and hatred from ever again uniting to overcome rationality, wisdom, and fairness to which our legal system aspires.

Given at the Executive Chamber in Boston, this nineteenth day of July in the year of our Lord one thousand and one hundred and seventy-seven and of the independence of the United States of America the two hundred and first.

A Chronology of Events
Related to the Sacco and Vanzetti Case
(1888–1977)

1888   Bartolomeo Vanzetti is born in Villafalletto, Italy.

1891   Ferdinando (Nicola) Sacco is born in Torremaggiore, Italy.

1892   Italian Socialist Party founded.

1901   Luigi Galleani arrives in the United States, settling in Paterson, New Jersey.

1903   Galleani launches the anarchist journal *Cronaca sovversiva* in Barre, Vermont.

1905   Galleani publishes *La salute è en voi!,* a manual for making explosives.

1907   Society for the Protection of Italian Immigrants established.

1908   Separately, Sacco and Vanzetti arrive in the United States from Italy.

1909   Vanzetti begins five years of working a series of unskilled jobs in New York, Connecticut, and Massachusetts, enduring periods of homelessness.

Sacco trains for three months to become a skilled shoemaker.

1912   Galleani moves *Cronaca sovversiva* to Lynn, Massachusetts.

Sacco is drawn toward anarchist politics during the Lawrence, Massachusetts, textile strike. Vanzetti also participates in the strike (although the two have not yet met), through his membership in an anarchist circle in Worcester, Massachusetts.

1913   Sacco begins attending meetings of an anarchist group in Milford, Massachusetts, and starts reading *Cronaca sovversiva.*

1916   Vanzetti meets Galleani and becomes an occasional contributor to *Cronaca sovversiva* during the Plymouth Cordage strike.

1917   *April:* The United States enters World War I.

May: Separately, Sacco and Vanzetti flee to Mexico to avoid being drafted. They meet there among a group of approximately sixty fellow *Galleanisti.*

June: Congress passes the Espionage Act, prescribing heavy fines and imprisonment for anyone interfering with the recruitment of troops or refusing to perform military duty.

The offices of *Cronaca sovversiva* are raided after Galleani publishes numerous articles denouncing the war; Galleani is arrested and charged with conspiracy to obstruct the draft.

September: Sacco and Vanzetti return to the United States.

November: The Bolshevik Revolution brings Communists to power in Russia.

1918   Congress passes the Sedition Act, making it a federal crime to criticize the government.

1919   Four million U.S. workers, from shipyard workers in Seattle to police officers in Boston, go on strike.

March: President Woodrow Wilson appoints A. Mitchell Palmer as attorney general. He immediately targets the Union of Russian Workers and the *Galleanisti.*

April: Thirty bombs are mailed to a series of prominent business and political leaders, including Attorney General Palmer; none reaches its intended victim.

June 2: Bombs explode in seven cities; copies of *Plain Words,* an anarchist pamphlet, are found at scenes of explosions. Federal authorities suspect the *Galleanisti.*

June 24: Galleani and eight *Galleanisti* are deported.

November 1919–January 1920: The Department of Justice begins a nationwide sweep for radicals, culminating in the Palmer Raids, in which ten thousand suspected radicals are brutally arrested and detained without due process.

December 24: An attempted robbery is committed in Bridgewater, Massachusetts (for which Vanzetti will later be convicted).

1920   *April 15:* The payroll robbery and two murders are committed in South Braintree, Massachusetts.

April 25–29: Galleanisti Andrea Salsedo and Roberto Elia are arrested in connection with pamphlets found at the scene of the June 1919 bombings.

May 3: Salsedo commits suicide while detained in New York.

May 5: Sacco and Vanzetti are arrested.

June 11–August 16: Vanzetti is indicted, tried, and convicted for the attempted robbery in Bridgewater.

September 11: Sacco and Vanzetti are indicted for the South Braintree robbery and murders.

1921 Congress passes the Immigration Restriction Act, limiting the number of immigrants entering the United States.

May 31–July 14: Sacco and Vanzetti are tried and convicted for the South Braintree crimes.

November: Defense attorneys make a motion for a new trial against weight of evidence.

Defense attorneys file first appeal (Walter Ripley).

December 24: Judge Webster Thayer denies the motion for a new trial.

1922 *May:* Defense attorneys file second appeal (Roy Gould and Louis Pelser).

July: Defense attorneys file third appeal (Carlos Goodridge).

September: Defense attorneys file fourth appeal (Lola Andrews).

1923 *February:* Sacco begins the first of several hunger strikes.

April–September: Physically and mentally exhausted, Sacco is admitted to the Bridgewater State Hospital for the Criminally Insane.

April: Defense attorneys file fifth appeal based on new ballistics testimony (Albert Hamilton).

October: Defense attorneys file a supplement to the first appeal based on new testimony concerning a biased juror (William Daly).

November: Defense attorneys file sixth appeal (William Proctor).

1924 Immigration Restriction Act passed.

August: Sacco fires his defense attorney, Fred Moore.

October: Judge Thayer denies all motions for appeal.

November: William Thompson agrees to defend Sacco and Vanzetti.

1925 *January–May:* Vanzetti is admitted to the Bridgewater State Hospital for the Criminally Insane.

November 16: Celestino Madeiros confesses to committing the South Braintree robbery and murders.

1926 *May:* Herbert Ehrmann becomes associate counsel for Sacco and Vanzetti.

May 12: The Massachusetts Supreme Judicial Court affirms Sacco and Vanzetti's convictions.

May 26: Defense attorneys file seventh appeal on basis of Celestino Madeiros's confession.

October 23: Judge Webster Thayer denies the Madeiros motion.

1927   *April 5:* The Massachusetts Supreme Judicial Court affirms the denial of the Madeiros motion.

April 9: Judge Thayer sentences Sacco and Vanzetti to death.

June: Defense attorneys learn of the existence of Pinkerton agents' reports on the South Braintree crime.

June 1: Under mounting pressure, Massachusetts Governor Alvan Fuller established the Advisory [Lowell] Committee to review the trial.

July 11–21: The Lowell Committee conducts its hearings.

July 27: The Lowell Committee issues its report, concluding both men are guilty.

August 3: Governor Fuller denies Sacco and Vanzetti clemency.

August 6: Defense attorneys file a final appeal to revoke Sacco and Vanzetti's sentences based on Judge Thayer's prejudicial behavior inside and outside the courtroom.

August 8: Judge Thayer rejects the final appeal.

August 10–20: Defense attorneys' efforts to convince Supreme Court justices Brandeis and Holmes to stay Sacco and Vanzetti's executions fail.

August 23: Sacco, Vanzetti, and Madeiros are executed.

1959   Massachusetts State Representative Alexander J. Cella's bill to exonerate Sacco and Vanzetti is debated, but fails to pass.

1977   Massachusetts Governor Michael S. Dukakis issues a controversial proclamation declaring that Sacco and Vanzetti did not receive a fair trial.

Massachusetts State Police files on the Sacco and Vanzetti case are released.

Questions for Consideration

1. How were immigrants received in the United States at the turn of the last century? What factors influenced their reception?

2. In what ways were Sacco and Vanzetti "typical" Italian immigrants? In what ways were they not?

3. What was anarchism, as practiced by Luigi Galleani and *Galleanisti* like Sacco and Vanzetti?

4. What was the Red Scare? Was the widespread concern about, and the reaction to radicals in the aftermath of World War I merited? Why or why not?

5. What role did concerns about the Red Scare play in Sacco and Vanzetti's trial?

6. Did Sacco and Vanzetti's anarchism justify the treatment they received during their trial?

7. Did their treatment during their trial provide a justification for their anarchism?

8. Why did their trial provoke such widespread protest? Should it have?

9. To what extremes can a nation go to defend itself during times of perceived peril? Should people who present a potential danger to a nation be stopped at any cost?

10. Why does this case still matter to people decades after the deaths of Sacco and Vanzetti?

Selected Bibliography

An immense—and, over time, increasingly contentious—body of literature exists on the Sacco and Vanzetti trial, which dates back to the last years of the appeals. A consensus on Sacco and Vanzetti's innocence characterized the early work by historians and other scholars. The scholarly production on the case has grown more complex, however, as time has passed. In fact, this case provides a useful window into how historiography—the history of how historians and other scholars have written about and analyzed a subject—evolves and develops. The issues involved are very clear cut; most of the historical writing on Sacco and Vanzetti has focused almost exclusively on whether they were guilty and on the fairness of their trial. Examining how historians and other scholars have written about the trial, it is relatively easy to see how they have engaged each other's arguments, and how historical knowledge has increased as more and more research has been conducted. Initial consensus on their innocence has been replaced by often vociferous debate about the nature of the two men and the conduct of their trial. It is in the world of scholarly production where the case and its implications are now most heatedly contested.

The most important primary sources—the starting point for any student of the trial—were generally produced by those most sympathetic to the two prisoners. Any careful examination of the case, however, must begin with the transcript of the trial and the appeals. *The Sacco-Vanzetti Case: Transcript of the Record of the Trial of Nicola Sacco and Bartolomeo Vanzetti in the Courts of Massachusetts and Subsequent Proceedings, 1920–1927,* vols. I–VI (Mamaroneck, N.Y.: Paul P. Appel, Publisher, 1969) includes testimony, depositions, and supporting documents from the trial, the appeals, and the investigations of the Advisory [Lowell] Committee. Volume VI is the transcript from Vanzetti's trial for the attempted Bridgewater robbery. A broad sampling of the poignant letters written by Sacco and Vanzetti during their imprisonment are contained in Richard Polenberg, *The Letters of Sacco and Vanzetti* (New York: Penguin Books, 1997). One of the earliest summaries of the case, written as an appeal for support for the two prisoners, is John Dos Passos, *Facing the Chair: Story of the Americanization of Two Foreignborn Workmen* (New York: Da Capo Press, 1927). This booklet also contains letters of support from liberal, labor, and Left leaders throughout the world. There are two personal memoirs written by liberal women who fought for Sacco and Vanzetti in the frenetic last weeks of their lives, Jeanette Marks, *Thirteen Days* (New York: Albert & Charles Boni, 1929), and Katherine Anne Porter, *The Never-Ending Wrong* (Boston: Little, Brown, 1977).

Two other important early works on the case shared a singular vantage point—that Sacco and Vanzetti were not guilty and that their trial was unfair. The first protest against the injustice of the trial in scholarly form was Felix Frankfurter, *The Case of Sacco and Vanzetti: A Critical Analysis for Lawyers and Laymen* (Stanford, Calif.: Academic Reprints, 1954 [1927]). At the time Frankfurter was a Harvard law professor; he later became a Supreme Court Justice. His book was followed quickly in 1927 by an even more demonstrative defense of the two men, Eugene Lyons, *Life and Death of Sacco and Vanzetti* (New York: International Publishers, 1927). Lyons, a member of the Communist party, portrayed the two anarchists as devoted advocates for the working class and presented compelling documentation of the worldwide protest that their prolonged imprisonment and ultimate executions provoked. His book was translated into several languages; a Russian edition apparently sold well over 100,000 copies. Nonetheless, it was not a careful analysis of the trial or of the men's lives.

Agreement about the case carried into the 1930s. The standard work of this early era is Osmond Fraenkel, *The Sacco-Vanzetti Case* (New York: Alfred A. Knopf, 1931). The New York attorney laid out the sequence of events during the trial and appeals in exhaustive detail, and he staked out the central issues about which controversy would continue to swirl. One of these was the Madeiros confession and the possible involvement of the Morelli gang. This was the subject of Herbert Ehrmann, *The Untried Case: The Sacco-Vanzetti Case and the Morelli Gang* (New York: Vanguard Press, 1960 [1933]). Ehrmann was part of the defense team and, even more than Frankfurter, Lyons, and Fraenkel, he was not only convinced of Sacco and Vanzetti's innocence, but he was determined to clear their names after their executions. Ehrmann was certain the Morelli gang were the real culprits.

The first crack in the consensus about Sacco and Vanzetti's inno- cence came from an unlikely source—Edmund M. Morgan and G. Louis Joughin, *The Legacy of Sacco and Vanzetti* (New York: Har- court, Brace and Company, 1948). This work was in many ways yet another staunch defense of the two anarchists. Split into two sections, the first part of the work, by Morgan, a Harvard law professor, was a critical examination of the flawed trial and appeals process. The last two sections, by Joughin, a literature scholar and ACLU advocate, dealt with the legacy of the case in popular and artistic terms. Although the authors clearly saw the case as unfair, Morgan sug- gested that the two men were innocent of the South Braintree crime, but that Vanzetti might have been guilty in the Bridgewater case. It is an unlikely argument, and Morgan's analysis seemed strained. It was, nonetheless, the first time any scholar had suggested that either man might be guilty of either crime.

Serious challenges of Sacco and Vanzetti's innocence came from a series of works in the 1960s that took up not only the trial but the furor that had surrounded it. The first of these was Robert Mont- gomery, *Sacco-Vanzetti: The Murder and the Myth* (New York: The Devin-Adair Company, 1960). Montgomery, a friend of Judge Webster Thayer's and a member of the reactionary John Birch Society, pre- sented what became a familiar theme among Sacco and Vanzetti detractors in future years. He argued that the case was a simple rob- bery and murder committed by two criminals who were turned into international celebrities by unscrupulous radicals.

The second in this triad of assaults against their innocence was scholar Francis Russell, *Tragedy in Dedham: The Story of the Sacco- Vanzetti Case* (New York: McGraw-Hill, 1962). Although largely a sym- pathetic treatment of the two anarchists, Russell's book was the first to suggest an argument that remains alive today: Vanzetti was innocent of the crime, but Sacco was guilty. Russell's logic was rooted largely in ballistics evidence. Tests run just before the executions in 1927 and again in 1961 seemed to indicate that Sacco's gun had fired the fatal shot into Berardelli. Russell also pointed to comments made by defense attorney Fred Moore, radical author Upton Sinclair, and for- mer Leftist Max Eastman that seemed to indicate Sacco's possible involvement in the crime. Russell would continue to argue Sacco's guilt for years.

The third work built on Montgomery's critique of the case as an international phenomenon again several years later. Scholar David Felix, *Protest: Sacco-Vanzetti and the Intellectuals* (Bloomington: Indiana University Press, 1965), argued that the case would have, and should have, been dealt with quickly and quietly. It gained its notoriety only because of Communists and misguided intellectuals who saw it as an opportunity to attack institutions with which they disagreed.

A rejoinder to these arguments came quickly from defense attorney Herbert Ehrmann, *The Case That Will Not Die: Commonwealth vs. Sacco and Vanzetti* (Boston: Little, Brown, 1969), the most exhaustive and convincing defense of the two men. Ehrmann went back through the trial and appeals process, addressing each issue raised by Montgomery, Felix, and Russell in preceding years. He reexamined the issue of the unfairness of the trial with the confidence and passion of someone who had been doing painstaking research for decades. He also raised doubt about the veracity of both post-trial ballistics tests. He argued that, in one test, the slugs had been marked sloppily and potentially incorrectly and, in the other, the men who conducted it asserted beforehand that they believed both men were guilty.

An extraordinary and disturbing breakthrough in the case came from rare book dealer William Young and historian David Kaiser, *Postmortem: New Evidence in the Case of Sacco and Vanzetti* (Amherst: University of Massachusetts Press, 1985). While unable to provide evidence that positively proved Sacco's innocence, they did uncover jarring new findings concerning Vanzetti. Much of the prosecution's case hinged on its assertion that the gun in his possession the night of his arrest had belonged to Berardelli, and that Vanzetti (or another robber) had taken it from him as he lay dying. The argument was weak to begin with; the prosecution had little success even establishing that Berardelli had his gun with him the day of the robbery.

What Young and Kaiser discovered when relevant Massachusetts State Police records were released in the late 1970s was that the police *knew* that they did not have the right gun. They had discovered the serial number of Berardelli's gun during the course of their investigation, and it did not match Vanzetti's. Nonetheless, neither the police investigating the crime nor the prosecuting attorneys exposed this finding. The trial proceeded with District Attorney Katzmann arguing that the gun had belonged to the murdered guard. This stunning revelation does more than cast serious doubt on Vanzetti's guilt. It also opens up the possibility of other forms of misconduct by the police and prosecution. It shows how far the police and prosecution would go to convict the two anarchists. Young and Kaiser also suggested that the police had substituted the bullet and shell that had supposedly come from Sacco's gun.

Most recently, though, following a 1983 investigation by a specially appointed commission, forensic expert James Starrs, "Once More Unto the Breech: The Firearms Evidence in the Sacco and Vanzetti Case Revisited," *Journal of Forensic Science* (April 1986): 630–54; (July 1986): 1050–78, argued that the substitution theory was unlikely. The commission, he pointed out, had been able to find evidence of similarities between shells found at the scene and cartridges ejected from Sacco's gun. The commission's findings and Starrs' presentation of them are hardly indisputable. But they do pose a challenge to straightforward assertions of Sacco's innocence—an issue that by this point will probably never be satisfactorily resolved.

The scholarly work in the first sixty years, all of the disagreements that emerged aside, focused almost exclusively on the trial process itself; recent scholarship has explored the backgrounds—especially the political backgrounds—of the two men. Nunzio Pernicone, "Carlo Tresca and the Sacco-Vanzetti Case," *The Journal of American History*, 66, no. 1 (December 1979), 535–47; Robert D'Attillio, "*La salute è in voi!:* The Anarchist Dimension," *Sacco-Vanzetti: Developments and Reconsiderations — 1979* (Boston: Boston Public Library, 1982), 75–89; and Paul Avrich, *Sacco and Vanzetti: The Anarchist Background* (Princeton, N.J.: Princeton University Press, 1991), have each examined Sacco and Vanzetti as anarchists, looking unflinchingly at the *Galleanisti*'s attempts to use violence to achieve their ends. Each of these historians has sought to debunk the long-standing image of Sacco and Vanzetti as singularly pastoral, gentle-souled men. Certainly that side of their personalities was there, but these scholars have sought to juxtapose and to reconcile the compassionate and combative sides of each man. What emerges in their work is a continued insistence that Sacco and Vanzetti did not receive fair trials, and a sympathetic but far more complex portrait of the two men and their political and personal lives. Although the question of guilt or innocence continues to tantalize, for historians the subject matter of these more recent works provide a much richer, and certainly more accessible, set of questions.

Cultural and Artistic Productions
Related to the Sacco and Vanzetti Case

The trial has inspired a truly extraordinary range of creative efforts. As with the scholarly works on the trial, cultural and artistic productions inspired by the case and by Sacco and Vanzetti's lives began to appear before the trial and appeals ended, and people continue to create them. Novels and other literary works began to appear just after Sacco and Vanzetti's execution. In the decades following the executions, a number of musicians drew inspiration from the two men. More recently, operas, films, and now dozens of Web sites on the anarchists and the trial have been created.

The first novel about the case—and, in many ways, the most important—was published just a year after their execution. Upton Sinclair, known for authoring *The Jungle,* his exposé on the meat-packing industry, earlier in the century, began *Boston* the night of Sacco and Vanzetti's execution. Written from the point of view of a Boston Brahmin woman who defied her family and her community in defending Sacco and Vanzetti, Sinclair's novel dealt in considerable detail both with the enormous gap between social classes in Boston—the "two nations," in Dos Passos's phrase—and with the trial itself. His perspective was clear: Sacco and Vanzetti were innocent and had been tried and executed unfairly. One of the most compelling aspects of Sinclair's novel was his unflinching look at the anarchist community with which Sacco and Vanzetti had associated themselves. He dealt frankly with their capacity for violence in the name of their ideals in ways that few others would for decades to come. His approach to the two men made most other fictional treatments, including Howard Fast's noble portraits in his 1953 *The Passion of Sacco and Vanzetti,* seem sentimental by comparison.

The trial and the two men also inspired a number of—usually bad—plays. Most of these were relentlessly romanticized; Sacco and Vanzetti often appeared as Christ-like figures. This was true of French playwright Pierre Yroudy's 1929 *Sept ans d'agonie: le drame Sacco-Vanzetti* (*Seven Years of Agony: The Sacco-Vanzetti Drama*). One critic, cruelly but not inaccurately, referred to "Seven Years of Agony" as "page after page of drool." The plays of American playwright Maxwell Anderson were much better as artistic productions. Anderson made Sacco and Vanzetti the subject of two of his plays, including the award-winning *Winterset* in 1935. He took considerable artistic license with each man, but he did manage to convey the blatant unfairness of the trial and the aura of fear and prejudice in which these men lived and ultimately died, with great success. Another exemplary theatrical production is Louis Lippa's 1998 *Sacco and Vanzetti: A Vaudeville*. Lippa took the unusual step of combining drama and comedy; the actors playing the two anarchists present their lives and their case through a series of songs, dances, and gags. This play has been staged in theaters throughout the United States, from Lippa's home state of Pennsylvania to the Bay area in California, and critics have lauded his effort to examine "how close farce and tragedy really are."

The case has been the subject of other artistic productions as well. At the time of their trial and just after, Sacco and Vanzetti became the subjects of a number of Leftist artists and illustrators. One of the best known was Hugo Gellert, who had been producing art for Leftist journals and magazines since 1916, and who created lithographs and posters used to promote defense efforts for the anarchists. The artist whose renderings have had the longest staying power is Ben Shahn; his artwork from the early 1930s, often based closely on photographs taken during the trial, is easily the most visually captivating. The Jersey City Museum in New Jersey produced a retrospective of his Sacco and Vanzetti art in 2001. In the late 1950s, composer Marc Blitzstein began work on a folk opera titled *Sacco and Vanzetti* based on the trial. It was going to be performed at the Metropolitan Opera House in New York City, but Blitzstein died before he could finish the project. The opera was finally completed by composer Leonard Lehrman, whose production of the opera opened in Connecticut in August 2001. Another opera, this one written by composer Anton Coppola and titled *Sacco & Vanzetti,* opened at the Tampa Bay Performing Arts Center in Tampa, Florida, in March 2001. Both presented Sacco and Vanzetti as profoundly sympathetic characters.

So too did movie and musical versions of their lives. Woody Guthrie, one of the most compelling and progressive folk singers in American history, wrote a series of ballads just after World War II, again simply titled "Sacco and Vanzetti." NBC presented a television movie written by Reginald Rose titled *The Sacco-Vanzetti Story* in June 1960. A more famous Italian film titled *Sacco e Vanzetti,* directed by Giuliano Montaldo, opened in 1971. The soundtrack for the latter film featured an unusual pairing of musicians: Italian composer Ennio Morricone, who has since established a considerable reputation writing film soundtracks, and Joan Baez, a folk singer who was deeply involved in the 1960s American Left. In 1998, A&E Television Networks produced a film on the trial for the History Channel's *In Search of History* series titled "The True Story of Sacco and Vanzetti." Courtroom Television Network produced a version of the trial in the same year.

Interest in the case and in the lives of the Italian immigrant anarchists continues to this day, manifesting itself most recently in the numerous Web pages devoted to them. Essays and book-length treatments written at the time of the trial and appeals by defenders, and even trial transcripts and FBI files on the two men are available online. There are Web sites devoted to evaluating ballistics evidence, to the trial as a whole, and to the continuing relevance of anarchism. There are others that examine the implications of the case for current debates on capital punishment, racial and radical identity and the judiciary, and the relationship between the state and immigrants and radicals. The best Web site is The Sacco-Vanzetti Project at www.saccovanzettiproject.org, which documents educational efforts and events, and provides a summary of the case, historical context, and an assessment of the controversies still surrounding the trials and executions. It also contains a bibliography, a chronology, and a place for interested parties to exchange ideas.

ACKNOWLEDGMENTS

Document 3. Luigi Galleani, *Anarchy Will Be!* Translated by Robert D'Attilio and reprinted with his permission.

Document 4. Luigi Galleani, *La salute é in voi!* From the private collection of Nuncio Pernicone and reprinted with his permission.

Documents 7, 8, 29, 30, and 38. From *The Letters of Sacco and Vanzetti* by Marion D. Frankfurter and Gardner Jackson, copyright 1928, renewed © 1955 by The Viking Press, Inc. Used by permission of Viking Penguin, a division of the Penguin Group (USA) Inc.

Documents 11, 18, and 32. Bartolomeo Vanzetti, *Background of the Plymouth Trial; Affidavit of District Attorney Frederick Katzmann;* and Frank Goodwin, *Sacco-Vanzetti and the Red Peril: Speech before the Lawrence Kiwanis Club.* Courtesy of Michigan State University Libraries, Special Collections Division, Digital & Multimedia Center.

Documents 16 and 25. Pinkerton Agent Henry Hellyer, *Reports,* April 19, 1920; May 11, 1920. *Celestino Madeiros' Statement,* April 8, 1926. Courtesy of Special Collections Department, Harvard Law School Library.

Document 28. Elizabeth Gurley Flynn, *Rebel Girl: An Autobiography, My First Life (1906-1926).* (New York: International Publishers, 1955). Reprinted with permission.

Document 33. Katherine Anne Porter, *The Never-Ending Wrong.* The Literary Estate of Katherine Anne Porter.

Document 36. Countee Cullen, *Not Sacco and Vanzetti.* Copyrights held by Amistad Research Center, Tulane University. Administered by Thompson and Thompson, Brooklyn, N.Y.

Document 37. "Justice Denied in Massachusetts" by Edna St. Vincent Millay. From *Collected Poems,* HarperCollins. Copyright © 1928, 1955 by Edna St. Vincent Millay and Norma Millay Ellis. "Letter 153 to Governor Alvan T. Fuller from Edna St. Vincent Millay," August 22, 1927. From *Letters of Edna St. Vincent Millay,* Harper & Brothers. Copyright © 1952, 1980 by Norma Millay Ellis. All rights reserved. Reprinted by permission of Elizabeth Barnett, literary executor.

Document 39. Benito Mussolini, *Letter to Governor Fuller.* Reprinted with permission from The University of Chicago Press, Chicago, Illinois.

Document 40. From the book *The Nation 1865-1990: Selections from the Independent Magazine of Politics and Culture,* edited by Katrina Vanden Heuvel. All other contents copyright © 1990 by The Nation Company. Appears by permission of the publisher, Thunder's Mouth Press, a division of Avalon Publishing Group.

Document 42. Vera B. Weisbord, *Remember Sacco and Vanzetti.* From www. weisbord.org. Courtesy of the Albert & Vera Weisbord Foundation.

Index